THE CONCEPT OF EXISTENCE IN
THE CONCLUDING UNSCIENTIFIC POSTSCRIPT

THE CONCEPT OF EXISTENCE IN THE CONCLUDING UNSCIENTIFIC POSTSCRIPT

by

RALPH HENRY JOHNSON

MARTINUS NIJHOFF/THE HAGUE/ 1972

© *1972 by Martinus Nijhoff, The Hague, Netherlands*
All rights reserved, including the right to translate or
to reproduce this book or parts thereof in any form
ISBN 90 247 1335 8

PRINTED IN BELGIUM

To my parents

"The aspects of things that are most important for us are hidden because of their simplicity and familiarity. (One is unable to notice something—because it is always before one's eyes.)"
—Wittgenstein, *Philosophical Investigations*

PREFACE

The writings of Kierkegaard continue to be a fertile source for contemporary philosophical thought. Perhaps the most interesting of his works to a philosopher is the *Concluding Unscientific Postscript to the Philosophical Fragments*. The *Fragments* is a brief, algebraic piece in which the author attempts to put forward the central teachings of Christianity in philosophical terminology. The work is addressed to a reader who has a philosophical bent and who may therefore be tempted to relate to Christianity *via* such questions as: Can the truth of Christianity be established? The analysis of the *Fragments* establishes that this way of relating to Christianity is misguided, since Christianity and philosophy are categorically different. Having done this, the author turns his attention in the *Postscript* to the question of how an individual human being can properly establish a relationship to Christianity. In order to become a Christian, one must first of all *exist*. "Nothing more than *that*!" one may be tempted to think. Yet at the very core of the *Postscript* is the notion that to *exist* as an individual human being is difficult. The author goes so far as to claim that men have forgotten what it means to *exist*. Thus while the larger purpose of the *Postscript* is to get clear on what it means to be a Christian, there is a narrower and more philosophical thematic devoted to a fundamental question which will surely engage any reflective individual: What does it mean to be a man? This thematic will be the focus of this study. Specifically, it will be our aim to clarify the meaning of the term *"exist"* in the above mentioned claim, for it is our contention that the forgetting-claim provides us with the hermeneutical key, so to speak, to the *Postscript's* concept of existence. If that be true, then there is ample justification for yet another work on Kierkegaard, since nowhere in the abundant secondary literature can one find an elucidation of this rather puzzling, though absolutely fundamental, claim.

The *Postscript* first appeared at a time when philosophy was under the dominance of speculative idealism and its pursuit of systematic knowledge. Its author very clearly holds this philosophy responsible for the fact that men have forgotten what it means to *exist*. Indeed, his treatment of human existence is best understood as contrasting the individual human being's mode of existence with that of philosophy. Thus to render that treatment accessible to the contemporary reader of the *Postscript*, two courses were open. Either it would be necessary to resurrect the spectre of speculative idealism (in order to grasp the contrast) or else to find a contemporary analogue or surrogate to stand in its stead. Science seemed to be a suitable candidate for a contemporary analogue. Hence in the second chapter, a contrast is developed between the individual human being's mode of existence and that of Science, or the scientific community. This chapter is important for two reasons. First, it prefigures the third chapter which is a straightforward textual analysis of what is said in the *Postscript* concerning human existence. Secondly, it serves as a basis for the fifth chapter in which the forgetting-claim is explained and illustrated with examples taken from the writings of scientists. (The claim is also explained as it relates to the speculative idealists.) It should be said that the account we have offered of the scientific community's mode of existence is not intended to be an exhaustive or definitive treatment of a highly complex and controversial subject.

In utilizing the scientific community as a contemporary analogue of the Hegelian speculative philosophical community, we are mindful of the fact that there are important differences between the two. The scientific community does not take itself with such metaphysical serious-ness as does the Hegelian. The business of the former does not require it to take a stand on the nature of the individual human being and his mode for existence. Hegel, on the other hand, has a carefully worked out philosophy of the nature of true (or absolute) individuality. Without losing sight of this important difference or denying that there may be others, we yet venture the opinion (hopefully rendered plausible by this study) that there is also an important similarity. Both science and philos-ophy are species of objectivity; both are instances of what the *Postscript* terms "the objective tendency." Both can become the occasion whereby an individual loses sight of his own mode of existence (and the tasks relating to it) and forgets thereby what it means to *exist*. We may mention one other similarity, too. Just as Hegelian philosophy was the dominant intellectual force of the nineteenth century, so it can reasonably be claimed that science is the driving intellectual force of this century. As such, both are highly respected disciplines whose dangers may easily go undetected.

It will hardly have escaped notice that we have regularly used the circumlocution, "the author of the *Postscript*," and have refrained from attributing the work to Kierkegaard himself. The reason, of course, is that the work is pseudonymous. The question of how the pseudonymous works are to be interpreted has been the focal point of much discussion and just as much disagreement. We have not therefore tried to settle this problem once and for all but rather have committed ourselves to the approach which, upon reflection, seems most satisfactory. This is discussed in detail in the first chapter.

This work is based on a dissertation submitted in partial fulfillment of the requirements for the Ph.D. degree at the University of Notre Dame. I would like to express my gratitude to Dr. Harry A. Nielsen who originally interested me in the writings of Kierkegaard, suggested the topic of this work, and read the various drafts. I would also like to thank my director, Dr. Ralph McInerny, for his suggestions and encouragement, and Dr. C. F. Delaney from whose criticisms this work has hopefully benefited. The University of Windsor, through an enlightened policy, made it possible for the author to have a year free from teaching duties in order to finish this work, and provided financial assistance as well. The Canada Council graciously provided additional and much-appreciated financial support. Finally, I must thank my wife, Maggie, who shared the burden, constantly providing both perspective and love, and who helped to prepare, type and proofread the manuscript.

R.H.J.
University of Windsor
June, 1971

ANALYTICAL TABLE OF CONTENTS

Chapter

I. INTRODUCTION

This chapter is an introduction to Kierkegaard's writings, generally, and to the *Concluding Unscientific Postscript,* specifically.

This book will investigate the concept of human existence in the *Postscript.* After summarizing the current attitudes about Kierkegaard, we outline the plan of our study.

Kierkegaard's authorship is susceptible of various interpretations. For purposes of this study, we accept Kierkegaard's own interpretation that the authorship is basically religious in its orientation. The *Postscript,* in particular, raises the problem of becoming a Christian. But the work is pseudonymous. Johannes Climacus claims that there is a misunderstanding between Christianity and modern philosophical thought. It is based upon the fact that men have forgotten what it means to exist. This is the fundamental claim of the *Postscript.*

In his first work, Climacus attempts to show that philosophy and Christianity are categorically different. This work is discussed in the context of its immediate historical background. Particularly important is the work of Lessing.

The *Postscript* must be understood in its relationship to the *Fragments.* Moreover, the point of view of its pseudonymous author must be explored. Climacus is not a Christian, but a humorist asking how one becomes a Christian.

II. DIFFERENCES

As a preliminary to the analysis of human existence and as a preparation for the elucidation of the claim that men have forgotten what it
means to exist, it is helpful to call to mind some of the differences
between the individual human being and the ongoing scientific
community.

Climacus' analysis of human existence is basically a protest against
idealistic philosophy—its manner of thought and expression. He reacts
to statements of the form, *"Philosophy says such-and-such,"* viewing
them as possible indicators that the person speaking may have confused
himself with philosophy. In contemporary culture, one often encounters
statements of the form, *"Science* says such-and-such." If such statements harbor a confusion, this can best be exposed and protected
against by calling to mind some of the differences between Science
(or the scientific community) and the individual. The task is amenable
to a "grammatical investigation" (in Wittgenstein's sense).

Both the scientific community and the individual have a beginning
in time. But the individual must face up to the prospect of death,
whereas the community does not. The community can therefore adopt
a relaxed view of time.

The scientific community is a cognitive entity. Its powers of understanding will display different features than those characteristic of the
individual human being.

The community exists solely for the purpose of understanding
phenomena. It cannot step outside this "posture." The individual,
however, has no one characteristic posture.

The community is essentially a public entity. The individual has both
a public and a private dimension to his existence.

Science is often compared to a living organism. The four differences
alluded to in this chapter may check the tendency to push such a
comparison too far.

III. HUMAN EXISTENCE

The question discussed in this chapter is: What, according to Climacus
in the *Postscript,* does it mean to exist as an individual human being?

Climacus' concern with this question arises out of his conviction
that there is widespread disregard for the individual human being
because of the great enthusiasm for knowledge.

Climacus distinguishes between a loose and a strict sense of "exists."
In the strict sense, to *exist* means to become a subject. The individual's
highest task is to understand himself. The task requires thought, passion,
and inwardness, and is sufficient to last a man for his entire life.

Climacus claims that subjectivity is the highest truth available to the
individual who becomes conscious of himself as existing. The claim
is not an unrestricted one, nor a denial of other kinds of truth. Neither
is it an affirmation of a privatism.

The requirements of a truly human existence can be met by every
man. Climacus' analysis of human existence must be appraised in light
of this consequence.

The results of the previous chapter are compared with those of George
Price (*The Narrow Pass*) and James Collins (*The Mind of Kierkegaard*).
Both of them distort the *Postscript's* analysis of human existence:
Price by *psychologizing* it; Collins by *metaphysicizing* it. Neither is
aware of the centrality of the forgetting-claim.

Since inwardness is an essential component of human existence, the
forgetting-claim must be applied tentatively and cautiously. A forgetting
is signalled when an individual thinker speaks or writes as though
his mode of existence displayed a different set of properties from
those which it in fact has.

Climacus takes the claim that an existential system is possible for
a human thinker as an indication that Hegel has forgotten what it
means to *exist*.

ACKNOWLEDGEMENTS

The author gratefully acknowledges permission to use quotations from the following works:

Philosophical Fragments, Søren Kierkegaard, original translation by David F. Swenson, new introduction and commentary by Niels Thulstrup, translation revised and commentary translated by Howard V. Hong, Copyright 1936, 1962 by Princeton University Press, reprinted by permission of Princeton University Press; *Concluding Unscientific Postscript,* Søren Kierkegaard, translated by David F. Swenson and Walter Lowrie, Copyright 1941 by Princeton University Press, reprinted by permission of Princeton University Press; *The Point of View for My Work as an Author,* Søren Kierkegaard, translated by Walter Lowrie, edited by Benjamin Nelson, Copyright 1962 by Harper & Row, Publishers; *The Structure of Scientific Revolutions,* Thomas Kuhn, Copyright 1962 by the University of Chicago; *Science, Faith, and Society,* Michael Polanyi, The University of Chicago Press, Copyright 1946 by Michael Polanyi, Introduction Copyright 1964 by the University of Chicago; *Lessing and the Enlightenment,* Henry E. Allison, University of Michigan Press, Copyright 1966 by the University of Michigan; *Open Vistas,* Henry Margenau, Yale University Press, Copyright 1961 by Yale University; *Scientific Research I-II,* Mario Bunge, Copyright 1967 by Springer-Verlag, New York; *Lessing's Theological Writings,* edited and translated by Henry Chadwick, Copyright 1956 by Adam & Charles Black, Publishers; *Science, Technology, and Human Values,* A. Cornelius Benjamin, Copyright 1965 by the Curators of the University of Missouri, reprinted by permission of the publishers, University of Missouri Press, Columbia, Missouri; *Philosophy of Science,* edited by Arthur Danto and Sidney Morgenbesser, The World Publishing Company, Copyright 1960 by Meridian

Books; *The New Obedience: Kierkegaard on Imitating Christ,* Bradley Dewey, Copyright 1968 by The World Publishing Company; *The Mind of Kierkegaard,* James Collins, Copyright 1953 by Henry Regnery Company, Publishers; Ziman, J.M.: *Public Knowledge* 1968, Copyright Cambridge University Press; *The Narrow Pass,* George Price, Hutchinson & Company Publishers, Limited, London; *Out of My Later Years,* Albert Einstein, Copyright 1950 by Philosophical Library Inc., reprinted by permission of the Estate of Albert Einstein.

A NOTE ON REFERENCES

Full title and bibliographic information on the editions of Kierkegaard's works used in this study are given in the first reference to any particular work. Thereafter references will utilize an abbreviated form of the title.

The manner of identifying references to Kierkegaard's journals and papers follows the internationally accepted method of the Danish edition, citing volume, part, and entry number. The source of the English translation used is also indicated. Thus, a citation may appear as: Dru, #413; IV B 1.

CHAPTER I

INTRODUCTION

A. THE DIFFICULTIES

Briefly stated, the aim of this study is to arrive at an understanding of the treatment of existence in the *Concluding Unscientific Postscript*.[1] The task proves to be a complicated one, however, not only because of the complexities of the work itself and the authorship in which it is imbedded, but also because of the climate of opinion which presently surrounds the very name "Kierkegaard." It may be helpful at the outset, then, to allude to some of the elements in this climate.

We often hear it said, for example, that to understand Kierkegaard's writings, one must look first to his private life. In his introduction to a collection of essays on Kierkegaard, Gill tells his reader:

> Philosophers often warn against committing the "genetic fallacy" of basing one's understanding and estimation of a thinker's work upon factors pertaining to his life. While this is good general advice, there are thinkers whose work cannot be understood or evaluated apart from an awareness of the events and quality of their lives. SK is one of these thinkers. His life and thought are so inextricably related that it is necessary to begin one's study of him with a consideration of the people who played central roles in the drama that was his life.[2]

Studies which begin with this presupposition have been known to become so fascinated with Kierkegaard's eccentricities that they never get to his writings. Thus does exegesis become psycho-analysis:

> The case of Kierkegaard—he forces the clinical term upon us—is instructive. He asked to be judged as a wild goose, by his indifference to the world. But he was one

---

[1] Søren Kierkegaard, *Concluding Unscientific Postscript to the Philosophical Fragments,* trans. David F. Swenson and Walter Lowrie (Princeton, 1941). Hereafter cited as: *Post.*

[2] Jerry H. Gill, ed., *Essays on Kierkegaard* (Minneapolis, 1969), p. 1. Book hereafter cited as: Gill, *Essays.*

of the most thin-skinned men ever to have lived, and he was *abnormally not* "indifferent" to the world. He held that his suffering constituted his superiority,... It is hard to escape the suspicion that he sought extraordinary suffering for its own sake and held it close in spite of every opportunity—marriage and career—to avoid it.[3]

It is difficult to name another thinker whose private life has been the object of so much scrutiny and speculation—all too often, it would seem, at the expense of confronting his writings.

The reader who manages to make his way to these writings will undoubtedly meet with the thought that Kierkegaard's method of communication is enigmatic, his prose obscure. Although his prose is not the easiest and the presence of pseudonymous writings compounds the difficulties, one must still question the wisdom of an observation like the following:

He [Kierkegaard] liked to construct intellectual Chinese puzzles, having one compartment cleverly concealed within another. In this penchant for raising dust for its own sake, he detected a feeling of inferiority and a need to compensate for it, by convincing himself of his ability to bemuse less agile minds. Although he brought this motive out into the open and sought to control it, Kierkegaard never succeeded completely in outgrowing or disciplining this secretive and obfuscating tendency. Many passages in the esthetic works and even in his religious discourses simply overwhelm one, with their straining after sheer virtuosity in the statement of difficulties and nuances. At times, this love of mystification defeats the primary aim of communicating truth, because it destroys the reader's confidence and produces an obscurity not dispelled by other means.[4]

For if the reader approaches Kierkegaard's writings expecting to be baffled by dense prose and Chinese puzzles, mightn't this expectation itself contribute to that result?

If, finally, the reader does confront Kierkegaard's ideas, he can hardly have avoided the notion that Kierkegaard was a seminal influence on Existentialism. After quoting several passages from the *Postscript* in her brief discussion of Kierkegaard in *Existentialist Ethics*, Mary Warnock states:

In these passages which I have quoted we have, it seems to me, the salient features of all subsequent Existentialist thought. This does not mean that all Existentialists deliberately derived all or any part of their thought from that of Kierkegaard; but

---

[3] Ralph Harper, *The Seventh Solitude* (Baltimore, 1967), pp. 9-10. (Italics mine except for "*not*.")

[4] James Collins, *The Mind of Kierkegaard* (Chicago, 1935), p. 36. Hereafter cited as: Collins, *Mind*.

rather that he first manifested the tendencies which are the mark of Existentialism, whoever practises it.[5]

One of these tendencies, according to Warnock, is "...the recognition that each person, in his own individual existence, must receive and understand a purely personal and subjective truth ... Just as the individual has his own passions and his own life to live, so he has his own truth." [6] Although it is indisputable that Kierkegaard's writings have influenced some now classified as Existentialists, one must beware the temptation to read back into his writings, thoughts and ideas which have emerged since his time.[7]

The composite picture that emerges from our brief survey of the present climate of opinion about Kierkegaard is that of an eccentric, enigmatic, proto-Existentialist who advocated a subjectivist view of life. It was perhaps the existence of this climate of opinion that provoked Bradley Dewey to observe:

On the whole, the misuse of Kierkegaard seems to be lessening. Perhaps the mere passage of time has rendered him less *a la mode*. But another factor, hopefully, is the growing awareness of how much is not yet known about his vast and labyrinthine literature. A thin, steady flow of well-researched books and articles in English has pointed out the intricate and puzzling nature of his thirty-five books and twenty large volumes of private papers. Kierkegaard's various pseudonymous masks, his indirect communication, not to mention his demanding prose, have discouraged close and thorough scholarship. *Consequently, many have been tempted to frame conclusions prematurely, to superimpose systems which are not there, and to supply word for him where he is intentionally silent.... What is needed first is a clearer understanding of what he himself said, not a multiplication of what others say about him.*[8]

We agree with this lucid appraisal of the current status of Kierkegaard-research and hope this study will meet the need that Dewey has articulated by providing a clearer understanding of what is said in the *Postscript* about existence. Dewey has also described well the road that leads to this goal:

[5] Mary Warnock, *Existentialist Ethics*, New Studies in Ethics, ed. W. D. Hudson (London, 1967), p. 9. Hereafter cited as: Warnock, *Ethics*. Cf. also Paul Roubiczek, *Existentialism: For and Against* (Cambridge, 1964) pp. 55-74. Roubiczek claims that Kierkegaard coined the term 'Existentialism' (*Ibid.*, p. 55).

[6] Warnock, *Ethics*, pp. 9-10.

[7] Warnock goes on to state that "Most characteristically, then, Existentialism will undermine the distinction between thinking and feeling, between the rational and the sentimental" (*Ibid.*, p. 10).

[8] Bradley Dewey, *The New Obedience: Kierkegaard on Imitating Christ* (Washington, 1968), p. xx. (Italics mine.)

Is not easy
to have or
to be familiar
with Kierkegaard
works, but is
important

Ideally, those engaged in research should possess a reasonable familiarity with the complete works, then focus on a limited area of Kierkegaard's thought, studying it for its own sake, and producing careful exposition and analysis. General theories about his life or writings must be held in check until the evidence has been presented as objectively as possible. Certainly the scholar has the right to interpret and criticize. But this right must not be usurped; it must be earned by the labor of diligent research, and the restraint of laudatory or pejorative inclinations when selecting, analyzing, and interpreting the material from primary sources. Perhaps this is unrealistic.... But given the unstable and transitional nature of Kierkegaard scholarship—especially in the English-speaking countries—*there seems to be a serious need for more basic research. Until this need is adequately met, the difficult counsel of patience and restraint appears to be in order.*[9]

In addition to the conditions laid down by Dewey, we would suggest that each study should make a forthright declaration of its interpretive principles and assumptions.

The plan of our study is as follows. In the next section, we begin with a brief discussion of the authorship as a whole.[10] We state also the interpretive principles to be used in this study. We shall find, however, that we cannot hope to understand the *Postscript* without some familiarity with its predecessor, the *Philosophical Fragments*. After treating the latter in the third section, we turn in the final section to the preliminaries necessary for understanding the *Postscript*.

B. KIERKEGAARD'S AUTHORSHIP

If we did not know otherwise, we might find it surprising that one author is ultimately responsible for both *Either-Or* and the *Postscript*; for both the *Works of Love* and the *Attack on Christendom*. So varied is this authorship not only in content and tone but also in style and point of view that it has quite rightly been said that "More so than with many other thinkers, an understanding of Kierkegaard involves a significant element of interpretation."[11] This statement opens the door to further

[9] *Ibid.,* p. xxi. (Italics mine.)

[10] We agree with T. H. Croxall who states, in his *Kierkegaard Commentary* (New York, 1956), that "In approaching Kierkegaard, it is essential to recognize that there is a definite and progressive plan in Kierkegaard's authorship, so that it is impossible to rightly understand any particular book unless it is seen in relation to the whole" (p. 1).

[11] George A. Martin, "An Interpretive Principle for Understanding Kierkegaard," (Unpublished doctoral dissertation, University of Notre Dame, 1969), p. 5. Hereafter cited as: Martin, *Principle.*

complications. For little reading is necessary to bring one to the realization that there is very little agreement among Kierkegaard's many interpreters. Thus the question arises as to which of the many styles of
interpretation one ought to adopt.

In his survey of the course of Kierkegaard-research in the Scandinavian
countries, Henriksen describes the three approaches which have dominated:

Of the many viewpoints adopted in the course of time three stand out as simple and
primary, the remainder being derivatives and combinations of them. The three main
points of view group themselves into two pairs of contrasts: opposed to the contention that the study of Søren Kierkegaard should aim at understanding the expression,
the literary form, stands the view that the contents of the production, the thoughts
and ideas, are the central thing. The group of enquirers who study the contents divide
into two formations, one of which maintains that the works should be understood as
parts of the totality of the production, the other, that it is the history of Søren
Kierkegaard's spiritual development which unites the production.[12]

For sake of easy reference, we shall refer to these respectively as the
monistic, the holistic, and the historical viewpoints.

Clearly, the historical viewpoint does not recommend itself to anyone
interested in a philosophical appraisal of Kierkegaard. For even if his
personal life were transparant to us, the task of understanding and evaluat-
ing the philosophical dimension of his writings would still remain.[13]

---

[12] Aage Henriksen, *Methods and Results of Kierkegaard Studies in Scandinavia*
(Copenhagen, 1951), pp. 10-11. Hereafter cited as: Henriksen, *Methods*. Other
discussions of the history of Kierkegaardian research can be found in: Walter
Lowrie, "Translators and Interpreters of Kierkegaard," *Theology Today*, XII (1955),
pp. 312-27; Niels Thulstrup, "Theological and Philosophical Kierkegaardian Studies
in Scandinavia, 1945-53," trans. Paul Holmer, *Theology Today*, XII (1955), pp. 297-
311; Harold A. Durfee, "The Second Stage of Kierkegaardian Scholarship in America," *International Philosophical Quarterly*, III (1963), pp. 121-39; George Price,
The Narrow Pass (London, 1963), pp. 11-32. Price, for example, begins his book
(cited hereafter as: Price, *Pass*) by listing some of the many views which have been
held about Kierkegaard (*Ibid.*, p. 11). While it is instructive to consult this list, it
does not of itself seem to justify Price's conclusion that "Obviously, we need a new
principle of interpretation,..." (*Ibid.*).

[13] Paul Holmer approximates this point in his carefully argued and incisive article,
"On Understanding Kierkegaard," *A Kierkegaard Critique*, ed. Howard A. Johnson
and Niels Thulstrup (New York, 1962), pp. 40-53. Signs point to a growing dis-
content with the various branches of this historical viewpoint. Cf. Paul Sponheim,
Kierkegaard on Christ and Christian Coherence (New York and Evanston, 1968),
pp. 13-7. Hereafter cited as Sponheim, *Coherence*. Cf. also Stephen D. Crites, "The
Author and the Authorship: Recent Kierkegaard Literature," *Journal of the American Academy of Religion*, XXXVIII (1970), pp. 37-54.

The monistic point of view, first adopted by Hermann Diem, stresses the importance of the individual reader's interaction with the individual works. It holds that:

It was in order to arrive at this result: that the person questioned, the reader, should be released from all external authorities and learn to think for himself, that Søren Kierkegaard, adopting a pseudonym, attempted to disappear behind his works in Socratic concealment. The work done to demonstrate the personal element in his production is therefore in conflict with Søren Kierkegaard's express wishes and an obstacle to the right understanding of his work.... We gain no understanding of or profit from Kierkegaard's books by talking of him...[14]

There is much that strikes one as sound about an approach that emphasizes the individual works in their integrity and scrupulously avoids historical and psychological questions. But curiously enough, though the practitioners of this approach can discern a rationale in the use of the pseudonyms, they fail to follow this insight through its logical conclusion by respecting the strictures which Kierkegaard placed on the use of the pseudonymous works.[15] Furthermore, too strong an emphasis on the individual works may prevent one from seeing how they cohere in the service of one ideal.

The virtue of the holists is their sensitivity to the entire authorship and their attempt to find a "totality view" which would integrate the parts:

...this totality view, which can be deduced from the works and described systematically, is the unity behind the multitudinous and varied production, against the background of which apparent inconsistencies in Kierkegaard's thinking, and contradictions between the individual publications, resolve themselves into a harmony.[16]

Each holist, of course, has his own candidate for the proper "totality view." For Price, it is the concept of man;[17] for J. Heywood Thomas, it is the principle of subjectivity;[18] for Gregor Malantschuk, it is the theory of the stages.[19]

Although it would seem that some combination of the monistic and holistic approaches holds the key, Henriksen yet states that "A point of

[14] Henriksen, *Methods*, pp. 11-12.

[15] These strictures will be discussed shortly. Here we simply note that Diem falls in with the practice of quoting from different pseudonymous works, attributing all the thoughts to Kierkegaard. Cf. Hermann Diem, *Kierkegaard's Dialectic of Existence*, trans. Harold Knight (Edinburgh, 1959), *passim*.

[16] Henriksen, *Methods*, p. 12.

[17] Price, *Pass*, p. 11.

[18] J. Heywood Thomas, *Subjectivity and Paradox* (Oxford, 1957), p. 12.

[19] Gregor Malantschuk, *Kierkegaard's Way to the Truth*, trans. Mary Michelsen (Minneapolis, 1963), pp. 21-22. Hereafter cited as: Malantschuk, *Way*.

view which neither violates the totality nor the separate parts does not seem to have been attained by anybody. The core of the authorship has not been penetrated." [20]

It is but one of many anomalies in the history of Kierkegaardian scholarship that although Kierkegaard himself provided the key, it has very rarely been used. One might well say, paraphrasing Chesterton, that Kierkegaard's explanation of his authorship has not been tried and found wanting. It has been found difficult; and left untried.[21] There are, of course, reasons for dismissing Kierkegaard's own views.[22] But in his careful study, Martin seems to have deflated most of them by a careful analysis which indicates that Kierkegaard's own explanation of his authorship is viable.[23] In view of the results of that study, we presume that it is now safe to adopt Kierkegaard's declaration: *"Without authority, to call attention* to religion, to Christianity, is the category for my whole activity as an author, integrally regarded." [24]

In deciding to accept Kierkegaard's own view of his authorship, we make our first commitment. Much work must be done, as Martin points out,[25] before this principle yields an understanding of any particular work. That will soon be our task. But keeping our eye, for the moment, on the whole authorship, we can perhaps best characterize it, using a phrase of Martin's, as a *"pastoral* endeavor." [26] This literary pastorate of

[20] Henriksen, *Methods, p. 10.*

[21] "The Christian ideal has not been tried and found wanting; it has been found difficult; and left untried." G. K. Chesterton, *What's Wrong with the World* (London, New York, Toronto, and Melbourne, 1913), p. 39.

[22] Kierkegaard's own views are found in the following: Søren Kierkegaard, *The Point of View for My Work as an Author,* trans. Walter Lowrie, ed. Benjamin Nelson (New York, 1962); and Søren Kierkegaard, *My Activity as a Writer,* trans. Walter Lowrie, in *The Point of View for My Work as an Author,* ed. Benjamin Nelson (New York, 1962). Hereafter cited respectively as: *POV* and *Activity.* Some of the reasons that have been given for discounting Kierkegaard's views are given by Henriksen (*Methods,* pp. 7-10) who observes, with a typically Kierkegaardian turn of phrase, that whether we accept or reject Kierkegaard's views, we shall regret it (*Ibid.,* p. 10). A recent challenge to the credibility of Kierkegaard's views is to be found in: Frederick Sontag, intro., *On Authority and Revelation* by Søren Kierkegaard, trans. Walter Lowrie (New York, 1966), pp. vii-x. Work hereafter cited as: *Adler.*

[23] Martin, *Principle,* Chapters II, IV, and V. See pp. 189-94 for Martin's critique of Sontag's challenge.

[24] *Activity,* p. 151.

[25] Martin, *Principle,* pp. 216-18.

[26] *Ibid.,* p. 34.

Kierkegaard's may be seen as dividing into three distinct but related phases.[27]

To the first phase of his authorship [28] belong all the published writings bounded, on one side, by *Either-Or* (published in 1843) and, on the other, by the *Postscript* (published in 1846).[29] The dominant motif in these writings (and we take this to apply to the acknowledged no less than to the pseudonymous works) is the problem of becoming a Christian. Kierkegaard supports this understanding of the works of this period when he says, referring to them, that "The problem itself is a problem of reflection: to become a Christian... when one is a Christian of a sort." [30]

The second phase of the authorship, which takes in all of the writings from the *Edifiying Discourses in Various Spirits* (published in 1847) to *For Self-Examination* (published in 1851), explores a question which is distinct from, though related to, that of the first phase, *viz*: What does it mean to exist as a Christian? [31] Again here we find both pseudonymous and acknowledged writings. But the edifying discourse is replaced by the Christian discourse, and Johannes Climacus (the pseudonymous author of the *Postscript*) yields to Anti-Climacus (the pseudonymous author of *The Sickness Unto Death* and *Training in Christianity*).

To the third and final phase belong the writings of the last two years of his life, most of them newspaper articles. In these, we find Kierkegaard protesting against the spiritless Christendom he sees about him and

---

[27] The overview which we here describe accords roughly with Kierkegaard's own (incomplete) description in *POV* and *Activity*.

[28] It may be noted here that there is some difficulty in giving a precise sense to the term "authorship"; that is, in elucidating it so as to include the important works while excluding those of less significance. For some of the important works (for example, the *Point of View* and *Adler*) were never published by Kierkegaard. But this is likewise true of a work like *Johannes Climacus or, De Omnibus Dubitandum Est*, which is of secondary importance at best. Kierkegaard displays some ingenuity in his discussion of some of the works and how they relate to the authorship, distinguishing, for example, between the works he produced *qua* critic and those produced *qua* author (*Activity*, p. 148); and between those works belonging "to" rather than "in" the authorship (*Ibid.*, p. 142). The difficulty is easily enough solved by simply using the term so as to include *everything*. Cf. George E. Argaugh and George B. Arbaugh, *Kierkegaard's Authorship* (London, 1968). Martin's approach (*Principle*, pp. 100-32 and 168-73) seems better.

[29] As the very title suggests, Kierkegaard intended to end his literary endeavors at this point and become ordained. Cf. Walter Lowrie, *Kierkegaard* (New York, 1962), pp. 366-69.

[30] *POV.*, p. 43.

[31] Thus Kierkegaard says that with the *Postscript* "began the transition to the series of purely religious writings" (*POV*, p. 53).

heaping scorn on an ecclesiastical establishment which has failed, in his judgment, to live up to the Christian ideal.

This completes our brief survey of the authorship as a whole. Without claiming that its development was clear to Kierkegaard from the beginning,[32] we can still acknowledge that there is continuity and that each of its phases can be understood as making a contribution to the author's declared purpose of calling attention to Christianity.

Having dealt briefly then with the authorship *in toto*, we now narrow the focus and return to the writings of the first phase, among which the *Postscript* is to be found. As previously noted, the works of this period have in sight the problem of becoming a Christian. In particular, they describe two paths which may be taken:

> The *Concluding Postscript* constitutes, as I have already said, the turning-point in my whole work as an author. It presents the 'Problem', that of becoming a Christian. Having appropriated the whole pseudonymous, aesthetic work as the description of *one* way a person may take to become a Christian (viz. *away* from the aesthetical in order to become a Christian), it undertakes to describe the other way (viz. *away* from the System, from speculation, etc., in order to become a Christian).[33]

From this text, one must conclude that Kierkegaard believes that the pseudonymous works of this phase provide an exhaustive analysis of the problem of becoming a Christian.[34] But having said this, we must once again narrow our focus, this time from the writings of the first phase to the *Postscript* and the path which leads from speculation, from philosophy to Christianity.

In doing so, we encounter a difficulty. Almost all interpretations of the *Postscript* share one trait—they all ascribe this work to Kierkegaard. Thus Warnock writes that "It is the myth of objective truth which Kierkegaard above all wanted to explode. Hence was derived his hostility to science; for his *Concluding Unscientific Postscript* is not so much unscientific as anti-scientific." [35] Yet the title-page of the *Postscript* lists

---

[32] Not only does Kierkegaard acknowledge the role played by Providence (*POV*, Chapter III), he admits that "I now understand the whole in such a way, that I myself by no means have so surveyed the whole from the beginning,..." X[3] A 258; cited in Sponheim, *Coherence*, p. 33, note 96. Cf. also X[5] B 145.

[33] *POV.*, pp. 41-2.

[34] In our view, Kierkegaard is not quite so modest as Martin thinks (*Principle*, p. 134).

[35] Warnock, *Ethics*, p. 7. Two apparent exceptions to this are: Herbert M. Garelick, *The Anti-Christianity of Kierkegaard* (The Hague, 1965) and Henry E. Allison, "Christianity and Nonsense," *Review of Metaphysics*, XX (1967), pp. 432-60. The last-mentioned article cited hereafter as: Allison, *Nonsense*.

the author as Johannes Climacus, though Kierkegaard adds his name as one "responsible for publication." The *Postscript* is a pseudonymous work.[36]

In a note attached to the *Postscript*, Kierkegaard acknowledges that he is "the author, as people would call it," [37] of the pseudonymous works. But he adds that "in the pseudonymous works there is not a single word which is mine" [38] and addresses a plea to his reader: "My wish, my prayer is that, if it might occur to anyone to quote a particular saying from the books, he would do me the favor to cite the name of the respective pseudonymous author...." [39]

Clearly, then, Kierkegaard wished us to exercise restraint in quoting from and interpreting the pseudonymous works. In this study, we shall abide by these strictures and from this point on, with few exceptions shall make no claims about Kierkegaard. This constitutes our second interpretive assumption and its import needs to be made clear.

In the first place, it means that we shall be studying Climacus' treatment of existence; or, if one prefers, the treatment of existence in the *Concluding Unscientific Postscript*—not "Kierkegaard's" concept of existence. In effect, we are giving Kierkegaard the benefit of the doubt in attributing the *Postscript* to Johannes Climacus. This is a decision which, frankly, seems to us long overdue in the history of Kierkegaard-research. Perhaps for the first time, an investigation of an important concept (existence) in a pivotal work (the *Postscript*) is being carried out using

---

[36] Discussions of the problem of pseudonymity in Kierkegaard's writings are abundant. The reader should consult first Kierkegaard's own statements in *Point of View, Activity* and the note at the end of the *Postscript*. In addition, we mention the now-classic discussions of the problem itself and Kierkegaard's explanations in Lowrie, *Kierkegaard*, pp. 286-90; and in Henriksen, *Methods*, pp. 8-10. Collins (*Mind*, pp. 34-42) and Price (*Pass*, pp. 14-32) both discuss at length the motives which may have led Kierkegaard to adopt pseudonyms. Also worth consulting is Sponheim, *Coherence*, pp. 28-43. Martin's views (*Principle*, pp. 54-59) most closely parallel our own.

Climacus, too, has some views about the pseudonyms (*Post.*, 255-66). Two of his remarks are worth noting. He mentions that "The pseudonymous works are generally ascribed to a single origin,..." (*Ibid.*, p. 241); and apparently includes himself among the pseudonymous authors when he states that "...people could not persuade themselves that the pseudonymous authors, including myself, Johannes Climacus,..." (*Ibid.*, p. 249).

[37] *Post.*, "A First and Last Declaration," signed by S. Kierkegaard and unpaged (at his request), p. 551. Hereafter cited as: *Declaration.*

[38] *Ibid.*

[39] *Ibid.*, p. 552.

the frame of reference suggested by Kierkegaard himself (referring the work to the pseudonym). Such a study will necessarily lack the scope of others which refer now to this work, now to that, attributing all the texts to "Kierkegaard." It is our hope that what is lost in scope will be recovered in accuracy and intelligibility.

Now it is possible, of course, that our assumption is gratuitous and that no significant differences exist between Søren Kierkegaard and Johannes Climacus. But certainly this claim cannot reasonably be made a priori, though this seems to have been the practice in most Kierkegaard-research. If such a claim is to be justified, it will have to be on the basis of studies like this one. For it will only be when we know what Climacus thinks about such-and-such that we will be able to compare his point of view with Kierkegaard's. Until such results are available, the practice of attributing the *Postscript* to Kierkegaard must be regarded as uncritical. (The same argument can be made, *mutatis mutandis,* in connection with the other pseudonymous works.) For it is based on the *assumption* that Kierkegaard's strictures may be safely disregarded. Our study is also based on an assumption. Not only does our assumption seem to us more reasonable, but it has the virtue of being open and declared.[40]

Our decision to interpret the *Postscript* as the work of Climacus has a second consequence. For although we have heard Kierkegaard's views about this work, we have not yet heard from the author. Our decision suggests that we allow Climacus the rights that are usually associated with being an author and permit him to state how and why he wrote this work. The story is related in consecutive chapters of the *Postscript* [41] and may be capsulized as follows.

One Sunday afternoon, while sitting idly on a bench outside a cemetery, Climacus inadvertently found himself an unseen witness to a scene between an elderly gentleman and his young grandson. (He would have

---

[40] Kierkegaard's own view that the words of the pseudonymous authors are not his own has been substantiated, at least from a literary and stylistic point of view. Cf. Alastair McKinnon, "Kierkegaard's Pseudonyms: A New Hierarchy," *American Philosophical Quarterly,* VI (1969), pp. 116-26. "..., all our evidence shows that the pseudonymous selections are quite unlike the acknowledged ones and, equally important, quite distinct from one another... Indeed, [these results] show that each pseudonym is, as Kierkegaard said, a distinct literary personality. They show that Kierkegaard's warnings concerning his authorship are entirely justified and that there can no longer be any excuse for not taking them seriously." *Ibid.,* pp. 120-21. This result is likewise confirmed by Martin's ranking procedure. Cf. Martin, *Principle,* Chapter III.

[41] *Post.,* pp. 164-67, 210-16.

left immediately, Climacus tells us, but for his belief that the disturbance which his departure might have caused would have proven the more embarrassing.) The two have come to the gravesite of the man who was the son of the elderly gentleman and the young boy's father. Expressing his grief that his young grandson is without an earthly father, the old man assures the boy that he has a Father in Heaven. Then:

He told him that there was a wisdom which tried to fly beyond faith, that on the other side of faith there was a wide stretch of country, like blue mountains, an illusory land, which to a mortal eye might appear to yield a certainty higher than that of faith; but the believer feared this mirage...; that it was an illusion of eternity in which a mortal cannot live, but only lose his faith when he permits his gaze to be fascinated by the sight. He fell silent, and then once more spoke half aloud to himself: "Alas, that my unhappy son should have permitted himself to be deceived! To what end all his learning, which made it impossible for him to explain himself to me, so that I could not even speak to him about his error, because it was too high for me!" [42]

The scene ends with the grandfather's plea to the young boy to hold fast to his faith and not allow himself to be deceived as his father before him had been.

On a previous Sunday two months prior to this scene, Climacus had resolved to make something of his life, to make a contribution to humanity. That idle resolve, he tells us, found a focus as a result of his having witnessed this scene:

Fundamentally, I had understood the old gentleman at once, for my studies had in many ways led me to take note of *a dubious relationship between a modern Christian speculation and Christianity,* but the matter had not in any decisive manner enlisted my interest. Now it was invested with its own proper significance. The venerable old man with his faith seemed to be an individual with an absolutely justified grievance, a man whom existence had mistreated, because a modern speculation, like a change in the currency, had made property values in the realm of faith insecure. His sorrow over the loss of his son, not only by death, but as he understood it, still more terribly through speculative philosophy, moved me profoundly; while the contra-diction in his position, that he could not even explain how the enemy had conducted the campaign, became for me a decisive challenge to trace out a definite clue. The entire matter appealed to me as a very complicated criminal case, where the criss-crossing of many trails made it difficult to find the truth. This was something for me. And I thought to myself: "You are now tired of life's diversions, you are tired of the maidens, whom you love only in passing; you must have something fully to occupy your time. Here it is: *to discover where the misunderstanding lies between speculative philosophy and Christianity."* [43]

---

[42] *Ibid.,* p. 213.
[43] *Ibid.,* pp. 215-16. (Italics mine.)

His studies had already prepared him for his investigation. And whenever he felt the temptation to transform his researches into "an erudite learning," the figure of the old gentleman flashed before his mind [44] —a reminder that the problem has its roots in "life's *casibus*" rather than in philosophical or theological journals.

We come, finally, to the text which we take to be *fundamental* for a proper understanding of the *Postscript*. Climacus says that:

> Chiefly I sought by reflection to trace the misunderstanding to its roots. My many failures, I need not here recite, but finally it became clear to me that the misdirection of speculative philosophy and its consequent assumed justification for reducing faith to the status of a relative moment could not be anything accidental, but must be rooted deeply in the entire tendency of the age. *It must, in short, be rooted in the fact that on account of our vastly increased knowledge, men had forgotten what it means to exist, and what inwardness signifies.*[45]

This text contains two important claims. First, Climacus claims that the relationship between Christianity and speculative philosophy is based upon a misunderstanding. Secondly, he claims that this misunderstanding is rooted in the fact that men have forgotten what it means to *exist*. This forgetting-claim (as we shall hereafter refer to it) emerges then as bedrock in Climacus' investigation into the misunderstanding between Christianity and philosophy. Our analysis thus suggests that no study of Climacus' treatment of existence can be satisfactory unless it accords primacy to the forgetting-claim. The aim of our study may now be stated more precisely. We shall be attempting to understand, first, the sense of "exist" operative in the forgetting-claim;[46] and, secondly, the forgetting-claim itself.[47] In order to have a better insight into the precise nature of the "dubious relationship" which the forgetting-claim seeks to explain, we turn next to the *Philosophical Fragments*.[48]

---

[44] *Ibid.*, p. 216. ⟨ 242

[45] *Ibid.* (Italics mine, except in the last sentence. "Exist" and "inwardness" are both underlined in the original.)

[46] The fact that Climacus italicizes the word signifies that he attaches a special significance to it.

[47] The fact that the relevant sense of "exist" is such that men can be said to have forgotten what it means to exist contains an important clue as to the kind of treatment of existence that the reader of the *Postscript* may expect. More of this in Chapter III.

[48] Søren Kierkegaard, *Philosophical Fragments or a Fragment of Philosophy*, 2nd ed., trans. and intro. David F. Swenson, new intro. and commentary Niels Thulstrup, trans. revised and commentary trans. Howard V. Hong (Princeton, 1962). Work hereafter cited as: *Frag.* Swenson's introduction hereafter cited as: Swenson,

C. THE PHILOSOPHICAL FRAGMENTS

The relationship between philosophy and Christianity, between reason and faith, is problematic for the entire modern tradition from Descartes to Hegel. To appreciate the place of the *Fragments* in this tradition would require us to discuss in depth:

(1) The assumptions that Descartes makes about Christianity and becoming a Christian when he states that:

..., it certainly does not seem possible ever to persuade infidels of any religion... unless to begin with, we prove these two facts that the human soul does not perish with the body, and that God exists by means of natural reason.[49]

(2) The presuppositions of and arguments in John Locke's *On the Reasonableness of Christianity as Delivered in Scriptures* (1695), John Toland's *Christianity not Mysterious* (1702), and Matthew Tindal's *Christianity as Old as the Creation* (1730).

(3) Leibniz's attempts to justify the ways of God to men in his *Theodicy,* in which he states:

Likewise concerning the origin of evil in its relation to God, I shall offer a vindication of his perfections that shall extol not less his holiness, his justice and his goodness than his greatness, his power and his independence.... Most important of all, however, I show that it has been possible for God to permit sin and misery, and even to co-operate therein and promote it, without detriment to his holiness and goodness: although, generally speaking, he could have avoided all these evils.[50]

(4) The traditional apologetic, which attempted to prove the truth of Christianity by demonstrating that Jesus Christ fulfilled the Old Testament prophecies, that he worked miracles, and that the expansion of the early Church was miraculous.[51]

(5) Lessing's belief that his historical distance from Jesus Christ puts him at a disadvantage with respect to becoming a disciple.[52]

Introduction. Thulstrup's introduction and commentary cited respectively as: Thulstrup, *Introduction,* and Thulstrup, *Commentary.*

[49] Rene Descartes, *Meditations on First Philosophy,* trans. Elizabeth S. Haldane and G. R. T. Ross, in *The Philosophical Works of Descartes* (New York, 1955), I, p. 133.

[50] Gottfried Wilhelm von Leibniz, *Theodicy,* trans. E. M. Huggard, ed. and intro. Austin Farrer (London, 1951), p. 61.

[51] Cf. Henry Chadwick, intro., *Lessing's Theological Writings,* trans. Henry Chadwick (London, 1956), p. 10 and pp. 34-36. Hereafter cited as: Chadwick, *Introduction.*

[52] Gotthold Ephraim Lessing, *On the Proof of the Spirit and of Power,* trans.

(6) Hegel's view, in the words of Thulstrup, that:

... religion in its highest form, Christianity, and philosophy in its highest form, Hegel's own Speculative Idealism, have the same content, only that it appears in different forms, in the lower, imperfect, representational form of religion and in the higher, perfect adequate conceptual form of Speculative Idealism.[53]

We would, in short, find ourselves in the very situation described by Climacus in the *Fragments:*

The monks never finish telling the history of the world because they always begin with creation; if in dealing with the relations between philosophy and Christianity we begin by first recounting what has previously been said, how will it ever be possible—not to finish but to begin, ...[54]

Climacus appears to have solved this dilemma in his *Fragments* by posing three questions on the title-page:

Is an historical point of departure possible for an eternal consciousness; how can such a point of departure have any other than a merely historical interest; is it possible to base an eternal happiness upon historical knowledge?[55]

Why did Climacus choose to begin with these questions?

In the first draft of the work (*Pap.* V B I) the problem is formulated in this way: "How do I arrive at an historical point of departure for my eternal consciousness; how can such a point of departure have more than historical interest?" This is explained further (*Pap.* V B I, 2): "*This is and remains the main problem with respect to the relationship between Christianity and philosophy. Lessing is the only one who has deal with this.* But Lessing knew considerably more what the issue is about than the common herd of modern philosophers."[56]

Instead of attempting to relate its entire history, Climacus seems to have thought that this trio of questions would focus attention on "... the main problem... between Christianity and philosophy." Lessing helped to crystallize his judgment as to "just what the issue is about."[57]

If we were to proceed to a detailed historical exposition of the six issues raised in the above paragraphs, "how would it ever be possible...

Henry Chadwick, *Lessing's Theological Writings* (London, 1956), pp. 51-2. Hereafter cited as: Lessing, *Proof.*

[53] Thulstrup, *Introduction,* p. 1v.

[54] *Frag.,* p. 138.

[55] *Ibid.,* p. iii.

[56] Thulstrup, *Commentary,* p. 149. (Italics mine.)

[57] On Kierkegaard's knowledge of Lessing's works, see Thulstrup, *Commentary,* pp. 149-52.

to begin" with the work of Climacus? On the other hand, we cannot abstract altogether from the historical context. Suppose, however, that we were to limit our historical exposition to the immediate background of the *Fragments*. If we understood just what Climacus thinks "the main problem" is between Christianity and philosophy, and how the work of Lessing figured in his thinking, then it seems that we would have an understanding of the historical situation sufficient for the purpose of this study.[58]

It is best to begin in 1754—the year in which Hermann Samuel Reimarus, a professor of Oriental languages in Hamburg, published his *Treatise on the Foremost Truths of Natural Religion*.[59] In this work, Reimarus presents natural religion as a clear and sufficient body of knowledge about Nature, the purpose of God, and the eternal destiny of man. For Reimarus (as for many of his predecessors in the Enlightenment) Creation itself is the only miracle and Nature the only revelation. Next to this natural revelation, any "positive" revelation is at best superfluous.

Reimarus put these ideas to work in a monumental work to which he gave the title, *Apology for the Rational Worshippers of God*.[60] Using his linguistic and critical acumen, he attempts to show that many Scriptural accounts are unreliable. More important for later theological investigation, Reimarus argues that Jesus Christ did not intend to found

[58] For a more comprehensive view of the historical and intellectual background of the *Fragments*, the reader may consult Thulstrup, *Introduction*, pp. xlvi-lx, for the essential leads. Cf. also Walter Ruttenbeck, *Søren Kierkegaard: Der Christliche Denker und sein Werk* (Berlin and Frankfurt, 1929), pp. 42-100. For an understanding of the theological situation in Denmark during Kierkegaard's student years, cf. Torsten Bohlin, *Kierkegaards dogmatische Anschauung* (Gütersloh, 1927), Chapter I. In English, very helpful historical discussions can be found in J. Heywood Thomas, *Subjectivity and Paradox* (Oxford, 1957), Chapter II; and T. H. Croxall, intro. *Johannes Climacus or, De Omnibus Dubitandum Est* by Søren Kierkegaard, trans. T. H. Croxall (London, 1958), pp. 15-54.

[59] Our account of the background to Lessing's work is based primarily upon Henry E. Allison's informative work, *Lessing and the Enlightenment* (Ann Arbor, 1966), Chapters I and III. Hereafter this work is cited as: Allison, *Lessing*. To a lesser extent, we have also drawn upon Chadwick, *Introduction*.

[60] The complete text of this work has never been published in English. Most accounts of Reimarus' thought are based upon David Friedrich Strauss, *Hermann Samuel Reimarus, und sein Schutzschrift für die vernunftigen Verehrer Gottes* (1862). In English, in addition to Allison's discussion, we have Rev. Charles Voysey, trans. and ed., *Fragments from Reimarus* (London and Edinburgh, 1879).

a new religion.[61] But before he could ready his manuscript for publication, Reimarus died.

In 1766, on a visit to Hamburg, Lessing had met Reimarus and his family. Upon his death, Reimarus' daughter Elise passed the manuscript on to Lessing who was then the chief librarian at the Duke of Brunswick's library. Although he immediately recognized the importance of Reimarus' work, Lessing judged that both its size and content made it impossible for the work to be published in its entirety. He decided rather to publish the work anonymously in his series of *Contributions to Literature and History from the Ducal Library at Wolfenbüttel.* Claiming that he had been unable to discover how or when the material had come into the library, Lessing published parts of the manuscript—along with his own "Editor's Counter-propositions"—over a five-year period under the title, *Fragments of an Unnamed.*

The first fragment, published in 1774, attracted no attention. But the five fragments issued in 1777 provoked a furious and many-sided controversy which found Lessing's "counter-propositions" even more in dispute than the fragments themselves. The five fragments of that year had one common theme: Scripture is not reliable. In his counter-propositions, however, Lessing asked:

But what are this man's hypotheses, explanations, and proofs to the Christian? To him this Christianity, which he feels to be true and in which he feels so blessed, exists forever. When the paralytic experiences the beneficial shocks of the electric sparks, what does he care whether Nollet, or Franklin, or neither of them, is right?[62]

Lessing's point is clear. The Christian has nothing at all to fear from the attacks of the unnamed author. He has his own certainty. Both the unnamed author and his attackers have confused the Bible with religion, the letter with the spirit:

The letter is not the spirit and the Bible is not religion. Hence objections to the letter and the Bible are not likewise objections to the spirit and religion.

For the Bible obviously contains more than belongs to religion and it is a mere hypothesis that it must be equally infallible in these extras. Moreover, religion existed before the Bible.... The religion is not true because the evangelists and apostles taught it, but they taught it because it is true. The written traditions must be explained according to their inner truth, and no written tradition can give it any inner truth if it has none.[63]

---

[61] Cf. Albert Schweitzer's assessment of Reimarus in his famous work, *The Quest of the Historical Jesus,* trans. W. Montgomery (New York, 1957), Chapter II.

[62] Gotthold Ephraim Lessing, *Gesammelte Werke,* ed. Paul Rilla (Berlin, 1956), VII, pp. 812-13, cited in Allison, *Lessing,* p. 95.

[63] Lessing, *Gesammelte Werke,* VII, p. 813, cited in Allison, *Lessing,* pp. 95-96.

Allison's comment on this passage is pertinent:

This, Lessing suggests, is the attitude one may assume even if Reimarus' objections are unanswerable, that is, even if the factual claims of the Christian religion are insupportable and the Biblical accounts of these alleged facts hopelessly contradictory. In short, this is the standpoint from which Christianity may be appreciated irrespective of its historical foundation. *Thus, for the first time in the eighteenth century the question of the facticity of the Christian revelation was held to be irrelevant for the truth of the Christian religion.*[64]

One of the first to take issue with Lessing was J.D. Schumann, the director of the Hannover Lyceum, who issued a pamphlet entitled *On the Evidence for the Proofs of the Truth of the Christian Religion.* Schumann here defends the orthodox theory of the verbal infallibility of Scripture. Referring to Origen's *Contra Celsum,* Schumann reaffirms the traditional apologetical arguments for the truth of the Christian religion: that Jesus worked miracles and fulfilled prophecies, and that the expansion of the early Church was miraculous.[65]

Lessing replied to Schumann in 1778 in his *On the Proof of the Spirit and of Power.* Lessing begins his work by distinguishing between prophecies whose fulfillment one experiences oneself and those which one knows of only from the testimony of others:

If I had lived at the time of Christ, then of course the prophecies fulfilled in his person would have made me pay great attention to him. If I had actually seen him do miracles; if I had had no cause to doubt that these were true miracles; then in a worker of miracles who had been marked out so long before, I would have gained so much confidence that I would have submitted my intellect to his, and I would have believed him in all things in which equally indisputable experiences did not tell against him.[66]

But eighteen century's have intervened between Lessing and Christ. Even if the reports in Scripture were as reliable as any historical reports could possibly be, why are they treated by some as if they were infinitely more reliable? For those who advance the traditional historical arguments for the truth of the Christian faith are in fact proposing that one stake one's eternal destiny on these historical matters. Lessing refuses the gambit in these words:

... *accidental truths of history can never become the proof of necessary truths of reason.*[67]

[64] Allison, *Lessing,* p. 96.
[65] *Ibid.,* p. 101.
[66] Lessing, *Proof,* pp. 51-52.
[67] *Ibid.,* p. 53. It was this saying of Lessing's that seems to have inspired the trio of questions on the title page of the *Fragments.*

Where one's eternal destiny is at stake, Lessing maintains, nothing less than necessary truth suffices.

Lessing continues:

… What does it mean to accept an historical proposition as true? to believe an historical truth? Does it mean anything other than this: to accept this proposition, this truth as valid? to accept that there is no objection to be brought against it? to accept that one historical proposition is built upon one thing, another on another, that from one historical truth another follows? to reserve to oneself the right to estimate other historical things accordingly? Does it mean anything other than this? Anything more? [68]

Both the traditional apologetical arguments and Reimarus' critique of them assume that, with respect to one particular class of historical proposition (those in Scripture), something more than this is implied by accepting them as true. Both hold that the acceptance or rejection of certain historical facts can be the basis for the acceptance or rejection of Christianity. But Christianity claims to have decisive significance for the individual's eternal destiny. Thus it would seem that an historical proposition can have more than simply historical consequences.

Lessing balks at this thought. We all believe, says Lessing, that Alexander the Great conquered Asia. This fact is probably as reliable as any historical fact could be:

But who, on the basis of this belief, would risk anything of great, permanent worth, the loss of which would be irreparable? Who, in consequence of this belief, would forswear forever all knowledge that conflicted with this belief? Certainly not I.[69]

It is not unlikely that the "something" of great worth which Lessing refers to here is his own eternal destiny. Lessing stubbornly refuses to base this destiny on anything merely historical, especially when this "historical fact" is—as we shall see—repugnant to his intellect.

Lessing continues:

If on historical grounds I have no objection to the statement that Christ raised to life a dead man; must I therefore accept it as true that God has a Son who is of the same essence as himself? [70]

The former is a statement of historical fact which Lessing is willing to accept as true. But the second proposition is no mere historical fact:

---

[68] *Ibid.*, pp. 53-54.
[69] *Ibid.*, p. 54.
[70] *Ibid.*

What is the connection between my inability to raise any significant objection to the evidence of the former and *my obligation to believe something against which my reason rebels?* [71]

Let us pause here to notice two points which might have attracted Climacus' attention. First, Lessing has called attention to the "subjective" element in this debate. The disputants have, in a sense, asked *him* to stake *his* eternal destiny on the result of an historical investigation. Second, Lessing's intellect rebels against the thought that an eternal God could have a Son who was a human being.[72] Climacus' own discussion of Christianity will give a prominent role to subjectivity and to the paradox of the God-man.

We return to Lessing:

That the Christ, against whose resurrection I can raise no important historical objection, therefore declared himself to be the Son of God; that his disciples therefore believed him to be such; this I gladly believe from my heart. For these truths, as truths of one and the same class, follow quite naturally on one another.
But to jump with that historical truth to a quite different class of truths, and to demand of me that I should form all my metaphysical and moral ideas accordingly; to expect me to alter my fundamental ideas of the Godhead because I cannot set any credible testimony against the resurrection of Christ: if that is not a μετάβασις εἰς ἄλλο γένος, then I do not know what Aristotle meant by this phrase.[73]

Lessing willingly grants everything that the traditional apologetic seeks to establish. He concedes the reliability of Scripture. Yet he refuses to allow such a concession to alter his "metaphysical and moral ideas"— his eternal destiny. Where upholders of the traditional apologetic see a smooth transition, Lessing can see only a ditch:

This, then, is the ugly, broad ditch which I cannot get across, however often and however earnestly I have tried to make the *leap*. If anyone can help me over it, let him do it, I beg him, I adjure him. He will deserve a divine reward from me.[74]

We leave Lessing, standing at the edge of this "ugly, broad ditch," and unable to make the leap. For we have reached the point of contact between Lessing and Climacus.

---

[71] *Ibid.* (Italics mine.)

[72] A later tradition, operating with a fortified concept of Reason, will come to see in the historical the very embodiment of intelligibility and necessity. Hence Lessing's objection will be overruled. The situation which results, however, is the one that Climacus will label a "forgetting."

[73] Lessing, *Proof*, p. 54.

[74] *Ibid.*, p. 55.

With an eye to what Lessing has stated in his *Proof,* Climacus claims that "Lessing opposes what I would call an attempt to create a *quantitative transition to a qualitative decision.* He attacks the direct transition from historical trustworthiness to the determination of an eternal happiness."[75] By a "quantitative transition," Climacus means the kind of conclusion or consequence that results from an historical investigation. Such investigation typically yields *more* knowledge, *greater* accuracy, etc. By a "qualitative decision," he means a decision which would result in a significant or drastic change in the life of an individual human being. The decision to become a Christian would be one example of a "qualitative decision"— in Climacus' view. Lessing "opposes" the attempt to create a quantitative transition to such a decision by insisting, as we have seen, that there is a "ditch" between historical knowledge and *his deepest beliefs* about God and himself. The ditch cannot be filled in by stockpiling historical arguments about the reliability of Scripture or by establishing that Jesus worked miracles and fulfilled prophecies. To understand the role played by Lessing's opposition in Climacus' analysis of the misunderstanding between Christianity and philosophy, we must turn next to a brief consideration of the *Fragments.*

In the *Fragments,* Climacus takes Socrates and Socratic thought as representative of the standpoint of speculative philosophy. He begins with a description of the Socratic teaching about Truth.[76] The doctrine of recollection is interpreted as an affirmation of the view that the Truth is always within the individual. For this reason, Socrates held that the maieutic relationship was the correct one between man and man. "From the standpoint of the Socratic thought, every point of departure in time is *eo ipso* accidental, an occasion, a vanishing moment. The teacher himself is no more than this;..."[77] The description of the Socratic viewpoint reaches the conclusion that:

... the underlying principle of all questioning is that the one who is asked must have the Truth in himself, and be able to acquire it by himself. The temporal point of departure is nothing; for as soon as I discover that I have known the Truth from eternity without being aware of it, the same instant this moment of occasion is hidden in the Eternal, and so incorporated with it that I cannot even find it so

---

[75] *Post.,* p. 88. (Italics mine.)

[76] Climacus does not spell out what he means by "Truth." The fact that he capitalizes the term throughout suggests, however, that he is not thinking about scientific or historical truth; but rather about "the essential truth about man." The meaning of the latter phrase is clarified in the *Postscript* (pp. 169-86).

[77] *Frag.,* p. 13.

to speak, even if I sought it; because in my eternal consciousness there is neither here nor there, but only an *ubique et nusquam*.[78]

Having thus delineated the essentials of the Socratic point of view, Climacus next develops an hypothesis which is contrary to the Socratic view at every point:

Now if things are to be otherwise, the Moment in time must have a decisive significance, so that I will never be able to forget it either in time or eternity; because the Eternal, which hitherto did not exist, came into existence in this moment.[79]

We cannot here trace the dialectical development of this alternative hypothesis. But implicitly throughout the book and explicitly at its conclusion, this hypothesis is identified with Christianity.

On the title-page, it was asked whether there could be an historical point of departure for an eternal happiness. From the Socratic point of view, the answer must be "No." But from the point of view of the hypothesis developed in contrast to the Socratic, the answer is, paradoxically, "Yes." As we have just said, the content of the hypothesis is Christianity—though it has been stripped of its terminology and its historical costume:

That an eternal happiness is decided in time through the relationship to something historical was the content of my experiment [the hypothesis in the *Fragments*], and what I now call Christianity. I scarcely suppose that anyone will deny that it is the Christian teaching in the New Testament that the eternal happiness of the individual is decided in time, and is decided through the relationship to Christianity as something historical.[80]

We can now state Climacus' view as to the nature of the "dubious relationship" between Christianity and speculative philosophy.

If the analysis of the *Fragments* is correct, it is a mistake to think that either historical or philosophical reflection can play a decisive role in the decision to become a Christian:

Even the longest of introductions cannot bring the individual a single step nearer to the absolute decision. For if it could, the decision would not be absolute, would not be a qualitative leap, and the individual would be deceived instead of helped. But the fact that the introduction does not even in its maximum bring anyone a single step nearer, is again an expression for its inevitably repellent character. Philosophy offers an immediate introduction to Christianity, and so do the historical and rhetorical introductions.[81]

---

[78] *Ibid.*, pp. 15-16.
[79] *Ibid.*, p. 16.
[80] *Post.*, p. 330.
[81] *Ibid.*, p. 343.

Lessing, by his stubborn refusal to be moved by any "immediate introduction," brings to the fore "the issue" between Christianity and speculative philosophy.[82] Neither Lessing nor speculative philosophy can acknowledge a Moment which is decisive for the eternal happiness of the individual. The failure to notice this decisive difference with respect to "the
historical" is the basis of the misunderstanding between modern Christian
speculation and Christianity.

For the modern tradition has assumed that a quantitative transition to
Christianity is possible. Various forms of this assumption seem to be
discernible in each of the six points listed on pages 14 and 15. The
Fragments opposes this common assumption as well as the individual
expressions of it. Against (6), the *Fragments* contends that Christianity
and philosophy cannot be said to have the same content.[83] Against (5),
the *Fragments* shows that becoming a disciple of the Teacher (i.e., Jesus
Christ) is equally difficult for the contemporary disciple and the disciple
at second hand.[84] Against (4), it is seen that not having doubts about
what the Teacher did is not the same thing as becoming his disciple.[85]

---

[82] Our view of Lessing's influence on Climacus' thought thus differs in important
respects from that of Richard Campbell, "Lessing's Problem and Kierkegaard's
Answer," in Gill, *Essays*, pp. 74-89. According to Campbell, the significance of
Lessing's work for Climacus or Kierkegaard (Campbell is ambivalent) is that it
pointed out a logical gap between historical and theological assertions (*Ibid.*, pp.
80-82). Climacus' "sheer leap of faith" (*Ibid.*, p. 78) is, for Campbell, an attempt
to bridge that gap. He then argues that Lessing's logical gap is an outgrowth of his
rationalism (*Ibid.*, p. 82). If theological assertions are not identified with necessary
truths of reason, the gap disappears and no Kierkegaardian "leap of faith" is needed
(*Ibid.*, p. 83).
It seems to us that Campbell has not understood the way in which Lessing
influenced Climacus. What Lessing's ditch signifies to the author of the *Fragments*
is not so much the difference between theological and historical assertions as the
irreconcilable differences between Christianity and philosophy with respect to "the
historical," the Moment. Nor is the doctrine of a "sheer leap of faith" to be found
in the *Fragments,* which mentions "leap" just once (*Frag.*, p. 53) in a different
connection and which denies that faith is an act of the will (*Ibid.*, p. 77). Campbell's
mistake is his assumption that the matrix shared by Lessing and Climacus was a
theological one. The problem for Climacus is *not* the justification of theological
statements. It is rather to understand what had gone wrong in the relationship
between philosophy and Christianity. Lessing helped him to understand the differences between the two and hence helped in the solution.
[83] *Frag.*, pp. 137-38.
[84] *Ibid.*, p. 134.
[85] *Ibid.*, pp. 68-81.

Against (3), the *Fragments* insists that God is the Unknown.[86] Against (2), Climacus' analysis shows that Christianity involves the Absolute Paradox of the God-man and that any attempt to remove the Paradox and make Christianity "reasonable" is mistaken. It can succeed only by changing Christianity into something else.[87] Against (1), the *Fragments* suggests that no proof can transform a non-believer into a believer.[88]

Although the *Fragments* has characterized the misunderstanding between philosophy and Christianity, it does not analyze its *source*. Looking ahead to the explanation offered in the *Postscript,* we shall here allude briefly to a general attitude toward the concept of miracle. Lessing, for example, does not deny that miracles are possible, though he is inclined to delimit sharply the credibility of their actual occurrence.[89] He shares the general attitude of the time that the supernatural is an hypothesis which ought not be readily invoked. Miracles and prophecy, once heavy artillery in the apologist's arsenal, have become a most embarrassing asset. Chadwick comments on this about-face:

What underlies this is the growing feeling that the world can be explained from within itself; it is a closed system, and the supernatural is an unnecessary or even dangerous hypothesis. For long centuries Christian apologists had talked as if God were virtually another name for the sum of hitherto undiscovered knowledge; as if religion were merely a matter of "filling in logical gaps with devotional material"; as if it were some consolation to believers that the Fellow of the Royal Society had not yet explained everything, and there was thus still some room left for God in the general scheme of things; as if in miracle and phophecy they could point to events which were incapable of being understood by any reasonable man except as proving the decisive intervention of God in nature and history and so vindicating the truth of the Christian revelation.[90]

The advances in the natural sciences are partly responsible for this "growing feeling." Nature is no longer being conceived of as the arena of Divine activity, but rather as a self-contained whole which the human mind can study and comprehend. As thinkers begin to turn their attention to History, it will also disclose itself as intelligible. Climacus will admire the herculean efforts required to understand Nature and History. He will, however, point out a dangerous side-effect of these efforts (and the increased knowledge accompanying them) which he calls "forgetting what it means to exist."

[86] *Ibid.,* pp. 46-60.
[87] *Ibid.,* pp. 61-67.
[88] *Ibid.,* pp. 49-57.
[89] Lessing, *Proof,* p. 53; Chadwick, *Introduction,* p. 34.
[90] Chadwick, *Introduction,* p. 36.

D. THE CONCLUDING UNSCIENTIFIC POSTSCRIPT

Having characterized the nature of the misunderstanding between Christianity and philosophy, Climacus was still faced with two tasks. First, since he had shown that no quantitative or direct transition to Christianity was possible, he had to show what was involved in becoming a Christian. Second, he had yet to indicate the *source* of the misunderstanding.

He takes up these two tasks in the *Postscript* at the point of their convergence, namely, the problem of what it means to exist as a human being. For, he claims, "If men had forgotten what it means to exist religiously, they had doubtless also forgotten what it means to exist as human beings." [91]

Our concern in this study is not with Climacus' analysis of becoming a Christian nor yet with his view of the *source* of "the dubious relationship" between philosophy and Christianity. We believe that Climacus' treatment of human existence is both intelligible and valuable apart from the purposes which it serves in the *Postscript*. But to understand it, we shall have to know more about its author's point of view. This is, of course, all the more important and necessary in view of our decision to attribute the *Postscript* to Climacus.[92]

Few studies interpret the *Postscript* as we do. None has yet provided a satisfactory analysis of Climacus' viewpoint as an author.[93] The standard approach to this problem (when it occurs at all) is that of Walter Lowrie:

The choice of the pseudonym, Johannes Climacus, is interesting and important. It may be a matter of only curious interest that S. K. found this name applied to a Greek monk who was celebrated as the author of a book entitled "The Ladder of Heaven." S. K. adopted it as a denomination for himself when in 1842 he started to write a polemic against the followers of Descartes, entitled *Johannes Climacus; or, de omnibus dubitandum est*... This work was left unfinished—perhaps because he began to realize that the real adversary was Hegel, perhaps only because he was diverted by the urge to write two more books for Regina. But when, with the *Fragments*, he returned again to philosophy, Johannes Climacus again appears as his pseudonym. A glance at the earlier work, which was in large part autobiographical...,

---

[91] *Post.*, p. 223.

[92] Let us observe in passing that Climacus' attempt to discover the misunderstanding between philosophy and Christianity coheres with Kierkegaard's view of the *Postscript* as describing the path which leads from speculation, from philosophy, to Christianity (*POV*, pp. 41-42). For presumably one step on this journey would be the recognition *that* philosophy and Christianity are very different.

[93] The most concerted effort is made by Allison. Cf. *Nonsense*, pp. 432-33. Cf. also Josiah Thompson, *The Lonely Labyrinth* (Carbondale, 1967), pp. 190-94. Thompson has the right idea, but overlooks the important texts.

will make it evident that this was S. K.'s most personal pseudonym. Whereas each of the other pseudonyms may be taken to represent one or another side of S. K.'s character, or a possibility which he discovered in himself, Johannes was neither more nor less than the young man Kierkegaard as he was in his twenty-fifth year, before his conversion in 1838, a young man thoroughly informed about Christianity, who had meditated profoundly upon its dialectical positions, was attracted to it like a moth to the candle, but, still critical, unresolved as yet to make the leap of faith. Hence, Climacus affirms emphatically that he is not a Christian.[94]

Typically, Climacus is characterized either by referring to the monk who previously bore the name and then speculating as to why Kierkegaard might have chosen it; or by referring to entries in his papers.[95] Either procedure is totally extraneous when one realizes that Climacus has given sufficient information about his point of view in the text of the *Postscript* itself.

In the first place, Climacus states that he is *not* a Christian:

As for my own humble person, the reader will please remember that it is I who find the matter and the task so extremely difficult,... I, who do not even profess to be a Christian; but please note that this is not to be taken in the sense that I have ceased to be a Christian in consequence of having gone further.[96]

Nor, secondly, would Climacus call himself a philosopher. "How fortunate that I am not a serious man, an asseverating philosopher..." [97] He is "...anything but a devilish good fellow at philosophy, one who is called to direct it into new paths." [98]

---

[94] Walter Lowrie, Introduction to *Post.*, p. xvi. Lowrie is one of the leading practitioners of the historical method of interpreting Kierkegaard. Not content to historicize Kierkegaard himself, Lowrie would historicize the pseudonyms also.

[95] Cf. Thulstrup, *Commentary*, pp. 148-49; and Price, *Pass*, p. 73. Price calls Climacus "urbane" (*Ibid.*, p. 30).

In the matter of journal references to Climacus. In *The Journals of Søren Kierkegaard*, ed. and trans. Alexander Dru (London, 1959)—hereafter cited as Dru—there are the following references to Climacus: #413 (IV B 1); #589 (VII A 99); #936 (X^1 A 510); #994 (X^2 A 163); #1021 (X^2 A 299); #1051 (X^2 A 428); #1054 (X^2 A 439); and #1238 (X^6 B 145), in which Kierkegaard castigates the practice of lumping together quotes from various pseudonymous authors. But none of these references is very helpful in understanding Climacus' point of view. In *The Last Years*, ed. Ronald Gregor Smith (New York, 1965) there is one reference to Climacus on p. 77 (XI^1 A 184). All of these references support Martin's observation that "... Kierkegaard himself rarely refers to the pseudonymous works as being his own, even in notes written in his private Journals.... He rarely refers to a statement made pseudonymously as one of his own statements, or quotes it as such" (*Principle*, p. 57).

[96] *Post.*, p. 417; cf. also pp. 404, 431, 457, 545.

[97] *Ibid.*, p. 378.

[98] *Ibid.*, p. 545.

So much for what Climacus (says he) is not. "I am," he says, "a poor individual, existing man, with sound natural capacities, not without a certain dialectical dexterity, nor entirely destitute of education." [99] He says further that he is *"essentially a humorist"* who has his life in "immanent categories";[100] and elsewhere refers to himself as "merely a *humoristic, experimenting psychologist.*" [101]

To understand Climacus' point of view, then, we must understand the sense that he attaches to these designations: existing man, experimenting psychologist, and humorist. In the third chapter, we shall deal with the phrase "existing man." But for the other terms in Climacus' self-description, since there is no literature to which we can refer the reader, we shall have to present an account of them which will be sufficient for purposes of our study.

A moment's reflection should serve to caution us about the danger of reading into Climacus' use of the term "psychologist" a sense which it has acquired only in the last half century. Climacus does not mean by "psychologist" one who is engaged in empirical and scientific study of human behavior and the human personality. Nor does he mean by it someone engaged in a philosophical study of human nature and the soul —a sense widely employed during his time.

Although Climacus does not state explicitly what the term "psychologist" means, its sense can be deduced from the following passage:

The introduction that I propose to offer to becoming a Christian will be repellent, making it difficult to become a Christian. It will not conceive of Christianity as a doctrine, but as an existential contradiction and an existential communication. It is not historical but *psychological, calling attention to how much must have been lived before the problem can have any significance for the individual, and showing how difficult it is to become aware of the difficulty of the decision involved.*[102]

In this passage, a "psychological" introduction to the problem of becoming a Christian is contrasted with an "historical" one. The latter would presumably set out to show that Scripture is reliable; that Jesus worked miracles, fulfilled prophecies, etc. The frame of reference of Climacus' introduction, on the other hand, is the individual human being in daily life—rather than history. Such an introduction would require that its author have a keenly developed sense of everyday life—in order to be

---

[99] *Ibid.,* (Italics mine.)
[100] *Ibid.,* p. 404. (Italics mine.)
[101] *Ibid.,* p. 431. (Italics mine.)
[102] *Ibid.,* pp. 341-42. (Italics mine.)

able to call attention to the kind of difficulty that an individual might encounter in deciding to become a Christian. Elsewhere Climacus writes:

Since I am now compelled to make the sad admission that I cannot speak about China, Persia, the System, the astrological or veterinary sciences, I have, in order to hit upon something to do in my embarrassment, exercised my pen within the powers bestowed upon me, *in imitating and describing, as concretely as possible, the affairs of daily life,* which are often enough something quite different from the Sunday-go-to-meeting atmosphere....
But what all is not required to present a human being as he is in daily life! [108]

We conclude, then, that a psychologist, in the sense in which Climacus uses the term, is someone aware of the difficulties posed by existential tasks and able to describe them concretely. His context is "the affairs of daily life."

Thus when he hears of a task, a psychologist might well inquire: "And now what does the task look like in daily life? For I always have my favorite them *in mente.*" [104] To discover what the task would look like in daily life, a psychologist might resort to an experiment. That is, he might attempt to describe what would happen if a hypothetical individual set out to perform the task. For example:

Last Sunday, the clergyman said: "You must depend upon God alone, and not upon men, and not upon yourself, but only and alone upon God." And we all understood it, myself included; for the ethical and the ethico-religious are so very easy to understand, but on the other hand so very difficult to do. [105]

In the twenty-eight pages that follow, Climacus describes very concretely the kinds of difficulty an individual might encounter if he were to incorporate this "Sunday thought" into his life on Monday, Tuesday and Wednesday.

The *Postscript* contains many such "experiments" which show that a task which seems easy on paper may prove very trying in life itself. [106] The *Postscript* is itself an experiment. [107] Climacus is using himself by way of illustration to elucidate what is involved in the decision to become a Christian. He attempts to describe as accurately as possible, to approximate in thought, to imitate, the movements involved in becom-

---

[108] *Ibid.,* p. 415. (Italics mine.)
[104] *Ibid.,* p. 417.
[105] *Ibid.*
[106] *Ibid.,* pp. 147-61.
[107] The *Fragments* was also an experiment, though in a different sense. The term "experiment" will be discussed again in Chapter VI.

ing a Christian.[108] His standpoint as an "experimenting psychologist" is thus an appropriate one—given his purposes.

This brings us to the key term in Climacus' self-description: *humorist*. This designation is not easy to explain briefly, since it is imbedded in the well-known theory of "existence-spheres" or "stages of existence." [109] Climacus offers the following terse summary of this theory:

> There are three spheres of existence: the aesthetic, the ethical, the religious. Two boundary zones correspond to these three: irony, constituting the boundary between the aesthetic and the ethical; humor, as the boundary that separates the ethical from the religious.[110]

We offer here only the briefest possible account of this important theory.[111]

The term "sphere" is, of course, metaphorical. Its sense is roughly equivalent to what is now called a "life-style." Climacus would claim,

---

[108] This is the key to understanding the sense in which the *Postscript* is a "mimic" work. This also is treated in Chapter VI.

[109] It should be said that this "theory" is not presented as such in either of Climacus' works. It is implicit throughout the *Postscript* and explicit discussions of it can be found on pp. 448-68; pp. 489-93; pp. 506-08; and pp. 225-66 *passim*, as Climacus presents his views of the pseudonymous works. The theory of the existence-spheres is the frame of reference of his review.

[110] *Post.*, p. 448.

[111] This theory has come to be very closely associated with Kierkegaard, so much so that almost any introductory study will call attention to it. Of the many treatments of this theory, we may mention Malantschuk, *Way*, pp. 23-78; and H. Reidar Thomte, *Kierkegaard's Philosophy of Religion* (Princeton, 1949), pp. 16-109.

Virtually every account of this theory assumes that there is a homogeneous version of this theory to be found in all the pseudonymous works and that this theory may be referred to Kierkegaard. Thus Malantschuk writes that "The theory of the stages, which is the basis of Søren Kierkegaard's whole authorship, is constructed on the premise that man is a synthesis of two different qualities" (*Way*, p. 22). In his presentation, Malantschuk refers to all of the pseudonymous works; he treats them as if they were all Kierkegaard's.

In our view, the existence of a homogenous theory of the spheres in all the works has yet to be proven, though it may well exist. The mere fact that the pseudonymous authors all use the terms "aesthetic" and "ethical" and "religious" would seem to indicate that each of them subscribes to some version of this theory. But it may well be that there are differences in their respective understandings of it. This is something which has yet to be investigated.

Climacus' version of the theory seems to be the most thoroughly articulated. But even though Climacus perceives important areas of agreement between himself and the other pseudonymous authors (*Post.*, pp. 225-66), there is not total agreement. See, for example, his comments about Johannes de Silentio (*Ibid.*, p. 446, *n.*).

In what follows, therefore, we take ourselves to be sketching "Climacus" theory of the existence-spheres—not Kierkegaard's.

apparently, that every individual inhabits (or exists in) one of these three spheres.[112] He means his classification to be exhaustive. Very roughly, the aesthetic sphere is characterized by the pursuit of pleasure—either sensual or intellectual. The ethical sphere is characterized by one's having an absolute concern for and interest in his own existence. (The third chapter will explain this.) The religious sphere is characterized by one's concern for his eternal happiness and by the transformations which this demands in his life.[113]

Humor, says Climacus, is the boundary separating the ethical from the religious. To live on the boundary, one might suggest, is to live on the extreme edges of the ethical sphere, thoroughly conscious of the requirements of an ethical mode of existence and yet aware of the possibility of "the religious." Discussing "Magister Kierkegaard's" *Edifying Discourses,* Climacus says:

> ...it was to me a striking and significant thing that the four last discourses took on a *carefully modulated humoristic* tone. This is doubtless the sum of what can be reached within the sphere of the immanent. While the ethical requirement is maintained, while life and existence is accentuated as a toilsome way, the decision is not posited in a paradox, and the metaphysical retirement by way of recollection into the eternal is always possible, and gives to this immanent sphere the color of humor, in the form of an infinitude's recall of the whole in an eternal decisiveness from behind.[114]

By "immanent" Climacus means the sphere governed by human reason. The humorist, like the ethicist, takes his own existence seriously, yet he does not treat his existence as decisive for his eternal destiny. He holds

---

[112] Climacus is very ambiguous both about the actual number of spheres or stages and their characteristics. In the text that we have quoted on page 29, he speaks of three. Elsewhere, he says that "...in spite of this triple division [aesthetic, ethical, and religious] the book [*Stages on Life's Way*] is nevertheless an either-or. The ethical and the religious stages have in fact an essential relationship to one another" (*Post.,* p. 261). This suggests that there are really two stages: the aesthetic and the ethico-religious. But then the distinction between religiousness A and religiousness B poses further difficulties. Cf. below footnote 113.

Now although it is clearly Climacus' view that an individual may move from one sphere to the next, this movement is not automatic. And there is the further question whether the movement to another sphere "dethrones" the previous one. On these points, cf. Alastair McKinnon, "Kierkegaard's Irrationalism Revisited," *International Philosophical Quarterly,* IX (1969), pp. 165-76; and T. H. Croxall, *Kierkegaard Studies* (New York, 1956), pp. 67-70.

[113] On the distinction between religiousness A and B, cf. *Post.,* pp. 493-98.

[114] *Post.,* p. 241.

out for the possibility that his eternal destiny has already been decided "from behind," as it were.

In another passage about humor, Climacus says:

Apparently, humor gives to existence a greater significance than irony does, but the immanent is predominant, and the more or less is a vanishing quantitative determination over against the qualitative decisiveness of the Christian position. Humor therefore becomes the last *terminus a quo* in connection with the problem of determining the Christian.... It [humor] can come deceptively close to the Christian position; but where decisiveness takes hold; where existence captures the existing individual so that he must remain in existence, while the bridge of immanence and recollection is burned behind him; where the decision comes to be in the moment, and the movement is forward toward a relationship with the eternal truth which came into being in time; there humor does not follow.[115]

The humorist does not accept the (paradoxical) thought that his own existence in time is decisive for his eternal destiny; he cannot accept the (paradoxical) thought that the eternal truth has come into being in time. At the same time, the humorist emphasizes the importance of existing and hence is at the last possible *terminus a quo* for becoming a Christian. The humorist, though not religious in the strict sense, stands at the doorway:

The humorist constantly... sets the God-idea into conjunction with other things and evokes the contradiction—but he does not maintain a relationship to God in terms of religious passion *stricte sic dictus,* he transforms himself instead into a jesting and yet profound exchange-center for all these transactions, but does not himself stand related to God.[116]

Climacus sometimes contrasts humor with speculation.[117] For there is a similarity between the two in that neither the speculative thinker nor the humorist takes his own existence in time as a matter of utmost seriousness. For the humorist, "the temporal life is... a fugitive episode having a very dubious significance;..." [118] The speculative philosopher does not think of his own existence as decisive for his eternal happiness. Indeed, he dismisses the very notion of an eternal happiness as jejune.[119] He is continually abstracting from his own existence in order to think things through *sub specie aeterni*. The difference between the humorist

---

[115] *Ibid.,* pp. 242.-43.

[116] *Ibid.,* p. 451. The first sentence of this passage is an excellent description of what Climacus himself attempts to do in *Post.,* pp. 417-45. Cf. pages 24-29 above.

[117] *Post.,* pp. 241-44.

[118] *Ibid.,* p. 242, *n.*

[119] *Ibid.,* p. 323.

and the speculative thinker is that the humorist knows what it means to exist, knows the seriousness of existing in time. The speculative thinker, on the other hand, has forgotten what it means to exist as an individual human being.

We can now summarize briefly the main features of Climacus' point of view. He is not a Christian; nor, therefore, a theologian. He is not a philosopher, although he is acquainted with philosophical discourse. He is essentially a humorist, living at the boundary of the ethical sphere, thoroughly familiar with the requirements of an ethical mode of existence and aware of the difficulties of living in time. But he does not treat his existence as decisive for his eternal destiny. He knows how to describe the affairs of everyday life. In short, he is well-situated for the task which he has taken upon himself of describing what it involved in becoming a Christian, and of understanding what has gone wrong in the relationship between philosophy and Christianity.

Lastly, we ought to say a word about the audience Climacus has in mind for his efforts. In terms of the theory of the existence-spheres, his reader would be one in the aesthetic sphere, although this would not necessarily be the way such a reader would describe himself. Specifically, he would be a person who takes delight in the life of ideas and the pursuit of intellectual pleasures:

What is developed in these pages does not concern the simple-minded, who bear feelingly the burdens of life,... On the other hand, it does concern those who deem themselves possessed of the leisure and talent for a deeper inquiry.[120]

And he says of the *Fragments*:

And yet the book is so far from being written for the uninformed, to give them something to know, that the one I introduce into the book as my interlocutor is precisely a *well-informed person*, which seems to indicate that the book is written for informed readers *whose misfortune is that they know too much*.[121]

If we recall the scene in the cemetery which prompted Climacus to become an author, it would seem that Climacus has written these works for somebody like the dead man, the elderly man's son, whose talent and learning resulted in his giving up his faith.

In the original Preface to his *Fragments,* Climacus has compared himself to "...a poor lodger who has a little room in the attic of a huge

---

[120] *Post.*, p. 152, *n.* Cf. also p. 342. Climacus states that he hopes to "render a service to the cultured classes,..." *Ibid.*, p. 446.

[121] *Ibid.*, p. 245, *n.* (Italics mine.)

building which is constantly being enlarged and beautified..." [122] The "huge building" may very well be the House of *Wissenschaft,* symbolizing the hopes and the achievements of the "speculatively significant nineteenth century." For Climacus considered that the philosophers of his day were totally preoccupied with enlarging and beautifying this edifice. That is, they were forever busy increasing the store of human knowledge. It is unlikely that Climacus believed that his two works (a "fragment" of philosophy and an "unscientific postscript" to it) would command the attention of such men.

But presumably, in addition to the builders themselves, there would be another group near this huge building—the apprentices. This group would be composed of those whose talents would enable them, at some future time, to make a contribution to the renovation of the building. But until that time, the members of this group might have a spare moment.

Climacus did not expect his works to usher in a new era, to be greeted with "...noisy acclaim, huzzahs at midnight, torchlight processions, and other similar encroachments..." [123] When a man has readied his palate for a systematic banquet, he cannot very well be expected to be overjoyed when he is offered, instead, a morsel. So the *Fragments* had a very favorable reception from Climacus' point of view, i.e., none at all. Now he is back at work:

> Encouraged in this manner by fortune's favor, I now propose to carry on with my project. Without let or hindrance from the outside, with no overhasty concern for what the times demand, following solely my own inner impulse, I shall proceed to knead the thoughts, so to speak, until in my opinion the dough is a good one.[124]

Hopefully this introductory chapter has served to clarify why Climacus is in the kitchen. Having sampled briefly his first offering (the *Fragments*) and having found out what kind of chef he is, we must now discover what he has cooked up for his reader in the *Postscript.*

---

[122] V B 24, cited in Thulstrup, *Commentary,* p. 153.
[123] *Post.,* p. 4.
[124] *Ibid.*

CHAPTER II

DIFFERENCES

A. INTRODUCTION

In this chapter, we deviate from the course set out in the last chapter. The rationale for this is our belief that Climacus' treatment of existence must be seen against its background. The following passage alludes to that setting:

But perhaps philosophy will say: "These are popular and simple reflections, which theologues and popularizing philosophers are fit to expound; but speculative philosophy has nothing to do with such things."... *It seems strange to me that people are always talking of speculative philosophy as if it were a man, or as if a man were speculative philosophy.* It is speculative philosophy that does everything, that doubts everything, and so forth.[1]

There is, Climacus observes, a way of talking about philosophy in which it is likened to an individual human being. If we can find out why Climacus regards this way of talking as "strange," we will have made an important step towards understanding his treatment of existence.

Some few sentences later, Climacus writes:

Socrates says that when we posit flute-playing we must also posit a flute-player; and so if we posit speculative philosophy we must also assume the existence of a philosopher, or of several philosophers.[2]

Regardless of one's views about the kind of reality philosophy has, it must be recognized that it is a human activity requiring human beings. Yet no matter how intensely a human might immerse himself in philosophy, in the life of ideas and the life of the community which gathers for the purpose of pursuing them, he does not cease to be an individual human being. There always remains that residue that Climacus calls

---

[1] *Post.*, p. 50. (Italics mine.) "There is constant talk of mediation and mediation; is mediation then a man, as Peter Deacon believes that *Imprimatur* is a man?" *Ibid.*, p. 177.

[2] *Ibid.*, p. 50.

"the existing individual." "If a man occupied himself, all his life through, solely with logic, he would nevertheless not become logic; *he must therefore himself exist in 'different categories.'*[3] Climacus' own treatment of existence can be best understood as an attempt to *italicize these categories,* to draw his reader's attention to those obvious truths about his existence which make it different from the kind of existence which, for example, philosophy or logic has. The strange thing about the way of speaking noted on the previous page is that it pays no heed to these differences. And when these are neglected, philosophy becomes an essay in absent-mindedness:

It is from this side... that objection must be made to modern philosophy; not that it has a mistaken presupposition, but that it has a comical presupposition, occasioned by its having forgotten, in a sort of world-historical absent-mindedness, what it means to be a human being. Not indeed, what it means to be a human being in general; for this is the sort of thing that one might even induce a speculative philosopher to agree to; but what it means that you and I and he are human beings, each one for himself.[4]

When this happens, it becomes necessary to "separate the philosopher from the philosophy"[5] in order to give these differences their due.

When Climacus wrote the *Postscript,* the influence of philosophy was as powerful as the waves at high tide. But some would say that the tide has ebbed:

It is by now hardly disputed that the peculiar mark of contemporary culture is science. Science is not only the foundation of technology,... but is moreover becoming *the centre of culture* and is even continually absorbing subjects that were formerly regarded as philosophical:...[6]

If it is true that the position of science in contemporary culture approximates closely that of philosophy during Climacus' time, then the aim of this study may better be served if we focus on science in the twentieth century rather than on philosophy in the nineteenth.

There is no one characteristic manner of speaking about science. But the following passages, selected randomly from several contemporary works on science, give evidence that there is a way of talking about science which is quite similar to the one which caught Climacus' eye over a century ago:

[3] *Ibid.,* p. 86. (Italics mine).
[4] *Ibid.,* p. 109.
[5] *Ibid.,* p. 324. What this formula means will be explained in Chapter VI.
[6] Mario Bunge, *Metascientific Queries* (Springfield, 1959), pp. 17-18. (Italics mine.) Hereafter cited as: Bunge, *Queries.*

What science *has to say about* distant times and places is said with hesitation; it is set forth as what is most probable on the existing evidence, but any day new evidence may lead to new conclusions on this point or that.[7]

For science, as it advances, *does not rest content with* establishing simple generalizations from observable facts: it *tries to explain* these lowest level generalizations by deducing them from more general hypotheses at a higher level.[8]

What science *observes,* what science *predicts* has all the shortcomings of fact... It does not read the future, it forecasts it;... The future is as it were always a little out of focus, and everything that we foresee in it is seen embedded in a small area of uncertainty. It is the human situation and the situation of science.[9]

Science starts from notions that seem clear to the non-initiated, and complicates, purifies, and eventually *rejects* them;...[10]

Reviewing some of the predicates (those we have italicized) in these passages, we may observe that they are often applied to the individual human being. It may be said of someone that he "has something to say"; that he "does not rest content with" something; that he "tries to explain"; that he "observes," "predicts," or "rejects" something. The fact that predicates denoting human activities can be applied to science suggests that there is some measure of likeness between science and the human individual. This suggestion gets added confirmation when one considers that science has a language,[11] that it has been called "a severe task-master," [12] and it has been proposed for the role of savior.[13]

Someone will be certain to remind us, however, that we ought not infer too much from the mere existence of such a manner of speaking. "... everybody should know," writes Harold Schilling, "that no one thinks of science as a metaphysical entity or objective reality, and that linguistic personification does not necessarily imply it."[14] In a similar vein, Quine has argued that one ought not draw simplistic inferences from the fact that a word can stand in the subject position of an

---

[7] Bertrand Russell, *The Art of Philosophizing and Other Essays* (New York, 1968), p. 17. (Italics mine.)

[8] R. B. Braithwaite, *Scientific Explanation* (New York, 1960), p. vii. (Italics mine.)

[9] Jacob Bronowski, *The Common Sense of Science* (Harmandsworth, 1960), p. 134. (Italics mine.) Hereafter cited as: Bronowski, *Common.*

[10] Bunge, *Queries*, p. 42. (Italics mine.)

[11] Albert Einstein, *Out of My Later Years* (New York, 1950), p. 108. Hereafter cited as: Einstein, *Years.*

[12] A. Cornelius Benjamin, *Science, Technology and Human Values* (Columbia, 1965), p. 5. Hereafter cited as: Benjamin, *Values.*

[13] George Lundberg, *Can Science Save Us?* (New York, 1947).

[14] Harold K. Schilling, *Science and Religion* (New York, 1962), p. 15. Hereafter cited as: Schilling, *Religion.* Cf. also Julian Huxley, *Man in the Modern World* (New York, 1948), p. 116.

intelligible sentence.[15] Still, as Schilling observes, the fact that people speak the way they do about science is not insignificant.[16]

These reminders raise a difficult question: What is the nature of science? What is its ontological status? Happily it is no part of our task to answer these questions. We say "happily" in light of the fact that no one answer to these questions seems to have as yet gained widespread acceptability. Indeed, Bunge claims that "No single philosophical school can claim to have contrived a consistent and realistic picture of actual science."[17] Bunge's claim is supported by Thomas Kuhn's provoking study, *The Structure of Scientific Revolutions,* in which he argues that contemporary views about science are innacurate and unrealistic precisely because they are unhistorical.[18]

We have come to an impasse. We have been developing the idea that we might best capture the flavor of Climacus' treatment of existence if we were to contrast science and the individual human being. For as we have seen, what apparently energized Climacus' thinking was his detection of a manner of speaking which likened philosophy to the individual without ever adverting to the *differences* between the two. And so he seems to have set himself the task of bringing some of these differences to light. Now we have noticed that a similar situation obtains today. We have produced texts in which science is likened to the individual human being. We should like to bring out some of the differences. But since no one seems to know exactly what science is, the task would be very difficult.

We can, however, avail ourselves of an assumption which would break the impasse and enable us to proceed with a similar task. Let us say,

[15] In "On What There Is," Quine argues that we make an ontological commitment *only when we* decide about the range of our bound variables. The simple fact that we talk about Pegasus does not itself commit us ontologically. And so, the point would be here, the simple fact that we speak about science does not commit us to including it among the things that exist. This is the force of Quine's aphorism that "To be is to be the value of a variable." Cf. Willard Van Orman Quine, *From a Logical Point of View,* 2nd ed. (New York and Evanston, 1963), pp. 1-19. Cf. especially p. 15.

[16] Schilling, *Religion,* p. 15: "The fact is that many people—and very intelligent ones too—do speak that way, and that it conveys important meaning. The reason why it does, and why, moreover science *is* spoken of in a variety of ways, is that it actually has many aspects and exists in a variety of modes."

[17] Bunge, *Queries,* p. 26.

[18] Thomas S. Kuhn, *The Structure of Scientific Revolutions,* 2nd ed., International Encyclopedia of Unified Science, ed. Otto Neurath, II (Chicago, 1970), pp. 1-3. Hereafter cited as: Kuhn, *Structure.*

with Socrates and Climacus, that if we posit science, we must also posit the existence of a scientist, or several scientists, or, better still, a community of scientists. Let us assume that any satisfactory answer to the question "What is science?" must recognize that science is a human activity which requires a community of human beings. Hence we shall focus on the scientific community rather than on science. The previously cited passages on page 36 lose none of their validity if we replace "science" by "the scientific community." Hence those same quotes may be said to suggest that there are similarities between the scientific community and the individual human being. Presumably there are also *differences;* and presumably, if he were alive, Climacus would wish to bring some of them to light. By taking this task upon ourselves in this chapter, we hope to accomplish two things. First, we shall have an excellent point of entry into Climacus' own treatment of existence. Second, we will have prepared ourselves for the analysis of the forgetting-claim. To anticipate that latter task for a moment, we may consider the following brief account of how one becomes a scientist:

It is not enough to be intellectually acquainted with the current consensus; he must learn how to behave like a scientist; indeed, he must learn to 'think scientifically.' *He must internalize the scientific attitude* so that he cannot even conceive of, say, writing a scholarly paper in Zen, or recording the epoch of an eclipse by reference to the age of the reigning monarch, or pay a claque to abuse the reading of his opponent's papers.[19]

Let us suppose that there are differences between the scientific community's mode of existence and the individual's, and that the community has developed over time an attitude in line with its mode of existence. If this is true, then the individual runs a risk in undertaking this "internalization." For he may be so successful in taking on the community's attitude (and the mode of existence which goes with it) that he loses contact with his own attitudes and the tasks which they may pose for him. This is the situation which Climacus calls "forgetting what it means to exist." It was for the purpose of exposing such forgettings that Climacus undertook his analysis of human existence. To prepare for that analysis, then, and to ready ourselves for an elucidation of the forgetting-claim, we shall endeavor in this chapter to understand the mode of existence of the scientific community with a view to noting some of the ways in which it differs from that of the individual human being.

[19] John Ziman, *Public Knowledge* (Cambridge, 1968), pp. 77-78. (Italics mine.) Hereafter cited as: Ziman, *Knowledge*.

Recent works on science evidence increased consciousness of the role that the community as a community plays in scientific endeavors.[20] But according to Kuhn, our ignorance about the community still outweighs our knowledge:

Every civilization of which we have records has possessed a technology, an art, a religion, a political system, laws, and so on. In many cases those facets of civilization have been as developed as our own. But only the civilizations that descend from Hellenic Greece have possessed more than the most rudimentary science. The bulk of scientific knowledge is a product of Europe in the last four centuries. No other place and time has supported *the very special communities* from which scientific productivity comes.
What are the essential characteristics of these communities? Obviously, they need vastly more study.[21]

To be sure, the scientific community will have the usual attributes of human communities: a language of its own, its own means of communication, group ideals, ethical and moral codes, sanctions, institutions, etc.[22] A good deal more than this needs to be said.[23]

Having indicated both the nature of our task in this chapter and its relevance to this study, it remains to settle on an approach. To what discipline does this task belong? Does it, for example, belong to the philosophy of science? Consider:

Although the label "philosophy of science" is of fairly recent vintage, the subject it designates is by no means novel.... The designation as commonly employed actually covers a miscellany of problems that are only faintly related to one another,... For example, the catalogue of themes often classified under that heading includes: Traditional issues in the epistemology of sense perception; problems concerning the genesis, the development, and the social effects of scientific ideas; projected philosophical syntheses of specialized scientific findings,...; moral evaluations of the accomplishments and the likely future fruits of the scientific enterprise; axiomatizations of various branches of theoretical inquiry; proposed justifications

[20] Cf., for example, Ziman, *Knowledge,* p. ix; Schilling, *Religion,* pp. 50-56; William G. Pollard, *Physicist and Christian* (New York, 1959), p. 39. Hereafter cited as: Pollard, *Physicist.*

[21] Kuhn, *Structure,* pp. 167-68. (Italics mine.)

[22] Schilling, *Religion,* pp. 54-55.

[23] In his "Postscript" to the second edition, Kuhn says that if he were to rewrite his book, "it would open with a discussion of the community structure of science, a topic that has recently become a significant subject of sociological research and that historians of science are beginning to take seriously." *Structure,* p. 176. Even more significant are Kuhn's last words: "Scientific knowledge, like language, is intrinsically the common property of a group or else nothing at all. To understand it we shall need to know the special characteristics of the groups that create and use it." *Ibid.,* p. 210.

of inductive procedures; criteria for meaningful discourse and types of definitional techniques; the structure of scientific laws; and the status and function of theoretical ideas.[24]

We may pause here long enough to note that the task we have in mind does not occur in this list. Nagel goes on to say:

This list is by no means exhaustive. But the items mentioned suffice to indicate that despite the supposition that the designation "philosophy of science" marks off a specialized area of philosophical analysis, the term does not at present denote a reasonably well-defined domain of inquiry.

It would certainly be profitless to dispute whether, and if so which, items in the above list "really belong to the philosophy of science. [sic] Nevertheless, although a certain breadth of conception is essential for fixing its scope if the philosophy of science is to contribute to illuminating the character of the scientific enterprise, it is doubtful whether any coherent conception underlies an indiscriminate lumping together under a common name of themes whose only bond is a reference in some way or other to science. But in any event, much is gained in the way of clarifying the aims of philosophical analysis by limiting the philosophy of science to a group of related questions that arise in attempting to understand the intellectual products of scientific inquiry as embodied in explicitly formulated statements.[25]

Since our interest is not with "the intellectual products of scientific inquiry," but rather with the mode of existence of the community which brings them into existence, it would seem that our task does not fall to philosophy of science.

Would it then fall to either the psychology or the sociology of science? Consider:

...the study of science can be approached scientifically and is done so on occasion: we have, in fact, a number of immature sciences of science. If science is viewed as a peculiar activity of individuals and teams, the psychology of science can emerge; this discipline will study, among other things, the cognitive drive, the psychological processes of hypotheses [sic] generation, mental rigidity among scientists, etc. Viewing science in its social context can lead to the sociology of science, i.e. the study of the social factors that prompt and those which inhibit research, the role of science in the planning and control of human action, and so on. And if science is studied as an aspect of cultural evolution, the history of science emerges,... The above are *external* approaches to science, in the sense that they do not analyse and criticize either the method or the outcome of research but take them for granted. Moreover, the psychology, the sociology and the history of science are factual (empirical) sciences of science: they handle large masses of empirical data.[26]

[24] Ernest Nagel, Preface to *Philosophy of Science,* ed. Arthur Danto and Sidney Morgenbesser (Cleveland, 1960), p. 12.

[25] *Ibid.,* p. 13.

[26] Mario Bunge, *Scientific Research I: The Search for System,* Studies in the Foundations, Methodology and Philosophy of Science, ed. Mario Bunge, III (New York, 1967), p. 31. Hereafter cited as: Bunge, *Research.*

It would seem, on the basis of the above descriptions, that our task would not fall to either the psychology or the sociology of science. For we are not interested in the behavior either of the individual or of the community, but rather in certain very general features which may be said to characterize its mode of existence.

In short, it does not seem that our task falls either to "metascience" or to "the science of science." [27] This is, however, as it should be, since the framework of this study is not scientific but rather philosophical. What we need is a philosophical approach which will enable us to come to an understanding of the mode of existence of the scientific community and its differences from that of the individual.

Wittgenstein suggests a plausible approach in his *Philosophical Investigations*. He states there that "Grammar tells us what kind of object anything is," [28] that "*Essence* is expressed by grammar." [29] If we were to apply these thoughts to the task at hand, our strategy would be to take notice of the kind of thing that is said about science (or the scientific community); for if Wittgenstein is right, the kind of thing that is said about science will serve to clarify what kind of being it is. By comparing those results with what we say about human beings, we should be able to arrive at some clarity about the differences between the two. This then is how we shall conduct our investigation.

The decision to adopt a Wittgensteinian approach perhaps warrants a brief comment. Several writers have alluded to important resonances between Kierkegaard and Wittgenstein.[30] While any detailed discussion

---

[27] In *Queries* (1959), Bunge, borrowing the term from J. O. Wisdom (p. 5), proposed the name "metascience" as a generic term to denote that inquiry which would be concerned "not... with the actual production of scientific results but with an examination of the nature of scientific problems and procedures, and even with an analysis of that very examination" (p. 3). At that time, it appears that he considered the terms "metascience" and "the science of science" synonymous. But in *Research* (1967), he has reserved "metascience" for one specific branch of "the science of science"—namely, for that branch which takes an internal rather than an external approach (p. 32).

[28] Ludwig Wittgenstein, *Philosophical Investigations*, 2nd ed., trans. G. E. M. Anscombe (Oxford, 1958), Part I, #373. Hereafter cited as: Wittgenstein, *Investigations*.

[29] *Ibid.*, #371.

[30] To mention two, cf. Stanley Cavell, "Existentialism and Analytic Philosophy," *Daedalus*, XCIII (1964), pp. 946-74; and Paul Holmer, Intro. to *The New Obedience: Kierkegaard on the Imitation of Christ* by Bradley Dewey (Washington, 1968), pp. vii-xii.

of such would take us beyond the bounds of our study, the following remark by Wittgenstein harmonizes with some notes struck by the author of the *Postscript:*

Here again we get the same thing as in set theory: the form of expression we use seems to have been *designed for a god,* who knows what we cannot know; he sees the whole of each of those infinite series and he sees into human consciousness. For us, of course, *these forms of expression are like pontificals which we may put on, but cannot do much with, since we lack the effective power that would give these vestments meaning and purpose.*

In the actual use of expressions we make detours, we go by sideroads. We see the straight highway before us, but of course we cannot use it, because it is permanently closed.[31]

Using Wittgenstein's own metaphor, we can say that our aim is to understand the kind of vestments and regalia that belong to the ongoing scientific community and how these differ from the dress of the individual human being. The hazard that Climacus calls a forgetting occurs when an individual becomes so used to strutting about in the vestments of the community (in "systematic buskins," as Climacus would say) that he forgets that these are not his own personal wardrobe. The consequence of such an occurrence is that his own clothes become, through neglect, moth-eaten and tattered.

B. THE COMMUNITY AS "TIMELESS"

Perhaps the way to begin this investigation is by citing some of the obvious characteristics of the human mode of existence. Each human being has a first day; each will have a last day. Between these two poles, the drama of life is played out. The human mode of existence is therefore a limited one, bounded on one side by birth and on the other by death. "I'm limited to just this stretch of history from —— to ——." An individual might use some such sentence to describe his mode of existence.

Let us consider, for a moment, death. It is one characteristic of the human mode of existence. Man's being, it has been said, is a being towards death.[32] Although death is a surety for every human, very few

---

[31] Wittgenstein, *Investigations,* #426. (Italics mine.) Compare with this *Post.,* pp. 277-78.

[32] Martin Heidegger, *Being and Time,* trans. John Macquarrie and Edward Robinson (New York, 1962), p. 303.

know the hour of its coming. "Death comes like a thief in the night," says an old maxim. The human mode of existence has an essential element of uncertainty and it therefore a precarious one. "Death is in the offing for me, though I don't know when." This is the sort of thing that a human might say about himself.

Equally characteristic of the human mode of existence is the fact that human beings react to these basic facts. "If I must someday die, what can I do to satisfy my desire to live?" [33] Some find the thought of death so distressing that they snuff it out of their conscious thinking, content to gather what rosebuds they may until the thief overtakes them. Some find solace in the promise of a life after this one; others in the belief that they are destined to be reborn again and again. Others still, and Plato saw this in his *Symposium,* seek immortality in their offspring. Although there is no typical reaction, then, to these basic facts, it is characteristic of human beings to think about death. "I wonder what, if anything, is on the other side of death." Humans wonder about such things.

Let us turn our attention to the scientific community. Like the individual, the community may be said to have a date of birth:

Science as a process consciously directed toward achieving knowledge that is explicitly formulated, general in scope, systematically ordered, and dependable, is less then three thousand years old; and science as a continuing institutionalized inquiry, integrally woven into the social fabric, is of still more recent origin.[34]

It does no violence to this text to construe it as assigning a date of birth to the scientific community. Other dates can be assigned; but whatever date one honors as marking the birth of the community, the community had a beginning in time and is now centuries old. Hence although the community may be compared to the individual in so far as both have a beginning in time, there is also a difference. The community reckons its age in centuries, whereas the individual will reckon his in decades. By human standards, the scientific community is a veritable Methuselah.

There is another difference. When the individual reflects on his future, he must surely see—however vaguely—his own death. But when the community looks at its future, death is conspicuous by its absence. To be sure, if there should be a nuclear holocaust or an ecological disaster, the community would perish along with everything else. But George

---

[33] John S. Dunne, C.S.C., *The City of the Gods: A Study in Myth and Mortality* (New York and London, 1965), p. v.

[34] Ernest Nagel, *op. cit.,* p. 11.

Sarton is not uttering total nonsense when he says of science that "It is immortal." [35] His point can be put grammatically (in Wittgenstein's sense) by noticing that while one speaks about the birth of the scientific community, and of its progress and maturation,[36] one does not speak about its death. This grammatical fact reveals one aspect of the community's mode of existence; i.e., it is the kind of being which has a beginning in time but—it seems—not an end. We can say, then, that the community's mode of existence is a "timeless" one. Its future appears to be open-ended. Since death, for the community, is a non-reality its mode of existence is theoretically interminable. Such a mode of existence is importantly different from that of the human being.

The individual scientist must face death, to be sure. But the community, precisely because it is a community, transcends this limitation. "Death itself," writes Sarton, "does not interrupt the scientist's work. Theories once unfolded are eternally living and acting." [37] The scientist's task, the community's task is to "... diminish the unknown which surrounds us everywhere." [38] To this end, the scientist labors to produce a theory. If death should interrupt him in the effort, the community stands ready to carry his work through to completion if it is deemed important. Once formulated, a theory stands on file, ready to be of service.

In its efforts to diminish the unknown, the community must undertake projects, pose questions, and traffic in problems whose solution may require decades, even centuries. We quote two texts which describe the shaping of scientific opinion:

Still, to say that resistance is inevitable and legitimate, that paradigm change cannot be justified by proof, is not to say that no arguments are relevant or that scientists cannot be persuaded to change their minds. *Though a generation is sometimes required to effect the change,* scientific communities have again and again been converted to new paradigms.[39] There are filtering mechanisms by which the most blatant errors are kept from publication, but these could never be made perfectly efficient. The general procedure is to allow all work that is apparently valid to be published: *time and further research will eventually separate the true from the false.*[40]

---

[35] Georges Sarton, *The Life of Science* (New York, 1948), p. 55.

[36] Mario Bunge, "The Maturation of Science," *Problems in the Philosophy of Science,* Proceedings of the International Colloquium in the Philosophy of Science, ed. Imre Lakatos and Alan Musgrave, III (Amsterdam, 1968), pp. 120-47.

[37] George Sarton, *op. cit.,* p. 43.

[38] *Ibid.*

[39] Kuhn, *Structure,* p. 152. (Italics mine.)

[40] Ziman, *Knowledge,* p. 55. (Italics mine.)

Although these texts are describing the formation of scientific opinion at different levels, there is a common denominator. In both cases, the community is pictured as free from the pressures of time. It has no deadlines of a relative sort; and it does not have to reckon with that ultimate deadline which the individual faces in death. The scientific community, it may be said, has a relaxed view of time. Ziman alludes indirectly to this attitude:

But there comes a time in the history of a discovery or hypothesis when it is finally accepted or rejected by the scientific community. *This may take a long time,* as with the theory of Continental Drift, *or it may occur almost overnight,* as in the theory of the Non-conversation of Parity in Weak Interactions.[41]

When one recalls that it took the community roughly fifty years to make up its mind about the theory of Continental Drift, the disjunction (fifty years or overnight) is illuminating. It suggests that fifty years and one night are pretty much the same thing, from the community's point of view. It makes no real difference how long or how short a period elapses between the proposal of a theory and its acceptance or rejection. The community is in no hurry; it has, almost literally, all the time in the world.

The individual human being, on the other hand, cannot take time so casually. His time is limited. He may feel the pinch of time and express it in a sentence like: "If only I had more time!" And to the degree that he is aware of the uncertainty of his own existence, he must reckon his future in the smaller temporal units: in days, weeks, and months. Such reckoning will contrast sharply with the community's tendency to reckon the future in the larger units. That is, it sounds perfectly natural for someone to say, when speaking on the community's behalf: "We look forward to great progress in the next hundred years."

Science is often described as an endless quest.[42] Among the items in a creed which he believes expresses "the new faith of science," Henry Margenau includes the following: "I believe that the search for truth is a never-ending quest; yet I pledge myself to seek it." [43] Is Margenau speaking with his own voice or with the community's? The pronoun "I" suggests the former. Interpreted in this fashion, his words might be an

---

[41] *Ibid.,* p. 123. (Italics mine.)

[42] Cf. Jacques Barzun, *Science: That Glorious Entertainment* (New York, 1964), p. 97. Hereafter cited as: Barzun, *Glorious.*

[43] Henry Margenau, *Open Vistas: Philosophical Perspectives of Modern Science* (London and New Haven, 1961), p. 76. Hereafter cited as: Margenau, *Vistas.*

affirmation of his own commitment to the search for truth. Since, however, the mode of existence of the individual human being is limited and thus does not allow for a "never-ending question," we would have to interpret Margenau to be affirming a life-long commitment. If, on the other hand, we take Margenau to be speaking for the scientific community, his words make good sense. For the community has the kind of existence, i.e., a timeless one, which permits an endless quest.

The following table summarizes the differences alluded to in this section.

TABLE 1

	The individual can say:	But the community
A)	"I'm limited to this stretch of history from —— to ——."	is (theoretically) interminable and possesses a "timeless" mode of existence.
B)	"Death is in the offing for me, though I don't know when."	does not face death and hence has no reason to be troubled by uncertainty.
C)	"I wonder what, if anything, is on the other side of death."	has no occasion to wonder about a possible after-life.
D)	"Next week, God willing, I'll..."	reckons its future in decades and centuries.
E)	"If only I had more time."	has all the time in the world.

The mode of existence of the individual human being is rooted in time, whereas the community's mode of existence is "timeless." The individual human may find himself repeating the words of poet Ralph Hodgson: "Time, you old gypsy man, will you not stay? Put up your caravan, just for one day." The scientific community, on the other hand, might prefer to sing a chorus of Cole Porter's "Time on My Hands."

C. THE COMMUNITY AS COGNITIVE

In this and the following section, we shall discuss what Kuhn refers to as "the knowledge-mediated relationship between the scientist and nature." [44] Speaking of the scientific community, Ziman states:

It is not a tribe, or an industrial corporation, trying to maintain its own stability and continuance as a social entity; it is a voluntary association of individuals dedicated to a *transcendental aim—the advancement of knowledge.*[45]

The scientific community came into existence in order to advance knowledge. This goal continues to attract its members:

The future scientist is attracted by popular scientific literature or by schoolwork in science long before he can form any true idea of the nature of scientific research. The morsels of science which he pikcs up...instil in him the intimation of intellectual treasures and creative joys far beyond his ken. His intuitive realization of a great system of valid thought and of an endless path of discovery sustain him in laboriously accumulating knowledge and urge him on to penetrate into brain-racking theories....
At every stage...he is urged on by the belief that certain things as yet beyond his knowledge and even understanding are on the whole true and valuable, so that it is worth spending his most intensive efforts on mastering them.[46]

The aim of advancing knowledge, then, is "transcendental" in that it is constitutive of the community's very existence. As Michael Polanyi has said, "Scientists who would suddenly lose all their passion for science and take up instead an interest in greyhounds would instantly cease to form a scientific society." [47] The community's mode of existence cannot accommodate such interests. Its purpose is univocal. Thus Polanyi writes:

Scientific life illustrates...how the general acceptance of a *definite* set of principles brings forth a community governed by these principles—a community which would automatically dissolve the moment its constitutive principles were repudiated.[48]

With these observations in mind, we shall say that the scientific community's mode of existence is a *cognitive* one.

A better understanding of this aspect of the community's mode of existence will require us to answer these two questions. First, what does the scientific community seek to understand? Second, what kind of under-

---

[44] Kuhn, *Structure*, p. 141.

[45] Ziman, *Knowledge*, p. 96. (Italics mine.)

[46] Michael Polanyi, *Science, Faith and Society* (Chicago, 1964), pp. 44-45. Hereafter cited as: Polanyi, *Faith*.

[47] *Ibid.*, p. 64.

[48] *Ibid.*

standing does it seek? The following quotes answer these questions sufficiently well for our purposes:

Science is a process of creating new concepts which unify our understanding of the world,...[49]
It would not be difficult to come to an agreement as to what we understand by science. Science is the century-old endeavor to bring together by means of *systematic thought the perceptible phenomena of this world into as thorough-going an association as possible.* To put it boldly, it is the attempt at the posterior reconstruction of existence by the process of conceptualization.[50]

The answer to the first question is implicit in these texts. The community endeavors to understand "the world" or "the perceptible phenomena of this world." The term "perceptible" does not here refer to what the unaided human eye or ear can take in. For the community's range of perception includes the microscopic world of sub-atomic particles and molecules as well as the macroscopic world of distant galaxies. And there is even more:

And finally, it should be added that scientific illumination of human experience is not confined to the area of inquiry about nature...., scientific understanding can be made to penetrate, not only the dealings of man with nature, but likewise the dealings of man with man.[51]

In sum, the answer to the question "What does the scientific community seek to understand?" the answer would appear to be "Anything and everything."

Although this is a very rough answer, it does bring out one very important feature of the community's mode of existence. For if it is true that the community is at least potentially interested in explaining any phenomenon, it must be able to perceive it. But this would mean that the community is possessed of a range of perception which far exceeds that had by any individual. The eye of the individual human can take in only a minute segment of "the perceptible phenomena of this world."

The answer to our second question ("What kind of understanding does the community seek?") can also be gleaned from the two quotations. Einstein would stress that it seeks a *systematic* and *complete* understanding. A general description of understanding in science would have to allude to the role of hypothesis, law and theory; to the role of models,

---

[49] Bronowski, *Common*, p. 140.
[50] Einstein, *Years*, p. 28. (Italics mine.)
[51] Margenau, *Vistas*, p. 76.

statistical correlation, observation, and prediction. Yet the question of what specifically constitutes scientific understanding is a complex one. Carnap writes:

If we demand from the modern physicist an answer to the question what he means by the symbol "ψ" of his calculus, and are astonished that he cannot give an answer, we ought to realize that the situation was already the same in classical physics. There the physicist could not tell us what he meant by the symbol "E" in Maxwell's equations. Perhaps, in order not to refuse an answer, he would tell us that "E" designates the electric field vector. To be sure, this statement has the form of a semantical rule, but it would not help us a bit to understand the theory. It simply refers from a symbol in a symbolic calculus to a corresponding word expression in a calculus of words. We are right in demanding an interpretation for "E," but that will be given indirectly by semantical rules referring to elementary signs together with the formulas connecting them with "E." This interpretation enables us to use the laws containing "E" for the derivation of predictions. Thus we understand "E," if "understanding" of an expression, a sentence, or a theory means capability of its use for the description of known facts or the prediction of new facts. An "intuitive understanding" or a direct translation of "E" into terms referring to observable properties is neither necessary nor possible. The situation of the modern physicist is not essentially different. He knows how to use the symbol "ψ" in the calculus in order to derive predictions which we can test by observations. (If they have the form of probability statements, they are tested by statistical results of observations.) Thus the physicist, although he cannot give us a translation into everyday language, understands the symbol "ψ" and the laws of quantum mechanics. He possesses *that kind of understanding which alone is essential in the field of knowledge and science.*[52]

Without pledging allegiance to Carnap's philosophy of science, we would agree with him that there is something which can rightly be called "*that kind of understanding which alone is essential in the field of knowledge and science.*"

"*That kind of understanding*" differs in important respects from what takes place when a man reads the evening newspaper. He possesses a kind of understanding, too. But for *this* kind of understanding, no special skill or talent or training is necessary. He uses the language of everyday life and he can explain himself in that language. But if an individual is to understand quantum mechanics, he will have to have special gifts.[53] Thus Polanyi says that:

---

[52] Rudolf Carnap, "Elementary and Abstract Terms," in *Philosophy of Science,* ed. Arthur Danto and Sydney Morgenbesser (Cleveland and New York, 1960), pp. 157-58. (Italics mine.)
[53] Polanyi, *Faith,* p. 65.

... a full initiation into the premisses of science can be gained only by the few who possess the gifts for becoming independent scientists, and they usually achieve it only through close personal association with the intimate views and practice of a distinguished master.[54]

As Carnap observes, understanding quantum mechanics will require familiarity with a specialized language which cannot be translated into everyday language. The task of elucidating the special features which characterize scientific understanding belongs to the philosophy of science. Our aim here is to point to general features which distinguish it from the kind of understanding characteristic of the individual human being in everyday life.[55]

Henry Margenau alludes to a very important feature of scientific understanding in this item of his scientific *credo*: "I recognize no subjects and no facts which are alleged to be forever closed to inquiry or understanding; *a mystery is but a challenge*." [56] The scientific community is devoted to the task of providing a *total and complete understanding*. It refuses to be satisfied with less. Hence what others (even other scientists) might call a mystery is, for the community, a phenomenon which has yet to be explained. It is, as Margenau says, a challenge to the community to come up with an explanation. (It does not follow from this that the community will take up every such challenge.)

Putting this same point grammatically, we could observe that words like "mystery" and "inexplicable" are conspicuously absent from the grammar of the ongoing scientific community. These words and all their cousins are by convention (the convention which brought the scientific community into existence and which continues to bind the community together) *out of place* in a finished work of science—i.e., in a journal article. The convention to which we refer is that acknowledged goal of seeking a full understanding. To recognize this goal as transcendental, as constitutive of the very being of the scientific community, is to recognize

---

[54] *Ibid.*, p. 43.

[55] Two observations are appropriate at this juncture. First, we are not suggesting that the term "understanding" has one determinate sense in ordinary language. Were we to attempt a detailed analysis of this term as it is used in ordinary language, we would follow the leads provided by Wittgenstein in his *Philosophical Investigations*. Secondly, we cannot here deal with an important question which is obviously raised by our characterization of the scientific community as cognitive: i.e., How do science and philosophy differ? For philosophy, too, seeks knowledge and understanding. The answer to this question requires a far more specific analysis than we can give here.

[56] Margenau, *Vistas*, p. 76. (Italics mine.)

that the community cannot—by its very nature—accord a place in its vocabulary to a word like "mystery."

Thus grammar not only helps us to understand what kind of being the scientific community is (i.e., a cognitive being in search of total understanding) but also shows us *that* it differs from the individual human being. For words like "mystery" and "inexplicable" do have a place in his vocabulary. An individual might easily find himself confronted by a phenomenon or a situation which would occasion this sentence: "It's a mystery to me; I'll never understand it." A human being can utter such a sentence; the community cannot. An individual can utter such a sentence without being unfaithful to his own nature. For his own cognitive powers will surely have limits, surely come to an end somewhere. Yet if the community were to say such a thing, it would be *eo ipso* untrue to its calling. This does not mean that the individual scientist could not proclaim something a mystery or that he could not point to something which he cannot understand. But the cognitive powers of the community transcend such limitations; the community itself regards every well-defined phenomenon as explicable all the way.

As one might expect, the scientific community (with its unlimited time, range of perception, and powers of cognition) will have a vision of the world which differs markedly from that of the individual human being (with his limited time, range of perception, and powers of cognition). An eminent physicist is reported to have said the following, on receiving an award:

I believe that these [discoveries] are but stepping stones leading to a deeper... understanding of nature. When we arrive at this understanding, we shall marvel how neatly all the elementary particles fit into the Great Scheme.[57]

All scientists would not agree with the notion that science will finally arrive at such an understanding. Still some allegiance to the idea of a "Great Scheme" is operative in the thinking of many scientists. Einstein, for example, writes:

Although it is true that the goal of science is to discover rules which permit the association and foretelling of facts, this is not its only aim. It also seeks to reduce the connections discovered to the smallest possible number of mutually independent conceptual elements. It is in this striving after *the rational unification of the manifold* that it encounters its greatest successes, even though it is precisely this attempt which causes it to run the greatest risk of falling a prey to illusions.[58]

[57] Words attributed to Mme. Wu, cited by Barzun in *Glorious*, p. 82. The insertion in brackets is Barzun's.

[58] Einstein, *Years*, p. 33. (Italics mine.)

The scientific community seeks more than an understanding of *particular* phenomena. It also seeks a total vision where everything fits into place, a point of view from which the flow of events will appear smooth and ordered. There are, at any given moments, dark patches, so to speak —phenomena which have thus far resisted incorporation into this total vision. But the community is committed to bringing these surds within that vision, to making them a part of the rationally unified manifold. To what degree this vision is operative in the mind of the working scientist is a question for the psychology of science. Benjamin writes:

Because man is unhappy in the presence of the mysterious and unexplained; because he is uncomfortable when he is unable to foresee and prepare for happenings in nature; and because he is basically curious and likes to solve problems and gain understanding and insight-because of all these factors in man's make-up he sets about through the use of his imaginative and rational capacities to create a world of formulas and laws in which mystery, irrationality, ignorance, and fear are minimized. This world, in its ideal form, is a utopia in which everything can be explained and accounted for, in which man has such complete control over his environment that unforeseen events can never surprise him, and in which the forces of nature are completely at his service.

Such a picture, of course, seldom enters consciously into the mind of any scientist, and when it does it is probably vague both in its outlines and in its details. But some such ideal seems to be the guiding factor in the development of science.[59]

This ideal, this unified vision belongs not to any one scientist, but to the ongoing scientific community as a whole.

Here then is another difference between the community and the individual. Not only does the individual have a much narrower range of perception, but that small portion of events which he does perceive will very likely appear to his eye as a mixture of the ordered and the chaotic, the routine and the surprising, the intelligible and the inexplicable. Presumably no one man could say, as Einstein has, that "the more a man is imbued with *the ordered regularity of all events* the firmer becomes his conviction that there is no room left by the side of this ordered regularity for causes of a different nature." [60] We must presume that Einstein is here speaking as a qualified spokesman on behalf of the ongoing scientific community, whose eye—as we have said—may take in all events and whose intellect is committed to bringing everything into the category of the explicable.

---

[59] Benjamin, *Values*, p. 15.
[60] Einstein, *Years*, p. 32. (Italics mine.)

Generally, the community will have a good idea of what its major tasks are at a given moment in time. It will know where the dark patches are which cloud its vision. In 1967, Mario Bunge drew up the following list:

A few instances of big unfinished tasks are: the building of a general theory of non-linear oscillations; the *n*-body problem; the investigation of the inners of fundamental particles; a detailed theory of the origin of life and the attempt to synthesize the grossest components of the protoplasm and eventually a whole unit of living matter; to set up neurological theories of thought processes; to build mathematical theories of basic social processes in large communities, enabling us to make accurate socio-logical forecasts. Such problems are ambitious and, at the same time, they seem within the reach of our century,...[61]

Notice, first, that these tasks—like all scientific tasks—are cognitive ones and can be undertaken only by those who have the special gifts which admit a man to the scientific community. Secondly, these tasks are not assigned to anyone in particular. Any interested scientist may attempt to solve them. Thirdly, these tasks are not subject to any temporal restriction. Bunge says that they "seem" to be within reach of this century, but there is no way of knowing this in advance. But as the community has no deadlines, it does not matter how long they may take. Fourthly, the community has developed a kind of decision-procedure which prevents it from undertaking pseudo-tasks and *insolubilia*:

According to obscurantism, not only are there inherently unsolvable problems (mys-teries) but the deeper a problem the more mysterious it is. The illuministic tradition, on the other hand, asserts the solvability of every problem subject to the following conditions: (i) that the problems be well-formulated; (ii) that the necessary means be available; (iii) that what is sought be not physically impossible (i.e., incompatible with natural laws), and (iv) that the term not be limited. In short, *qualified* solvability is asserted by illuminism: it does not say that every problem is solvable but rather that every *well-formulated* scientific problem is solvable *in principle*, i.e. if the adequate means (data, theories and techniques) are found. Clearly, this assertion is in keeping with the history of science, whereas the obscurantist thesis is refuted by the latter.[62]

Fifthly, because of its corporate nature, the community does not have to decide between these tasks but can proceed—through its various sub-communities—to attack them all simultaneously (unless there are relation-ships of logical dependence).

---

[61] Bunge, *Research*, p. 168.

[62] *Ibid.*, p. 209. We do not mean to imply, nor does Bunge, that the scientific community has the kind of decision-procedure which can be found in some areas of formal science.

Many of the tasks which occupy the individual human being display a different set of characteristics. In the first place, the individual is not always engaged in tasks which are cognitive; and he is engaged in tasks which do not require special gifts. Secondly, some of his tasks are tasks for him and for no one else. If, for example, he has pledged fidelity to another human in marriage, no one else can fulfill that task of being faithful for him. Thirdly, many of his tasks have a temporal parameter. In some cases, this will mean meeting a deadline (as in filing a yearly tax return); in other cases, the task will have time itself as its medium (as in being faithful *for life* to one's spouse). Fourthly, there is sometimes no way of knowing in advance whether one will be able to succeed or not. Not even the barest outlines of a decision procedure exists which would eliminate the factor of risk from some human tasks and problems. Fifthly, because he can only do so many things at one time and because he has limited time, the individual human being may have to decide between one task and another.

Scientific tasks, then, differ in several respects from the kind of task which may occupy the individual human being. The very fact that the community knows at a given moment what the important unfinished tasks before it are is itself significant. For where can an individual human being go to find out what his tasks are? Is such a list available to him? When an individual begins to wonder what his tasks are, he will very possibly have to confront the question "Who (or what) am I?" Such questions arise in the life of many individuals. And if they do, and if the individual finds that he has no answer, it may be difficult for him to settle the question of which tasks are his tasks.

The question "What is science?" is often asked. As we have noted, however, no satisfactory answer seems to have yet been given. But this does not interfere with the business of the community; it does not hamper its ability to define its tasks and to proceed to their solution:

What logic is and what it does has been the subject of much misunderstanding.... There are differences of opinion in which reasonable and knowledgeable experts are to be found on both sides; that is the way it goes with any attempt to answer basic questions,... We would meet with the same situation if we started by asking, "What is science?" or "What is mathematics?" Fortunately, it is possible to carry out many of the important functions of all these human activities without finding any ultimately satisfactory answer to such questions;...[63]
One can be zealous for Science, and a splendidly successful research worker, without

[63] D. B. Terrell, *Logic: A Modern Introduction to Deductive Reasoning* (New York, 1967), pp. 3-4.

pretending to a clear and certain notion of what Science really is. In practice it does not seem to matter.[64]

Certainly we have not shed any new light on this question. We have attempted to indicate that the scientific community has a cognitive mode of existence. The table below summarizes our results.

TABLE 2

	The scientific community:	But the individual:
A)	has an unlimited range of perception.	is witness to a small segment of all phenomena.
B)	regards every phenomenon as explicable all the way.	may expect to meet with things he cannot understand.
C)	views the flow of events as an ordered regularity.	will see as much disorder as order in that portion of all events which he views.
D)	knows exactly what its unfinished business is at a given moment.	may express his doubts as to which tasks are his.
E)	has not found that ignorance about the nature of Science prevents it from completing its tasks.	may find that ignorance about his own nature is an obstacle to carrying out his tasks.

The scientific community exists for the sake of knowledge. Given the fact that its corporate assets include some of the best minds in each generation, and given the fact that it is free from temporal restrictions, it is not surprising that its cognitive powers differ mightily from those of any individual human being.

D. THE COMMUNITY AS EXCLUSIVELY COGNITIVE

In the previous section, it was claimed that the scientific community has a cognitive mode of existence. In this section, we deal with the closely related point that its mode of existence is *exclusively* cognitive. To understand what is meant by this, consider the following passage:

[64] Ziman, *Knowledge*, p. 6.

As I see it, the duty of every active scientist requires him to stand back from his current research from time to time, to take a look at his subject as a whole. He ought to ask himself 'What major question are we asking of Nature? How far have we succeeded in answering it? What are the assumptions upon which our research has proceeded? Are all phenomena subservient to an intelligible theory, or are there major mysteries and contradictions? How does what we know in this field connect with our knowledge in other fields?... In short: what do we really *know* about our subject?' [65]

The questions on this list might be said to constitute one man's version of a "scientific examination of conscience." Note that all the questions are related to the community's attempt to advance knowledge. This is the community's only concern. It has no other posture towards the world, no other point of contact with phenomena than this cognitive one. This is what we mean by saying that the scientific community's mode of existence is exclusively cognitive.

At various times in his life, the individual human being will no doubt find himself engaged in the effort to understand something. But such efforts do not exhaust his mode of existence, as the following passage may indicate:

Another woman I met coming away from a funeral. It was a tragic case of a young married woman dying just after childbirth. To my surprise, this woman said, 'I have always gone to church and believed in God but I must admit that this has shaken my faith'. The reason for this was that her friend, a young married mother, had died, whereas a girl who had had an illegitimate baby about the same time had lived! What does one say to anyone in the street on such an occasion? [66]

In this passage, we meet two human beings, one sorrowing over the death of a close friend, the other wondering what to say to her. Both postures are characteristically human, though neither could be described as (primarily) cognitive. Sorrow and joy, suffering and ecstasy, tears and laughter —these and many more are all part of the human condition. The attempt to know is a natural part of any human life, for man is a being with a mind. But it will not be the only part of his life; for man's being also includes desire, affection, emotion and passion.

To bring out the contrast we have in mind here, let us suppose (*per impossibile*) that the scientific community could make contact with the sorrowing woman described above. The community has a language and it has (as we have indicated) tremendous cognitive powers. If the com-

---

[65] *Ibid.*, p. 124

[66] From a letter to Bishop John A. T. Robinson, cited in *The Honest To God Debate,* ed. David L. Edwards (Philadelphia, 1963), pp. 51-52.

munity could voice its thoughts, its speech would have to go something like this:

Granted what we know about how the human body functions, and given the respective physiological condition of the two women, it is perfectly understandable that your friend should have died and that the other woman lived. And given what we know about human behavior and your feelings for the dead woman, your own reaction to her death is also understandable.

Having pronounced this verdict of intelligibility, the community has exhausted its concern with this particular situation. It has said everything which can be said in character, everything that is possible for it to say as a cognitive entity. It cannot step outside of this posture in order to attempt to console the sorrowing woman. The scientific community is not the kind of being that can console and sympathize. It would be untrue to its nature if it attempted to do so. Its mode of existence is exclusively cognitive. It knows what suffering is, but does not itself suffer. It knows what joy is, but does not itself experience it.

If a human being met with such a sorrowing person, he might well attempt to sympathize with her. This would require intellect, though not necessarily the kind of total understanding which the community seeks. A human being might say to the woman:

I'm terribly sorry to hear of your friend's death; it's simply tragic. I, too, once lost someone very close to me just like that. I know what you must be going through, so if there is anything I can do, any way that I can help, please don't hesitate to call on me.

Of course, it would be equally possible just to ignore the woman, and say to oneself: "I just don't have the time or the energy to get involved with her grief; I have enough of my own." Both kinds of reaction are feasible for an individual human being, though neither falls within the compass of the scientific community. And when an individual examines his conscience, his reaction to such situations will be part of his material.

Our point can, once again, be seen from a grammatical point of view. The vocabulary of the scientific community, because it is geared exclusively to cognitive tasks, does not contain words like "tragic." Einstein observes:

The scientific way of thinking has a further characteristic. The concepts which it uses to build up its coherent systems are not expressing emotions. For the scientist, there is only "being," but no wishing, no valuing, no good, no evil;...[67]

---

[67] Einstein, *Years*, p. 110.

The scientific community is concerned only with "being," with what is, and with understanding it. Its vocabulary reflects this in that terms like "tragic" are absent from it. From its point of view, the death of the one mother is either "subservient to an intelligible theory" or it is not. But it is not tragic. Nor, from its point of view, could the other mother's baby be called "illegitimate." The fact that these terms and many others which have an emotional tone are absent from the community's vocabulary reveals what kind of being the community is: an exclusively cognitive one.[68] The fact that such terms do belong to the vocabulary of the individual human being shows in turn that there is an important difference between the two.

We may have created the impression that we believe the individual scientist to be a depersonalized being. Benjamin states:

Science does not go about the world disembodied, but is the activities of certain individuals, and the results of these activities exhibited in books, documents, and reports, on the one hand, and in inventions and objects of human ingenuity, on the other. It is common in discussions of science to regard scientists as a kind of Absolute Knower—a completely depersonalized being who makes observations, performs experiments, describes facts, invents theories, and creates symbolic schemes, and then promptly recedes into the background.[69]

This stereotype has been exploded time and again in the recent literature.[70] What Polanyi has said about the scientist seems true:

..., far from being neutral at heart, he is himself passionately interested in the outcome of the procedure. He must be, for otherwise he will never discover a problem at all and certainly not advance towards its solution. '... To solve a serious scientific problem (writes Polya) will-power is needed that can outlast years of toil and bitter disappointments....'[71]

Moreover, it is naive to think that a man who has worked for years and years on a project will have no emotional involvement with it. "An idea that one has nursed for years, until it has become the apple of one's eye,

---

[68] By "the community's vocabulary," we mean those terms which will occur in a finished work of science—a journal article, for example. We do not mean the terms which might occur in a work about science. If a study was done on the attitudes of a society towards a child born out of wedlock, the word "illegitimate" would occur; but it would not have the emotional tone that it might have in everyday speech.

[69] Benjamin, *Values*, p. 13.

[70] Cf. Michael Polanyi, *Personal Knowledge* (New York, 1964). Cf. especially Chaper 6, "Intellectual Passions." Cf. also James D. Watson, *The Double Helix* (New York, 1968).

[71] Polanyi, *Faith*, pp. 38-39.

becomes, when published to the world, an emotional attachment like one's own child." [72]

It may appear contradictory to admit that the individual scientist has, as does any other human being, an emotional aspect to his existence and yet maintain that the scientific community has an exclusively cognitive mode of existence. The apparent contradiction disappears, however, when a distinction is made between the scientific community as such and the individual scientist. Clearly the individual scientist has properties which are not characteristic of the community (he faces death), just as the community has properties (unlimited range of perception) which no individual scientist has. Kuhn invokes this distinction when he discusses the problem of rigidity:

Even though prolonged crises are probably reflected in less rigid educational practice, scientific training is not well designed to produce the man who will easily discover a fresh approach. But so long as somebody appears with a new candidate for a paradigm—usually a young man or one new to the field—the loss due to rigidity *accrues only to the individual.* Given a generation in which to effect the change, individual rigidity is compatible with a community that can switch from paradigm to paradigm when the occasion demands.[73]

Similarly, though individual scientists may be petty or intolerant, the community as a whole is able to transcend these imperfections, which suggests that it is more than the sum of its parts.

That the scientific community's mode of existence is an exclusively cognitive one is attested to not only by its vocabulary, but also by the kinds of sentence that are formulated in it:

Science searches for relations which are thought to exist independently of the searching individual. This includes the case where man himself is the subject. Or the subject of scientific statements may be concepts created by ourselves, as in mathematics. Such concepts are not necessarily supposed to correspond to any objects in the outside world. However, *all scientific statements and laws have one characteristic in common: they are "true or false" (adequate or inadequate). Roughly speaking, our reaction to them is "yes" or "no."* [74]

The individual human being, on the other hand, uses sentences which do not have one common characteristic. That is, the sentences of everyday life serve many purposes. They are used to tell jokes, to tease, to encourage a person, to chastise someone, and to make statements which are

---

[72] Ziman, *Knowledge*, p. 134.
[73] Kuhn, *Structure*, p. 166. (Italics mine.)
[74] Einstein, *Years*, p. 110. (Italics mine.)

"true or false." [75] Thus our reaction to sentences will vary. It may be laughter, irritation, uplift, repentance, and "yes" or "no". That the sentences of everyday life have this range, and that our reactions to them can vary so, again indicates that the mode of existence of the individual human being includes many postures besides the cognitive one which characterizes the scientific community's mode of existence.

Finally, the community's exclusive concern with knowledge is reflected in its form and style of communication:

> The official scientific paper in a reputable journal is not an advertisement, or a news item; it is a contributon to the consensus of public knowledge. ..., it is written in a special impersonal form, in somewhat abstract language, within a special convention of form and style.... A major achievement of our civilization is the creation of this form of communication, however clumsy and barbaric it may seem to those whose concerns are with poetry and feeling.[76]

The purpose of communication within the scientific community is to increase knowledge. The language in such communications is technical —intelligible only to those who have the special gifts which admit one to the community. The form is abstract, and the impersonal style of such communications reveals the fact that the whole enterprise of science is a corporate one:

> It is not merely, in Newton's incomparable phrase, that one stands on the shoulders of giants, and hence can see a little farther. Every scientist sees through his own eyes—and also through the eyes of his predecessors and colleagues. It is never one individual that goes through all the steps in the logico-inductive chain; it is a group of individuals, dividing their labour but continuously and jealously checking each other's contributions. The cliché of scientific prose betrays itself 'Hence *we* arrive at the conclusion that...' The audience to which scientific publications are addressed is not passive; by its cheering or booing, its bouquets or brickbats, it actively controls the substance of the communications that it receives.[77]

A scientific communication is addressed, as it were, to the community at large. There are only two appropriate responses: acceptance or rejection. Acceptance is usually signified by the fact that the communication is cited in a review article written by one of the community's acknowledged spokesmen.[78] The content of that communication is then fit for

---

[75] Cf. Wittgenstein, *Investigations*, #23.

[76] Ziman, *Knowledge*, p. 109. Chapter 6 of Ziman's work contains an informative discussion of the process of communication within the scientific community. Cf. also Derek J. de Solla Price, *Science Since Babylon* (New Haven, 1961), p. 95.

[77] *Ibid.*, p. 9.

[78] *Ibid.*, p. 122.

incorporation in the "mind" of the community; i.e., it is written into the textbooks; other scientists refer to it in their own work, etc.[79] In such fashion, the community appropriates the content of its communications.

Communication between individuals in daily life cannot be said to have any one purpose. Sometimes the aim will be to increase the recipient's knowledge, e.g., a family newsletter sent to friends at Christmas. But such would not be the primary purpose of sending a get-well card to a friend in the hospital. As there is no one purpose to communication in ordinary life, so there is not the strong convention of form and style that is found in the scientific community. Letters, phone-calls, a heart-to-heart talk, memos—all may be useful forms of communication. The language of daily life is all one needs to have mastered in order to be able to send and receive these. Some communications will be addressed to the individual in his own name, e.g., an invitation; while others will be addressed to him anonymously, e.g., a circular bearing only the name "Occupant." Finally, the kind of response which is appropriate varies from situation to situation. An invitation requires a "yes" or "no"; a subpoena requires the individual to appear in court; a "Dear John" letter expects no response at all.

Once again, we summarize our findings in a table.

TABLE 3

	The scientific community:	But the individual:
A)	has an exclusively cognitive mode of existence.	has many "postures" which are in keeping with his nature.
B)	is unable to console and sympathize.	may attempt to lighten the burden of another human.
C)	does not itself experience suffering or joy, though it may make them the object of investigation.	will in the course of his life experience suffering and joy, tears and laughter, and much else.
D)	has a language and a style of communication which has been perfected for its one purpose —increasing knowledge.	speaks the language of his country and is able to receive and respond to various kinds of communication.

[79] Kuhn, *Structure*, p. 137.

E. THE COMMUNITY AS ESSENTIALLY PUBLIC

In his illuminating work of the same title, John Ziman argues that the defining characteristic of scientific knowledge is that it is *Public Knowledge*.[80] Whether this formulation proves adequate or not, Ziman has certainly called attention to an *important* characteristic of scientific knowledge. He writes:

Science is not merely *published* knowledge or information. Anyone may make an observation, or conceive a hypothesis, and, if he has the financial means, get it printed and distributed for other persons to read. Scientific knowledge is more than this. Its facts and theories must survive a period of critical study and testing by other competent and disinterested individuals, and must have been found so persuasive that they are almost universally accepted. The objective of Science is not just to acquire information nor to utter all non-contradictory notions; its goal is a *consensus* of rational opinion over the widest possible field.[81]

A contribution to scientific knowledge must not only be public in the sense that it has been made public and hence is accessible to any qualified member of the community for appraisal. It must also be public in the sense that it has been ratified by the consensus. The solutions that satisfy the scientist "...may not be merely personal but must instead be accepted as solutions by many." [82]

Schilling gets to this point by means of an interesting question:

Science is not only a human, but more particularly a social enterprise—that is, one of sharing, cooperation, and of interaction of people. Among students the following question always generates considerable interest and discussion: Is a one-man physics possible? Could a completely isolated man with great intelligence and unlimited material resources, as well as unlimited time, develop a body of knowledge such as we now call physics? Almost invariably students reply with a *yes*.... Experienced physicists, however, reply with a *no*.[83]

Schilling's question is very closely related to our own investigation in this chapter. For in order to endow this hypothetical individual with the community's properties, one must first of all have become aware of them. Such an individual would have to be given the property of being "timeless." He would have to be isolated, i.e., free from any other concerns. He would have to have unlimited perception and vast intellectual powers.

---

[80] Ziman, *Knowledge,* Chapter 1.
[81] *Ibid.,* p. 9.
[82] Kuhn, *Structure,* p. 168.
[83] Schilling, *Religion,* pp. 50-51.

Yet it seems to many that such properties (all of which, we have seen, belong to the community) would not be enough. To whom would this one man publicize his results? To what consensus would he submit them for ratification? In short, the one essential commodity that our hypothetical one-man community cannot be endowed with is that of being public. This brings out the fact that science, as we know it, is essentially a public enterprise. A private science would simply not be science, as we know it. In *Physicist and Christian,* Pollard states: "I do not any more have a faith of my own than I have a physics of my own." [84]

Scientific knowledge must be public in the very same fashion as that which it seeks to explain—nature—is public. In *Science and Subjectivity,* Israel Scheffler writes:

To propound one's beliefs in a scientific spirit is to acknowledge that they may turn out to be wrong under continued examination, that they may fail to sustain themselves critically in an enlarged experience. It is, in effect, to conceive one's self of the here and now as linked through potential converse with a *community of others, whose differences of location or opinion yet allow a common discourse and access to a shared world.*[85]

The "standard view" of science understands it to be "...a systematic *public* enterprise, controlled by logic and empirical fact, whose purpose it is to formulate truth about the natural world." [86] Scheffler claims that the very existence of a consensus among scientists about this natural world testifies to the fact that there is a "codifiable methodology" underlying this enterprise, a methodology which "...makes possible the growth of tested scientific knowledge as a *public possession.*" [87] Scientific knowledge is public in this added sense that it does not belong to any one individual.

It is the public nature of scientific knowledge that renders national boundaries irrelevant. As Ziman says, "the manifest internationalism of Science is not a bourgeois or communist conspiracy;... Internationalism is a primary principle of Science demanded by *the inmost law of its being.*" [88] An atom is an atom, whether in Paris or in Moscow. An

---

[84] Pollard, *Physicist,* p. 13.

[85] Israel Scheffler, *Science and Subjectivity* (Indianapolis, New York, and Kansas City, 1967), pp. 1-2. (Italics mine.)

[86] *Ibid.,* p. 8. (Italics mine.)

[87] *Ibid.,* p. 10. (Italics mine.)

[88] Ziman, *Knowledge,* p. 93. (Italics mine.) This does not imply that scientists will, individually, be free from prejudices of a nationalistic sort. Cf. Derek J. de Solla Price, *op. cit.,* pp. 83 ff.

adequate theory about the atom will be acknowledged throughout the community. In Sarton's words, "Science is essentially international, or perhaps we should say supernational." [89]

In summary, then, scientific knowledge is public in the sense that it is published and therefore accessible to any qualified person. "*Scientific knowledge is communicable*: it is not ineffable but utterable, not private but public. Scientific knowledge conveys information to whomsoever has been trained to understand it." [90] Scientific knowledge is public in the sense that it must have been ratified by the consensus. And it is public in the sense that it does not belong to any one individual. Bronowski writes: "These are the marks of science: that it is open for all to hear, and all are free to speak their minds in it." [91] For all of these reasons, then, it seems reasonable to say that the scientific community's mode of existence is a *public* one. Its being is open, external, freely accessible to anyone with sufficient talent.

The mode of existence of the individual human being is also, to a certain extent, public. That is to say, certain aspects of his existence are external and open to view. His date and place of birth; his height, weight, and other vital statistics; his occupation and marital status—all of these are matters of public record in most societies today. In addition, many of his thoughts, ideas, and values may be known to other human beings.

At the same time, it is recognized that each individual has a dimension which is not external and public. Even those humans we think we know best often surprise us. "I've known him (her) for all these years and never had the slightest idea that he (she) felt that way." Most human beings have had occasion to utter some such sentence during their lives. The contrast between the outer and the inner is characteristically human. He is the kind of being that has both aspects to his existence:

Although to *outward view* he was a forthright and commanding figure, *this was only one aspect of the man. There was also an inner nature,...*[92]

The general formula applies to every human, although the details differ from one individual to the next. The outer and the inner, the exterior and the interior, the public and the private—human existence involves both.

[89] George Sarton, *The Life of Science* (New York, 1948), p. 26.

[90] Bunge, *Queries*, p. 43.

[91] Bronowski, *Common*, p. 154.

[92] T. A. Goudge, "Memorial for Fulton Henry Anderson, M.A., Ph.D., Ll.D., D.Litt., F.R.S.C." *Dialogue*, VII (1969), pp. 92-93. (Italics mine.)

Let us concentrate for a moment on the interior aspect of the human being. This interior may be said to contain an assortment of thoughts, attitudes, hopes, feelings, beliefs, and so on. The assortment varies from individual to individual. But it may be said to be private in at least two senses. First, the interior of one human is usually not known by another unless it is divulged. It can even be the case that the individual is himself only vaguely aware of what is contained in his own interior. The ability of one human being to penetrate the interior of another is extremely limited. Even when an individual chooses to reveal some aspect of his interior, allowances must be made for the possibility of deception, whether conscious or not. That is, lying and deception are phenomena often met with in the human mode of existence.

Secondly, even if the individual makes an honest revelation of some aspect of his interior, that which is revealed still remains a part of *his own interior*. The thought divulged still belongs to that person—even though someone else may have a similar thought. In this sense, the individual's interior is private; for it is *his*.

It is characteristic then of the mode of existence of the individual that it has both a public and a private dimension. Is there an interior or private dimension to the scientific community's mode of existence? What could its content be? We have already seen that the community has an exclusively cognitive mode of existence. Its only business is adding to the store of knowledge, so if there were to be anything "private" or "interior" it would have to be a thought or a piece of knowledge. It could not, it appears, be anything else. But we have just shown that scientific knowledge is public knowledge. Unpublished work cannot be assessed and ratified and therefore cannot truly play a role in the life of the community. It would seem fair to say, then, that the community has no "private" thoughts; indeed, that it is essentially a public being without an interior. But since its sole *raison d'être* is to produce public knowledge, this is not to be interpreted as deficiency.

Here then is another important difference between the community's mode of existence and the individual's. The community's mode of existence is public. Its tasks are public tasks. They can be undertaken by anyone with the necessary interest and talent. They can even be transferred from one scientist to another, from one generation of scientist to the next. And success or failure is a public affair.

The individual human being also has public tasks, e.g., paying his taxes. How he feels in his interior about this task is of no consequence. He may even appoint someone else to do it for him. But there are tasks which do make demands upon his interior as well. When a man pledges fidelity to his wife, he takes up a task which has both exterior and interior dimensions. Both are important, as indeed they are related. But such tasks are not the kind which he can transfer to someone else.

In light of the fact that the community's mode of existence is a public one, let us consider Einstein's words that "As long as we remain within the realm of science proper, we can never meet with a sentence of the type: 'Thou shalt not lie.'" [93] Although Einstein offers this observation in the context of distinguishing between scientific laws and ethical ones, it has significance for our own investigation. The sentence in question has no role to play in the life of the scientific community. Indeed, it cannot even be formulated in its specialized language. The fact that it is formulable in the language of everyday life and has, moreover, a role to play would again be an indication that the community and the individual have different modes of existence.

Since the scientific community is solely devoted to knowledge and truth, lying is *ipso facto* excluded from its mode of existence. But more to the point of this section, lying is possible only where there can be a disparity between what is said and what is thought. Since the scientific community has a public mode of existence, since in the last analysis what the community thinks and what it says are one and the same, it follows that, for the community as such, lying is impossible.

The situation of the individual scientist is different. He may attempt to lie to the community; he may even be, for a while, successful. But in doing so, he simply manifests his own failure to internalize the scientific attitude. Still there are reasons why lying and deception will be very infrequent in the scientific community. Some writers are amazed by the honesty of scientists:

Few professions impose a more rigorous set of ethics upon their members than does science. It is an amazing fact that the same man who may cheat on his income tax, be unfaithful to his wife, or play politics in the laboratory, will exercise the utmost honesty in the *public* profession of science.[94]

Precisely because science is *public*, we would suggest that this fact is not so amazing. For an intelligent man does not engage in a deception unless he believes he can be successful. And it is reasonable to believe that one may be unfaithful to one's wife and get away with it. One may

[93] Einstein, *Years*, p. 110.
[94] Richard H. Bube, ed., *The Encounter Between Christianity and Science* (Grand Rapide, 1968), p. 39. (Italics mine.)

even cheat on his income tax and get away with it. But before a result or a theory is ratified by the community, it must be made public and it must be scrutinized by very competent and intelligent men. What chances are there for a piece of successful deception in such conditions? Presumably, if a man is intelligent enough to have become a scientist, he would also be intelligent enough to understand that he has very little prospect of success.

The very fact that a human being might prefer something else to truth suggests again differences between the scientific community and the human being. For the community is understood to be devoted to the truth without reservation:

A community which effectively practices free discussion is therefore dedicated to the fourfold proposition (1) that there is such a thing as truth; (2) *that all members love it*; (3) *that they feel obliged and* (4) *are in fact capable of pursuing it.*[95]

But the individual human being has been known to rank many things above the love of the truth: pleasure, respect, security, money, success.

The differences between the individual and the community do not end here. For not only is the community fully devoted to the truth, it is also able to guard itself against error by, to use Barzun's phrase, "the communal sense of sight." [96] "In science," Margenau says, "an error does not remain undetected or forgotten;..." [97] "A mistaken observation will be repeated, and the discrepancy noted and corrected; a bad piece of logic or of calculation will be reworked and put right by some other person in due course." [98] But the individual human does not have the benefit of a communal sense of sight; nor does he have the community's freedom from the restraints of time which may be necessary to bring an error to light. Moreover, because his mode of existence has an interior dimension, his fellow human beings might not be able to detect an error which was located in that interior. It is possible for an individual human being to be in error without knowing it.

Not only is the community able to detect error, it is also able to correct it. This facility for self-correction is, according to Bunge, one of the most important features of the scientific method.[99] The following passage is a succinct summary of the community's situation:

---

[95] Polanyi, *Faith*, p. 71. (Italics mine.)
[96] Barzun, *Glorious*, p. 75.
[97] Margenau, *Vistas*, p. 74.
[98] Ziman, *Knowledge*, p. 55.
[99] Bunge, *Research*, p. 18.

What science claims is (i) to be *truer* than any non-scientific model of the world, (ii) to be able to *test* such a truth claim, (iii) to be able to *discover its own short-comings,* and (iv) to be able to *correct its own shortcomings,...*[100]

The scientific community has an exclusively cognitive mode of existence within which truth is an absolute value. Because its mode of existence is both timeless and essentially public, the community will eventually detect an error and correct it.

The individual human being's mode of existence is not exclusively cognitive. He cannot therefore assume that he is absolutely devoted to the truth. Because his mode of existence has an interior dimension, it is possible that *his* shortcomings dwell where no communal sense of sight can penetrate. Because he has a limited amount of time, it is possible that he might die before discovering *his* shortcomings. In short, the individual's mode of existence is just different enough from the community's that he, unlike the community, cannot claim with complete confidence the ability to discover and correct his own shortcomings.

Once the community has arrived at the truth, its public mode of existence insures that this truth will not be lost or forgotten. "The definitions of science, also a result of collective thought, are not supposed to be subject to individual variation.... Once understood, they do not slip away."[101] This applies not only to definitions, but to theories and laws as well. Once accepted, these are installed in the collective memory of the community—its textbooks and journals. They stand on file, ready to be cited, revised, corrected, ignored for a time; but they are never forgotten.

"With the affairs of active human beings," Einstein observes, "it is different. Here knowledge of truth alone does not suffice; on the contrary, this knowledge must *continually be renewed by ceaseless effort,* if it is not to be lost."[102] Because his mode of existence is varied, the individual is subject to distractions. He forgets things. If he wishes to honor a truth he must do more than just recognize it. He will have to hold fast to it. He must continually renew it, as Einstein says. The ceaseless effort that he must make contrasts sharply with the effortless ease with which the community installs a truth in its memory.

The scientific community is a public presence, a "we." "When a man is talking about scientific subjects, the little word 'I' should play no part

---

[100] *Ibid.*, p. 29. (Italics mine.)
[101] Barzun, *Glorious*, p. 75.
[102] Einstein, *Years*, p. 34. (Italics mine.)

in his expositions." [103] But the individual cannot, like the community,[104] dispense with the little word "I," which refers not only to his public presence but to an interior dimension as well. The results of this section are summarized in the table which follows.

TABLE 4

	The scientific community:	Buth the individual:
A)	has an essentially public mode of existence.	has a mode of existence that is both public and private.
B)	cannot lie or deceive.	may say one thing publicly, another thing privately.
C)	is understood to be devoted to the truth without reservation.	may in his heart rank many things above the truth.
D)	guards against error by a communal sense of sight.	may be in error without knowing it.
E)	is inexorably self-correcting in the long run.	may be unable to correct his error, once it is exposed.
F)	never forgets the truth; hence never needs reminding.	can forget important truths; will sometimes need to be reminded.
G)	installs the truth with effortless ease.	must make a ceaseless effort to hold to the truth.
H)	can dispense with the little word "I."	cannot do without this most personal of pronouns.

[103] Albert Einstein, *Essays in Science,* trans. Alan Harris (New York, 1950), p. 113.
[104] Cf. Robert Colborn, ed., *The Way of the Scientist* (New York, 1962), p. 48. In the marginal note, Colborn calls attention to the fact that a recent edition of a leading physics journal contained two articles, one of which listed fifty-one authors; the other listed no human author at all, only the laboratory where the research was done.

F. CONCLUSION

By observing the kinds of statement which may appropriately be made about the ongoing scientific community, we have thus arrived at four basic features of its mode of existence. The community is the kind of being which may be said to be timeless, cognitive, exclusively cognitive, and essentially public. Without claiming completeness for this list, we would maintain that any plausible account of the scientific community's mode of existence would have to include the characteristics noted in this chapter.

It is interesting to compare our list with Kuhn's:

A number of requisites for membership in a professional scientific group must already be strikingly clear. The scientist must, for example, be concerned to solve problems about the behavior of nature. In addition, though his concern with nature may be global in its extent, the problems on which he works must be problems of detail.[105]

But this criterion for membership in the scientific community reveals the fact that the community exists for the purpose of understanding nature. In alluding to "...*the unparalleled insulation* of mature scientific communities from the demands of the laity and of everyday life," [106] Kuhn evidences his awareness of what we have termed the community's exclusively cognitive mode of existence. Since we have already quoted Kuhn in our discussions of the community's mode of existence as timeless and public, it seems that Kuhn is also aware of these features.[107]

Many writers have compared science to a living organism. For example, Bunge writes:

Modern systems of scientific knowledge are like growing organisms: while alive, they change without pause.... Science, like the organism, changes both innerly and owing to its contact with it neighbors:...[108]

Another author states: "Like the society that supports it, the body of science is, in something more than a purely allegorical sense, a living thing." [109] The results of this chapter do not gainsay such comparisons.

---

[105] Kuhn, *Structure,* p. 168.
[106] *Ibid.,* p. 164. (Italics mine.)
[107] Cf. above pp. 44, 59, 62.
[108] Bunge, *Queries,* p. 55.
[109] Caryl P. Haskins, "The Two Faces of Science," *Ventures,* VI (1966), p. 23. Cited in Roussas John Rushdoony, *The Mythology of Science* (Nutley, 1967), p. 4. Cf. also Polanyi, *Faith,* p. 49.

But by drawing attention to a number of important *differences* between the scientific community and that very familiar organism which is the individual human being, our results might serve to check the tendency, endemic in quite a few comparisons, to push them too far. These results will be useful when, in a later chapter, we turn our attention to one exemplification of this tendency—the hazard which Climacus calls "forgetting what it means to *exist*."

CHAPTER III

HUMAN EXISTENCE

A. INTRODUCTION

In the first chapter, we argued that the forgetting-claim is the cornerstone of the *Postscript* and stated that our aim would be to elucidate the sense of *"exist"* operative in that claim.[1] That will be task of the present chapter. Although the forgetting-claim itself will not be dealt with until Chapter V, it is so crucial that unless we here consider its implications we shall fail to grasp the essence of Climacus' position.

In the first place, when he states that men have forgotten what it means to *exist,* he is thinking, not of all men, but of the idealist philosophers and theologians of the post-Hegelian era.[2] These thinkers were committed to the program of searching for the unity of all things. Nature, history, art, religion, philosophy—all are thought to be different manifestations of the same Absolute Spirit. The program owes much to Hegel, the most influential philosophical voice of the period. The following two passages indicate the philosophical temper of the times:

For the rest it is not difficult to see that our epoch is a birth-time, and a period of transition. The spirit of man has broken with the old order of things hitherto prevailing, and with the old ways of thinking, and is in mind to let them all sink into the depths of the past and to set about its own transformation. It is indeed never at rest, but carried along the stream of progress ever onward.[3]

Believing that a new epoch was about to begin, Hegel summons other thinkers to assist in bringing it to full term:

For the rest, at a time when the universal nature of spiritual life has become so very much emphasized and strengthened, and the mere individual aspect has

---

[1] Cf. Chapter I, p. 13.

[2] As the cause of the forgetting, Climacus cites the great increase in knowledge. Cf. *Post.,* pp. 216, 223. He himself is writing, not for the simple-minded, but for those who have "the leisure and talent necessary for a deeper inquiry" (*ibid.,* p. 152, *n.*).

[3] G. W. F. Hegel, *The Phenomenology of Mind,* 2nd. ed., intro. and trans. Sir James Baillie (London, 1964), p. 75.

become, as it should be, correspondingly a matter of indifference, when, too, that universal aspect holds, by the entire range of its substance, the full measure of the wealth it has built up, and lays claim to it all, the share of the total work of mind that falls to the activity of any particular individual can only be very small. *Because this is so, the individual must all the more forget himself, as in fact the very nature of science implies and requires that he should;* and he must, moreover, become and do what he can.[4]

Hegel calls for workers to forget themselves and advance the cause of *Wissenschaft.* Arriving on the scene thirty years later, Climacus judges that Hegel's summons has been heeded perhaps too well! Everyone now wants to go further. Every thinker wants to play the prophet and proclaim what the age demands![5] No one is content to be just an individual human being.[6] The age is so spoiled by the habit of contemplation [7] that philosophical reflection has become something queer and artificial.[8] As a result, the basic question has been ignored. This leads Climacus to ask:

Has the thing of being human become somewhat different from what is was in older times, are the conditions not still the same, namely, to be a particular existing being, for whom existing is essential so long as he continues to exist?[9]

We are not here concerned to defend Climacus' rather harsh judgment of his philosophical milieu but rather to point out that his analysis of human existence was prompted by his reading of it.

A second point which must be kept in mind is that Climacus does *not* diagnose the situation this way: These men simply do not know what it means to *exist,* and hence they must be told. Instead, he characterizes the situation as one of forgetting, and this provides an important clue about the nature of his analysis. If it were a case of just not knowing what it means to *exist,* then the proper response would be a new theory of human existence. Climacus, however, rejects the notion that what is needed is new knowledge.[10] If men have forgotten what it means

---

[4] *Ibid.,* p. 130. (Italics mine.)

[5] *Post.,* pp. 119, 129.

[6] *Ibid.,* p. 317.

[7] *Ibid.,* pp. 120, 283.

[8] *Ibid.,* p. 273.

[9] *Ibid.,* p. 192.

[10] Indeed, since there is already too much knowledge, some may have to be taken away. Cf. *ibid.,* p. 245, *n.* How Climacus can realistically hope to achieve this aim by becoming the author of book is an important question. We shall deal with this problem in Chapter VI.

to exist, it follows that they already know (in some sense) what it means. The proper response in this situation will be reminders.[11]

What sort of reminders? Climacus' focus in the *Postscript* is not the question of what it means to be a human being in general, but rather "what it means that you and I and he are human beings, each one for himself."[12] Climacus' reminders, then, have to do with what it means to exist as an *individual human being*.[13] Now there are just two roads open to the individual. Either he can do all in his power to forget the fact that he is an individual human being, or he can concentrate his entire energy upon this fundamental fact.[14] Because it seemed to him that his contemporaries were travelling the first road *en masse,* Climacus saw the need for someone to walk the second. He does this by occupying the standpoint of an individual human being, by showing what this involves, and by drawing out its implications. With this brief clarification of the genesis, nature, and focus of Climacus' reflections on human existence, we can now proceed.

B. HUMAN EXISTENCE: THE TASK OF BECOMING SUBJECTIVE

At the very heart of Climacus' position, we find a distinction between a loose and a strict sense of the predicate "exist":

It is easier to indulge in abstract thought than it is to exist, unless we understand by

---

[11] Such reminders are necessary just in so far as there are forgettings. Given the fact that the Hegelian sort of forgetting is no longer as prominent as it was in Climacus' time, it seemed advisable to attempt to produce other examples of this phenomenon. This we shall do in Chapter V.

[12] *Post.,* p. 109.

[13] Climacus' focus on the concept of existence is thus much narrower than the ontologist's. He is not analyzing how the predicate "exist(s)" functions in general. Nor is he attempting to itemize or classify the sorts of things that exist, as Aristotle *may* be doing in the *Categories* and as G. E. Moore is doing in *Some Main Problems of Philosophy* (New York, 1962), Chapter 1. It may be argued that Climacus' views about individual human existence nevertheless either presuppose or entail an ontology. Climacus would reply that ontology itself presupposes the existence of an ontologist, who is also an individual human being. Ontology requires him to abstract from his own existence and its concerns, an abstraction which is surely as questionable as Climacus' abstraction from ontology. Moreover, Climacus' focus is narrower than that of the philosopher of human nature, who is concerned to analyze human existence as such. But "existence has only individual human beings." *Post.,* p. 310. Cf. also pp. 149, 290, 294-95.

[14] *Ibid.,* p. 109.

the latter term what is loosely called existing, in analogy with what is loosely called being a subject.[15]

In the loose sense, the term signifies "merely that the individual having come into the world is present and is in process of becoming." [16] In this use, "exists" is hardly a predicate at all but is rather a prerequisite for significant or informative predications.[17] Climacus often refers to existence (in this loose sense) as the individual human being's *medium* whose basic feature is becoming.[18] Existence is, one might say, the individual human being's *status*, a status which is his whether he wills it or not.[19] Climacus' basic contention is that existing as a human being involves a great deal more than simply having a certain status or being present as an item in the spatio-temporal world.[20] In the *Postscript*, the loose sense of the predicate is not the target.[21] Moreover, the forgetting-claim obviously utilizes the strict sense. We shall therefore take our task to be an elucidation of the strict sense and shall herewith restrict attention to it.

[15] *Ibid.,* p. 273. Cf. also pp. 216, 223, 276 for other texts which implicitly or explicitly make this same distinction. The fact that Climacus here analogizes existing with being a subject is an important point which will be explained shortly. The fact that not every human being finds abstract thought easy confirms our earlier point that Climacus has the idealists in mind here.

[16] *Ibid.,* pp. 516-17.

[17] "...apart from this, 'to exist' is not a more sharply defining predicate, but is merely the form of all the more sharply defining predicates: one does not become anything by coming into being,..." *Ibid.,* p. 517.

[18] Referring to Socrates, Climacus says that he was "conscious of being a thinker, but he was also conscious that existence as his medium prevented him from thinking continuously." *Ibid.,* p. 274. On existence as the individual's medium, cf. *ibid.,* pp. 74-76, 405, 436, 442, 469-70. Sometimes Climacus contrasts existence as a medium with thought (*ibid.,* p. 278) or language (*ibid.,* pp. 398, 415). In the *Fragments* ("Interlude"), Climacus does analyze the concepts of contingency, possibility, and necessity. Cf. Charles Magel, "An Analysis of Kierkegaard's Philosophical Categories," (Unpublished doctoral dissertation, University of Minnesota, 1960), for an analysis of that material. In the *Postscript,* Climacus' focus is very different, as we have already indicated.

[19] "Existence has the remarkable trait of compelling an individual to exist whether he wills it or not." *Post.,* p. 109.

[20] "To have been young, and then to grow older, and finally to die is a very mediocre form of human existence; this merit belongs to every animal." *Post.,* p. 311. Swenson agrees with our interpretation. He says: "What then is existence, in Kierkegaard's use of this term as a category? It is first of all a synthesis of status and task. The task may be evaded or shabbily executed; but the existence of the individual remains to plague him and to render his situation comical. There are many who exist after a fashion, succeeding bestially enough in becoming objective, though they still remain subjects, also after a fashion; just as the

Many passages might have been selected as a starting-point for our exposition, but we have chosen the following. It is short and to the point. "Really to exist," Climacus states, "so as to interpenetrate one's existence with consciousness,... that is truly difficult." [22] In order to elucidate this brief formulation, we shall have to clarify the meaning of the term "consciousness" in it. Such clarification in turn requires that we analyze the term "the subjective thinker," the designation Climacus gives to the individual who really exists.[23]

The subjective thinker is Climacus' idealization of Socrates whom he conceives as an individual who took seriously the task of self-knowledge.[24] What this task entails is adumbrated in the following text which contrasts abstract thought with the subjective thinker:

drunken driver who lets the horses take him home is also a driver." David F. Swenson, *Something About Kierkegaard* (Minneapolis, 1945), p. 129. Swenson is clearly referring here to the *Postscript*. The distinction we have marked between a loose and a strict sense of the predicate "exist" corresponds to Swenson's distinction between existence as status and existence as task. The precise nature of the task of existing is what we are about to elucidate.

[21] Much traditional philosophical analysis has taken as its object what Climacus calls the loose sense. There are similarities between it and the Thomistic concept of *esse*. Thus, in his *In Aristotelis Librum De Anima Commentarium*, Aquinas states: "*Sed anima viventibus est causa essendi; per animam enim vivunt, et ipsum vivere est esse eorum: ...*" This is his gloss on "*Vivere autem viventibus esse est.*" Our reference is to the 4th Marietti Edition, ed. P. F. Pirotta, O.P., (n. p., 1959), p. 82. G. E. Moore analyzes the loose sense also in his "Is Existence a Predicate?" Cf. *Philosophical Papers* (New York, 1962), pp. 114-25. W. V. Quine is likewise analyzing the loose sense in his famous essay, "On What There Is." Cf. *From a Logical Point of View*, 2nd. ed. (New York and Evanston, 1963), pp. 1-19.

[22] *Post.*, p. 273. Cf. also *Adler* (p. 156): "When men who live thus religiously at a distance talk about religion,... one notices by their talk that they are not in it, just as though while existing they are not really existing, are not present to themselves." And: "To be entirely present to oneself is the highest thing, and the highest task for the personal life,..." *Ibid.*, p. 157. The idea that really being a human being is far from easy is one that Wittgenstein shares with Climacus: "A characteristic remark that Wittgenstein would make when referring to someone who was notably generous or kind or honest was 'He is a *human being!*'—thus implying that most people fail even to be human." Norman Malcolm, *Ludwig Wittgenstein: A Memoir* (Oxford, 1962), p. 61.

[23] On the subjective thinker, cf. Louis Mackey, "Kierkegaard and the Problem of Existential Philosophy," *Review of Metaphysics*, IX (1956), pp. 404-19; 569-88. Hereafter cited as: Mackey, *Existential*. Reprinted in Gill, *Essays*, pp. 31-57. Subsequent references to this article are to the version in Gill, *Essays*.

[24] "The subjective thinker has the task of understanding himself in his existence." *Post.*, p. 314. On Socrates as the paradigm case of an existing individual, cf. *ibid.*, pp. 183-85.

Abstract thought turns from concrete men to consider man in general; the subjective thinker seeks to understand the abstract determination of being human in terms of this particular human being.[25]

From this we may infer that the specific consciousness involved in existing, *stricte sic dictus,* is consciousness of what it means to be an individual human being.[26] It is one of the important lessons of the *Postscript* that developing this sort of consciousness, *i.e.,* becoming subjective, is by no means an easy task.[27] Nor is this the complete story. Once an individual has begun to interpenetrate his existence with this consciousness, he then faces the task of shaping his existence accordingly. "The task of the subjective thinker is to transform himself into an instrument that clearly and definitely expresses in existence whatever is essentially human." [28] This existential transformation will require both passion and inwardness. The essential determinants, then, in really existing are subjective thought, passion, and inwardness. We shall now consider each of these more fully in turn.

As has already been noted, Climacus describes subjective thought by contrasting it with its opposite, objective or abstract thought. The following text provides additional clarification of the contrast:

While objective thought is indifferent to the thinking subject and his existence, the subjective thinker is an existing individual essentially interested in his own thinking, existing as he does in his thought.[29]

---

[25] *Ibid.,* p. 315.

[26] Cf. above p. 76. "In all his thinking," says Climacus of the subjective thinker, "he therefore has to think the fact that he is an existing individual." *Post.,* p. 314.

[27] By becoming subjective, Climacus does not mean becoming eccentric or self-centered. He is aware that such a usage exists: "It is easy to see what this guidance understands by being a subject of a sort. It understands by it quite rightly the accidental, the selfish, the angular, the eccentric, and so forth, all of which every human being can have enough of." *Post.,* p. 117. He indicates his own usage of the term when he writes: "It is ordinarily assumed that no art or skill is required in order to be subjective. To be sure, every human being is a bit of a subject, in a sense. But now to strive to become what one already is: who would take the pains to waste his time on such a task,..." *Ibid.,* p. 116. And what is one? The most fundamental answer to this question is: an individual human being. Thus to become subjective means to become a human being, to *exist.* The difficulty of the task itself is perhaps exceeded only by the difficulty of taking it seriously as a task.

[28] *Post.,* p. 318. Cf. also pp. 76-78, especially p. 78 where the subjective thinker is described as one who "actually reflects existentially the structure of existence in his own existence,..."

[29] *Ibid.,* p. 67.

Objective thought is thought directed away from the thinker's own existence towards something else. What this "something else" is varies with the particular species of objective thought. In history, for example, thought is directed towards the past; in science, towards natural phenomena; in mathematics, towards number. In each case, objective thought will be interested in something other than the existence of the individual who does the thinking. A constitutive feature of objective thought is this simultaneous channeling of reflective energy *away from* the individual and *towards* an object, which object will be available to the thinking subject in somewhat the same way that a perceptible object is available to the perceiving subject. Since the purpose of objective thought is the comprehension of some object, the objective thinker turns his powers of reflection away from his own existence and its concerns. He "abstracts from" his own existence.[30] Objective thought, then, is indifferent to, or disinterested in, the thinker's own existence.[31]

If a human being is to understand himself (and were a man to understand everything but himself, this would surely be an egregious oversight [32]), then he cannot be disinterested. On the contrary, he must take an interest in his own existence.[33] Subjective thought is thought whose essential interest is existence. As the direction of objective thought is outward, so the direction of subjective thought is inward. It will thus be characterized by "a different type of reflection, namely, *the reflection of inwardness,* of possession, in virtue of which it belongs to the thinking subject and to no one else." [34] It would be a serious mistake to overlook

---

[30] This abstracting is similar in some respects to the *epoche* which is at the foundation of Husserl's phenomenology. In the *epoche,* the individual detaches himself, as it were, from the natural standpoint and its beliefs. He neither denies nor affirms them, but he makes no reference to them. In objective thought, the individual abstracts from his own existence, neither denying nor affirming it; but neither does he attend to it.

[31] Cf. *Post.,* pp. 173, 278, 290, 296.

[32] "To express existentially what one has understood about oneself and in this manner to understand oneself is in no way comical. To understand everything except one's own self is very comical." *Post.,* pp. 315-16. Cf. also p. 272, *n.*

[33] "Existence constitutes the highest interest of the existing individual, and his interest in his existence constitutes his reality." *Ibid.,* p. 279. Cf. also pp. 268, 278, 282-84, 289.

[34] *Ibid.,* pp. 67-68. (Italics mine.) The reflection of inwardness is the crucial step in subjective thinking. It is therefore surprising that it has not been more carefully elucidated in the extensive secondary literature. We hope to help remedy this deficiency shortly.

the fact that there is an objective dimension in subjective thought, as the next passage indicates:

The reflection of inwardness gives to the subjective thinker a *double reflection*. In thinking, he thinks the universal; but as existing in his thought and as assimilating it in his inwardness, he becomes more and more subjectively isolated.[85]

We propose the following interpretation of what Climacus means.

Every man is an *individual human being*. He may also be a carpenter or a salesman or a painter or a philosopher, but he becomes such by choice. No one chooses to be born a human being; yet once in existence, each man has the fundamental option of either ignoring this most basic fact or paying attention to it.[36] He cannot, however, escape it.[37] Every man is subject, as it were, to the *ethical imperative* which, simply put, is this: Become what you are.[38] Until this demand has been satisfied, all other tasks should be relegated to a secondary status.[39]

How is the ethical demand to be met? In the first place, since he is a *human being,* the individual must come to some understanding of the human mode of existence. That is, he must have a grasp of the basic attributes of human existence.[40] In thinking these, "he thinks the universal," because these attributes will apply to his existence in the very

---

[85] *Ibid.,* p. 68. (Italics mine.) Here again we find that the very important notion of a double reflection has not been adequately dealt with. H. M. Garelick makes an attempt at it. Cf. *The Anti-Christianity of Kierkegaard* (The Hague, 1965), p. 20.

[36] Cf. above p. 76. Cf. also *Post.,* p. 109.

[37] Even though a man throws himself totally into some task in the area of objective thought, he still remains an existing individual. "If a man occupied himself, all his life through, solely with logic, he would nevertheless not become logic; he must therefore himself exist in different categories." *Ibid.,* p. 86.

[38] The term "ethical imperative" is our own, but the basic idea can be found in many passages in the *Postscript*. Cf., for example, pp. 279; 284; 307, *n.*; 369; 377; 469. The ethical individual (in Climacus' sense of the term) is one who is responsive to this imperative and pays attention to the fact that he is an existing individual. Price uses the phrase "the existential imperative" but understands it somewhat differently. We discuss this in Chapter IV.

[39] "I do not doubt that even the most objective of men is at bottom in tacit agreement with what has been set forth here, that it is right and proper for the wise man first to understand the same thing that the plain man understands, and to feel himself obligated by the same considerations that obligate the simple— so that only after this has been done may he pass over to the study of world-history." *Post.,* p. 142. Cf. also p. 147.

[40] In the *Postscript,* Climacus emphasizes those attributes that idealism (so he thinks) obscures: being mortal; being in constant process of change; having limited time and powers of thought.

same way that they apply to the existence of every other human being. Since, however, he is not a human being in general ("like Soldin the bookseller" [41]) but rather an *individual* human being, his thought should reflect this as well. Having grasped the universal in a first reflection, he should then proceed to "assimilate" it.[42] The endeavor to understand how the universal applies to *his own existence* and what its implications are for him is the second half of the subjective thinker's double reflection, the reflection of inwardness.[43] Let us be clear about this: both reflections are needed if a man is to understand himself. Thought which remains at the level of the universal will result in a human being devoid of inwardness.[44] On the other hand, thought which revolves about the subject in his individuality but is not securely anchored in the universally human will result in aberrant inwardness: madness.[45] Subjective thought, combining as it does the individual and the universal, is then a mean between total objectivity and purely idiosyncratic reflection.

Because his contemporaries were preoccupied with the objective tendency,[46] Climacus emphasizes the need for and the difficulty of the reflection of inwardness. He assumes that there is no great difficulty in arriving at an awareness of the attributes which belong to the human mode of existence. Everyone knows these.[47] But what happens to this knowledge? Many will simply ignore it, convinced that what everyone knows is not worthy of any further attention. In the chapter entitled "Becoming Subjective," Climacus provides several examples of subjective thinking. His purpose is twofold. First, these examples help to illustrate the technique of thinking subjectively. Secondly, they show that a seemingly simple problem has, when it is situated in existence,[48] a way of becoming quite difficult. In following (and, where appropriate, amplify-

---

[41] *Post.*, pp. 149, 151.

[42] Cf. above p. 79. The reflection of inwardness resembles the logical operation of instantiating a universal proposition. The subjective thinker's task is to instantiate universal propositions about human existence with respect to his own existence. The process is similar to what G. E. Moore termed "translating a proposition into the concrete." Cf. *Philosophical Studies*, The International Library of Psychology, Philosophy and Scientific Method, ed. C. K. Ogden (Totowa, 1965), pp. 219 ff. Moore applies this tactic to assertions such as "Time is unreal."

[43] This should help to clarify the text quoted above on p. 77.

[44] Cf. *Post.*, p. 175.

[45] *Ibid.*, pp. 174-75.

[46] *Ibid.*, pp. 118-19.

[47] *Ibid.*, pp. 53, 80, 316, 550.

[48] *Ibid.*, p. 228.

ing) his discussion of death, we hope to be able to concretize the important points in the preceding remarks.

Climacus begins by reciting a number of facts about death. He knows, for example, that he will die if he takes a dose of sulphuric acid.[49] But isn't there more to thinking about death than simply compiling various facts about it? He pauses to reflect:

Before I pass over to universal history... it seems to me that I had better think about this, lest existence mock me, because I had become so learned and highfalutin that I had forgotten to understand what will some time happen to me as to every human being—sometime, nay, what am I saying: suppose death were so treacherous as to come tomorrow! [50]

Certainly every man knows that to be human means, *inter alia,* to be subject to death. The subjective thinker's task is to understand this abstract determination in terms of this particular human.[51] In the present context, this means understanding that death is in the offing *for him.* Moreover, death might come to him at any moment, and the subjective thinker is thus brought face-to-face with the fact that his existence is uncertain. To understand death subjectively (and thereby to understand, at least in part, what it means to be an individual human being) will require a man to have a firm grasp of the fact that his existence is uncertain.

To be sure, everyone knows that human life is uncertain. The tendency, however, is to think about this fact every so often,[52] as when a friend dies suddenly. Is this the way to achieve a firm grasp of the existential situation? If it is true at every moment that one's existence is uncertain, then the task is to accord this truth a status in one's own thought and existence which is commensurate with the existential situation. Does this mean that every moment is to be spent in thinking about the uncertainty of one's existence? No, but neither is it sufficient to think about it "once for all, or once a year at matins on New Year's morning." [53]

Climacus' point here is that a man should pause long enough to consider

---

[49] *Ibid.,* pp. 147-48.

[50] *Ibid.,* p. 148. There is a play here on the words "pass over" which in Hegel's philosophy denote the process by which a concept becomes its dialectical opposite. The implication of this text is that existential passing over is much less readily accomplished.

[51] Cf. above pp. 77, 80. The task is "to bring the general principle into connection with this particular moment, on this particular day, with these particular moods and states of mind, and under these particular circumstances." *Post.,* p. 442.

[52] "Every human being knows this, and at times gives it expression, especially on solemn occasions, and then not without tears and perspiration." *Ibid.,* p. 79.

[53] *Ibid.,* p. 149.

the fact and its implications. Though he does not give us an example, we suggest the following as one possible illustration of how an individual might reflect inwardly on the fact that human existence is uncertain:

"Nothing is certain," so the saying goes, "except death and taxes." Everyone knows this, but let me consider for a moment what this means for me as one individual human being. It means, for one thing, that I cannot count for sure on tomorrow. That is why it makes sense to have life insurance and a will. These things insure that my loved ones will be provided for, even if death were so treacherous as to come tomorrow. But what about myself? Am I prepared for that possibility? What, if anything, can I do to prepare for death? [54] Perhaps I should think about this.

In front of me, there is a calendar. Dates are filled in up to three and four months from now. What does this mean? How does this square with the fact that my existence is uncertain? Surely a man has to make plans; we all do. It would be very awkward if we did not. And I can imagine how others would react if I were to begin to speak about my future in only the most tentative of tones. When someone asks me to a gathering, he wants a definite "yes" or "no," not a hedge like "I'll come, if I'm still alive." People would think I was mad if I were to begin expressing myself in that way, even though this way of speaking is quite accurate and reflects their situation no less than my own.[55] Still I'm not sure that I want to be taken for a madman. At this point, I must confess that I just do not quite see how to square the fact that my existence is uncertain with some of my regular daily practices like making plans. Perhaps this deserves more thought, too.

This is only a beginning, yet it may serve to indicate how complacent ordinary habits of thought can be.[56]

For obvious reasons, Climacus does not predict what the specific contents of the reflection of inwardness will be. He does mention several general characteristics. For example, he says that it will *isolate* the individual.[57] The reason for this is that the individual's own thoughts and existence are the very focus of the reflection of inwardness. It would be inappropriate, in this connection, to ask others for their thoughts or to consult, for example, an encyclopedia. If he is essentially interested

---

[54] "We wish to know how the conception of death will transform a man's entire life, when in order to think its uncertainty he has to think it in every moment, so as to prepare himself for it. We wish to know what it means to prepare for death,... The question must be raised of the possibility of finding an ethical expression for the significance of death,..." *Ibid.*, p. 151.

[55] Cf. *ibid.*, pp. 80-82 to see how Climacus imagines that Socrates might express himself in such a situation.

[56] "To have one's daily life in the decisive dialectic of the infinite, and yet continue to live: this is both the art of life and its difficulty. Most men have complacent categories for their daily use, and resort to the categories of the infinite only upon solemn occasions;..." *Ibid.*, p. 79, *n.*

[57] Cf. above p. 74.

in his own thinking,[58] the subjective thinker must regard such sources as a possible distraction from his task of understanding himself. The reflection of inwardness is therefore also a reflection of *possession*.[59] The thoughts arrived at in this reflection carry the mark of the individual doing the thinking.[60] They are *his*. Because this is so, if the individual is to pursue this manner of thinking, he must make the decision to do so himself. No one else can do it for him. The decision will not be an easy one if he has been accustomed to according the highest value to objective thought. If a man were to announce his intention to undertake a study of the various ways in which human societies, past and present, have conceived death, he might well expect to receive the support and encouragement of others. If he were to die before completing his project, someone else might carry it through to completion.[61] When a man sets out to reflect about death subjectively, he would not receive and ought not expect that kind of support. Here the task concerns himself alone. His thoughts will have whatever value they have within his own existence. Their value is not here dependent upon their being publicly articulated, as is the case with objective thought. Indeed, as we shall see, such articulation may here be a false move. For this reason, then, Climacus characterizes this mode of reflection as a reflection of *inwardness*.[62] Having illustrated the reflection of inwardness and explained some of its characteristics, we may now return to Climacus' exposition in the *Postscript*.

The uncertainty which subjective reflection about death has brought to the fore will generate further difficulties. Specifically, Climacus suggests that it gives rise to this question which the individual thinker must ask of himself: "Suppose death were to come tomorrow. Would X be worth beginning today?"[63] By asking this question, one begins to assimilate

---

[58] Cf. above p. 77.

[59] Cf. above p. 78. This does not, of course, mean that someone else cannot have similar thoughts. The point is that they will be *his*.

[60] "The person of the abstract thinker is irrelevant to his thought. An existential thinker must be pictured as essentially thinking, but so that in presenting his thought he sketches himself." *Post.*, p. 319.

[61] This is an important difference between subjective tasks and objective ones. In the former, the individual is involved in his capacity as an individual human being; in the latter, he is involved in virtue of a certain background, training, and talent which he shares with others. This enables one man to carry on where another has left off, as often happens in scientific research.

[62] Cf. above p. 78.

[63] "Merely this one uncertainty, when it is to be understood and held fast by an existing individual, and hence enter into every thought, precisely because it is an

the fact that his existence is uncertain. Now suppose that for "*X*" one substituted "the study of world-history." Such an immense undertaking would, to be sure, require a great deal of time. However, the individual who raises the question is attempting to hold fast to the fact that his existence is uncertain by supposing that death may come tomorrow.[64] He cannot then suppose that he will have the time needed for such a study. Without denying that the study of world-history is worthwhile, Climacus implies that the answer to the above question is "No." This reveals something important about the nature of such tasks and the individual human being's relationship to them. That is, objective tasks intrinsically require a community of thinkers.[65] A community has, as an ongoing entity, a form of insulation against the uncertainty which afflicts the individual human being. It possesses a certain freedom from temporal pressures which is necessary to solve complex problems. The individual who undertakes such a problem becomes part of a community of thinkers which possesses, in common, a number of properties which no individual member can rightly claim as his own.[66] In doing so, however, the individual must forfeit, at least temporarily, his interest in his own existence.[67] He does not hold fast to the fact that his existence is

uncertainty entering into my beginning upon universal history even, so that I make it clear whether if death comes tomorrow, I am beginning upon something that is worth beginning—..." *Post.*, p. 148.

[64] Statistics concerning an individual's probable life-span are not relevant here, since the individual is, *ex hypothesi*, attempting to hold fast to the fact that his existence is uncertain. This is not to deny their utility in other contexts. Here, however, they are a distraction to be resisted.

[65] On this point, cf. Schilling, *Religion*, p. 51 where the question of whether a one-man physics is possible is discussed. There are several reasons why Schilling regards this as an impossibility, among which is the simple fact that no man has enough time. (Even if one hypothesizes a man with unlimited time, the answer is still "No.") The same reasoning would seem to apply to the study of world-history.

[66] This was the thrust of Chapter II.

[67] In other words, abstract or objective thought is disinterested. Cf. above p. 78. Climacus is surely right here, for this is just the obverse aspect of the situation Hegel describes when he says that the true nature of *Wissenschaft* requires the thinker to forget himself. Cf. above p. 73. The closest that abstract thought can come to existence is when it considers the notion of existence in general. It can consider the individual human being as the *terminus a quo* for the sake of developing a conception of man as its *terminus ad quem*. Since existence is always something particular (cf. *Post.*, p. 294), the subjective thinker has the opposite task. He takes the abstract determination of being human as his *terminus a quo*. His *terminus ad quem* is an understanding of this as it applies to himself.

uncertain, but rather lets it go in order to think objectively. This is a kind of forgetfulness of what it means to exist, although it becomes serious only when an individual becomes so thoroughly habituated to the community's tasks and its mode of existence that he loses sight of his own.[68]

Suppose, however, that for "X" (in the question on page 83) one were to substitute "the study of oneself as an individual human being." The answer now is "Yes." In the first place, the individual human being is in a constant process of becoming. Hence his study of himself can never be concluded so long as he exists.[69] Since there can be no final chapter to this study, it makes no essential difference whether the individual were to die tomorrow or in fifty years.[70] Secondly, the study of oneself is quite compatible with the attempt to hold fast to the uncertainty of existence, since the development of this awareness is itself part of the task.

The conclusion to be drawn from subjective thought about death is not that the only valid tasks for an individual are those which can be undertaken mindful of the fact that his existence is uncertain. It is rather that such tasks have a primacy in the existential order and should therefore be taken up first.[71] These tasks have an essential reference to the individual's very existence and require him to interpenetrate that existence with thought. He must first discover what he really thinks about his

[68] There is a difference between the kind of forgetfulness that eminates from Hegelianism and that which may occur in scientific work. The Hegelian position includes within itself a consciously articulated view of the nature of true or absolute individuality. Cf. *The Phenomenology of Mind*, pp. 374-416. The scientific position does not. But the existential result is the same.

[69] "How far the subjectve thinker has come along this road, whether a long distance or a short one, makes no essential difference. This is indeed only a finitely relative comparison; but as long as he is an existing individual, he is in process of becoming." *Post.*, p. 84.

[70] The question "What would you do if you had only one day left to live?" is not subjectively different from the question "What would you do if you had only fifty years left to live?" The man who can give the same answer ("Precisely what I am doing today.") to both has made a good start in the task of knowing himself.

[71] "And what then follows? Nothing, nothing at all. It is in fact my constant affirmation that between the simple man's knowledge and the wise man's knowledge of the simple there is merely this ridiculous little difference, that the simple man knows it, the wise man knows regarding it that he knows it, or knows that he does not know it. But on the other hand there does follow from this a certain consequence, namely the query whether it would not be best to check oneself a little in the matter of world-history when such is the situation with respect to one's knowledge of the simple." *Post.*, p. 162.

existence as an individual. Then he has the further duty to "really think what he thinks through making a reality of it." [72] He must transform his existence so that it reflects his thinking and expresses it.[73] The transformation requires passion and inwardness. Let us now consider what these terms mean and why they are involved in the task of existing, *stricte sic dictus.*

By "passion," Climacus does not mean intense emotion or feeling, though he would not deny that these have a role to play in human affairs.[74] The following is the most important text for an understanding of how he uses this term:

I have often reflected how one might bring a man into a *state of passion.* I have thought in this connection that if I could get him seated on a horse and the horse made to take fright and gallop wildly, or better still, for the sake of bringing the passion out, if I could take a man who wanted to arrive at a certain place as quickly as possible, and hence already had some passion, and could set him astride a horse that could scarcely walk—and yet this is what existence is like if one is to become consciously aware of it.[75]

The temptation is to think that the natural reaction of anyone in a situation such as the one described above will be fear, and to let it go at that. If we probe one step beyond this and ask why, we will be closer to Climacus' meaning. One will be afraid because his very existence seems to be threatened. Passion is not, then, some momentary impulse or episodic feeling,[76] but is rather a state of active concern for one's own existence.[77]

---

[72] *Ibid.,* p. 151.

[73] Cf. above p. 77.

[74] "But since we have in our time forgotten what it means to exist *sensu eminenti,* and since pathos is usually referred to the sphere of imagination and feeling, the dialectical being permitted to usurp it, instead of seeking a union of both in the simultaneity of existence, it has come about in our philosophical nineteenth century that pathos has been descredited and that dialectics has lost its passion; ..." *Post.,* p. 345. Cf. also *ibid.,* p. 311: "If thought speaks deprecatingly of the imagination, imagination in its turn speaks deprecatingly of thought; and likewise with feeling. The task is not to exalt one at the expense of the other, but to give them an equal status, to unify them in simultaneity; the medium in which they are unified is existence."

[75] *Ibid.,* p. 276. (Italics mine.)

[76] Climacus distinguishes earthly passion which, he says, "tends to prevent existence by transforming it into something merely momentary" from idealizing passion which is "an anticipation of eternity functioning so as to help the individual to exist." *Ibid.,* p. 277, *n.* Earthly passions come and go with great frequency.

[77] The historian has passion for his task, but it is objective passion. "As investigator

This is even clearer in the case of the man who wants to arrive at his destination quickly. Why does Climacus say that such a man already has some passion? Certainly, if he is impatient to arrive at some destination, we may assume that there is some concern which motivates him and which therefore distinguishes him from the man who takes his carriage out for a Sunday afternoon drive. The latter has no particular destination in mind and consequently is indifferent. If his horse is slow afoot, so much the better to view the scenery. But if a man is in a hurry and the horse can scarcely walk, this will heighten and intensify his concern. Yet if he allows himself to become emotional and excited, he may only make his journey more difficult. His best ally will be a steady concentration of will power, and Climacus' concept of passion includes this note as well.

Why does existing require passion?[78] In the first place, an element of self-concern and self-interest must already be present if a man is to take seriously the task of interpenetrating his existence with consciousness. Such self-concern or passion was anything but a given in Climacus' day when the problems of universal history had captured the fancy of many a thinker.[79] Once he begins the task of self-reflection, he will encounter not only the sorts of difficulties which are intrinsically connected with his task but also the many distractions that flesh is heir to.[80] He must face the future by way of action and decision.[81] He will be subject to

he takes part in a great endeavor carried on from generation to generation, to him it is always objective, scientifically it is important to come as near as possible to certainty, but it is not subjectively important." *Post.*, pp. 509-10. That is, it is important to the scientist *qua* scientist, not *qua* individual human being.

[78] "All existential problems are passionate problems, for when existence is interpenetrated with reflection it generates passion. To think about existential problems in such a way as to leave out the passion is tantamount to not thinking about them at all, since it is to forget the point, which is that the thinker himself is an existing individual." *Ibid.*, p. 313.

[79] "'What extraordinary presumption,' I seem to hear a thinker say, 'what egotistical vanity to dare to lay so much stress upon one's own petty self in this theocentric age, in the speculatively significant nineteenth century, which is entirely immersed in the great problems of universal history.'" *Post.*, p. 19.

[80] "... if his [the human being's] life is in time, then it is piecemeal; and if it is piecemeal, then it is *eo ipso* sprinkled with diversions and distractions: ..." *Ibid.*, p. 439.

[81] "Does he in fact exist? And if he does, is he then not in process of becoming? And if he is in process of becoming, does he not face the future? And does he ever face the future by way of action? ... But if he ever acts *sensu eminenti*, does he not in that case face the future with infinite passion? Is there not then for him an either-or?" *Ibid.*, p. 272.

either-or situations which involve his inmost being.[82] All of these factors give rise to passion.

Climacus uses the following metaphor:

Eternity is the winged horse, infinitely fast, and time is a worm-out jade; the existing individual is the driver. That is to say, he is such a driver when his mode of existence is not an existence loosely so-called; for then he is no driver, but a drunken peasant who lies asleep in the wagon and lets the horses take care of themselves. To be sure, he also drives and is a driver; and so there are many who—also exist.[83]

The existing individual has the goal of understanding himself as a human being. That is his destination. Existence (his medium) is the carriage in which he is seated, and it is drawn along by two rather different horses. One (eternity) is fast, while the other (time) is slow of foot. If the driver is to arrive at his destination, if he hopes to make any headway at all, he must know how to work the reins. He must be constantly vigilant. He must keep the demands of time from slowing him down to a crawl,[84] while at the same time he must prevent the demands of the future from running away with him. He must stay on the main road, in spite of the many interesting side-roads he will surely pass *en route*. Without passion, that is, without a healthy concern for his own existence and a firm resolve to maintain it, he will not be able to make the journey.

The last of the three determinants involved in the task of existing is inwardness. Basically, this term signifies the internal aspect of the individual human being, as the following text suggests:

Action outwardly directed may indeed transform existence (as when an emperor conquers the world and enslaves peoples), but not the individual's own existence; and

---

[82] Within the realm of abstract thought (*sub specie aeterni*), there is of course no becoming, no either-or, no action, and thus no passion. But the individual partakes of this realm only by virtue of his having abstracted from his own existence. "But where everything is in process of becoming, and only so much of eternity is present as to be a restraining influence in the passionate decision, where *eternity* is related as futurity to the individual in process of becoming, there the absolute disjunction belongs." *Ibid.* By "absolute disjunction" is meant either-or situations.

[83] *Ibid.,* p. 276.

[84] "In the passionate moment of decision, where the road swings away from objective knowledge, it seems as of the infinite decision were thereby realized. But in the same moment the existing individual finds himself in the temporal order, and the subjective 'how' is transformed into a striving, a striving which receives indeed its impulse and repeated renewal from the decisive passion of the infinite, but is nevertheless a striving." *Ibid.,* p. 182. The decision to understand oneself cannot be made once for all, but must be renewed again and again in time with its many distractions.

action outwardly directed may transform the individual's own existence (as when from having been a lieutenant he becomes an emperor, or from a street peddler becomes a millionaire, or whatever else of the sort may fall to his lot), but not the individual's inner existence.[85]

Every man has such an inner existence in the form of unspoken thoughts, desires, memories, and such. However Climacus also uses the term "inwardness" in a sense which is closely related to the term "passion." [86] It is difficult to drive a sharp wedge between them. Both terms refer to the "how" of existing, passion denoting its intensity, and inwardness its locus:

In the ethico-religious sphere, the accent is again on the "how." But this is not to be understood as referring to the demeanor, the expression, or the like: rather it refers to the relationship sustained by the existing individual in his own existence to the content of his utterance. Objectively, the interest is focussed merely on the thought-content, subjectively on the inwardness.[87]

Inwardness, in this sense, refers to the way that the existing individual relates to what he thinks. As we have already seen, his thought is always focussed on his own existence. Now how does he relate himself to his thoughts? Does he take them seriously and keep his task front and center at all times? This is inwardness, though it is very different from simply *saying*: "I always have the task in mind." [88] Just as inwardness in love does not consist in "consummating seven marriages with Danish maidens, and then cutting loose on the French, the Italians, and so forth, but in loving one and the same woman, and yet being constantly renewed in the same love," [89] so inwardness in existing means having one and the same task always before one's eyes and yet being constantly renewed in that task. Inwardness, then, is not a matter of the "how" in the sense of a man's speech and conduct. It is an affair of the inner man.[90]

To say that *existing* is a matter of inwardness is to take the view that being a human being does not demand any particular external manifesta-

---

[85] *Post.*, p. 387.

[86] "But essential existential pathos is essentially related to existence; and to exist essentially is inwardness,..." *Ibid.*, p. 388. Cf. also pp. 58, 181.

[87] *Ibid.*, p. 181.

[88] "I, for my part, am of the opinion that 'never to forget this impression,' is something quite different from saying once in a solemn moment: 'I will never forget it.' The first is inwardness. The second is perhaps only a momentary inwardness." *Ibid.*, p. 214.

[89] *Ibid.*, p. 211.

[90] Socrates, at seventy, is still attempting to understand with greater inwardness what a girl of sixteen already knows. *Ibid.*, p. 82.

tion. The important thing is for the individual, whatever his station in life and whatever blessings fortune may have conferred on him, to attend to the business of being a human being in the privacy of his own thoughts. He is to cultivate a steady mindfulness of what it means to be a human being and shape his life accordingly. Since this task must be compatible with *every* situation in which a human being may find himself, it cannot require any particular externality. It must be compossible with being a shoemaker or a surgeon; being single or married; being a European or an American. Since existing as a human being is primarily a matter of inwardness, it differs from those achievements which are visible to the human community. Whether a man is a surgeon or not depends upon certain public performances: his training, his conduct in the operating room, and others. What transpires in his inner existence is not a relevant factor here. Similarly, the scientist will be judged on the basis of his public utterances: what he writes in an article for a journal, and what he says at conferences. His inwardness, or lack of it, is not a factor. Being a human being, on the other hand, is primarily a matter of inwardness. "The real act is not the external act but an internal decision in which the individual puts an end to the mere possibility and identifies himself with the content of his thought in order to exist in it." [91]

Because "true inwardness demands absolutely no outward sign," [92] the situation is precarious.[93] This is as it should be:

It is unethical even to ask at all about another person's ethical inwardness, in so far as such inquiry constitutes a diversion of attention.... This is profitable preliminary training for an ethical mode of existence: to learn that the individual stands alone.[94]

---

[91] *Ibid.*, p. 302. Cf. also p. 284: "...; for the ethical, as being the internal, cannot be observed by an outsider. It can be realized only by the individual subject, who alone can know what it is that moves within him."

[92] *Ibid.*, p. 370.

[93] Climacus realizes this: "... it might seem as if communication between man and man were abandoned to unhampered freedom in lying and deception, if anyone so desires: for one need only say: 'I have done so and so,' and we can get no further with him. Well, what of it? But suppose that he has not really done it. What business is that of mine? Such a deception would be worst for himself." *Ibid.*, p. 151. This is the difference between subjectivity and objectivity which has safeguards against lying and deception. "In a certain sense, there is something fearful in speaking thus of the inner life, that it may be there and then again may not be there, without the fact being immediately apparent in any outward manner. But it is also glorious to be able to speak so of the inner life— when it is there: for this is the expression for its inwardness." *Ibid.*, p. 364.

[94] *Ibid.*, p. 287. Cf. also p. 222.

Existing as a human being is a one-man task wherein each man has to do with himself alone. If he concerns himself with another man's inwardness, he shirks his obligation to himself.

Climacus' position on the place of inwardness in human existence is perhaps easily misconstrued as a kind of solipsism. Such an interpretation appears to be confirmed by the following text:

All knowledge about reality is possibility. The only reality to which an existing individual may have a relationship which is more than cognitive is his own reality, the fact that he exists; this reality constitutes his absolute interest.[95]

Climacus is not here denying the existence of other human beings. This is clear if we keep in mind the distinction between the loose and the strict sense of existence and our discussion of inwardness. In order to *exist*, the individual must take seriously the fact that he exists. His own existence must be of primary concern. Because he has direct access to his own reality, and because he has the power to shape its innermost dimensions, his relationship is "more than cognitive." To any other existent, whether event or person, past or present, the individual stands in the role of an observer:

For the study of the ethical, every man is assigned to himself. His own self is as material for this study more than sufficient; aye, this is the only place where *he* can study it with any assurance of certainty. Even another human being with whom he lives can reveal himself to his observation only through the external; and in so far the interpretation is necessarily affected with ambiguities. But the more complicated the externality in which the ethical inwardness is reflected, the more difficult becomes the problem of observation, until it finally loses its way in something quite different, namely, the aesthetic.[96]

What Climacus is really claiming is that no man can know for certain about any other human being whether or not he *exists*. In order to know this, he would have to become that person. This is not only impossible,[97] but also ethically forbidden.[98] Climacus' solipsism is thus neither epistemological nor methaphysical in nature. It is (in his sense of the term)

---

[95] *Ibid.*, p. 280. "The only reality that exists for the existing individual is his own ethical reality. To every other reality he stands in a cognitive relation; but true knowledge consists in translating the real into the possible." *Ibid.* On this, cf. Mackey, *Existential*, pp. 31-42. Cf. also Paul Holmer, "On Understanding Kierkegaard," in Johnson and Thulstrup, *Critique*, pp. 44-47.

[96] *Post.*, p. 127.

[97] *Ibid.*, p. 285.

[98] *Ibid.*, p. 284.

ethical.[99] Although there is undeniably an epistemological substrate involved in his position,[100] we fail to grasp the distinctive thrust of Climacus'
views unless we recognize as pivotal his claim that epistemological
considerations are *secondary*.[101] The thinker's primary obligation is to
ethical concerns.

The modern philosophical tradition, beginning with Descartes, has
put epistemological problems in the forefront. The human subject has
thus been construed as the cognitive—or knowing—subject. Climacus
seeks to reinstate the ethical subject. "The real subject is not the cognitive

---

[99] At the same time, Climacus goes to some lengths to deny that his position
involves acosmism. "To assert the supremacy of thought is Gnosticism; to make
the ethical reality of the subject the only reality might seem to be acosmism.
The circumstance that it will seem so to a busy thinker who explains everything,
to a nimble mind that quickly surveys the entire universe, merely proves that
such a thinker has a very humble notion of what the ethical means to the subject.
If Ethics were to take away the entire world from such a thinker, letting him
keep his own self, he would probably regard such a trifle as not worth keeping,
and would let it go with the rest—and so it becomes acosmism. But why does
he think so slightingly of his own self? If it were our meaning that he should
give up the whole world in order to content himself with another person's ethical
reality, he would be justified in regarding the exchange as a dead loss. But his
own ethical reality, on the other hand, ought to mean more to him than
'heaven and earth and all that therein is,' more than the six thousand years of
human history, more than both astrology and the veterinary sciences or whatever
it is that the age demands, all of which is aesthetically and intellectually a huge
vulgarity. And if it is not so, it is worse for the individual himself, for in that
case he has absolutely nothing, no reality at all,..." *Ibid.*, p. 305. Socrates was an
ethical subject, yet this did not prevent him from taking part in the affairs of state
or becoming involved with other human beings.

[100] We get an inkling of his epistemology in a text such as this: "The apparent
trustworthiness of sense is an illusion. This was shown as early as in Greek
skepticism, and modern idealism has likewise demonstrated it. The trustworthiness
claimed by a knowledge of the historical is also a deception, in so far as it assumes
to be the very trustworthiness of reality; for the knower cannot know an historical
reality until he has resolved it into a possibility." *Ibid.*, p. 280. Cf. also pp. 38, 75.

[101] "That the content of my thought exists in the conceptual sense needs no
proof, or needs no argument to prove it, since it is proved by my thinking it.
But as soon as I impose a teleology upon my thought, and bring it into
relation with something else, interest begins to play a role in the matter. The
instant this happens the ethical is present, and absolves me from any further
responsibility in proving my own existence. It forbids me to draw a conclusion that
is ethically deceitful and metaphysically unclear, by imposing upon me the duty
of existing." *Post.*, pp. 282-83. The metaphysical lack of clarity is treated on p. 282.
The ethical deceit lies in the fact that in attempting to prove that he exists,
the thinker abstracts from the interest in existence which Ethics demands.

subject, since in knowing he moves in the sphere of the possible; the real subject is the ethically existing subject." [102] As we have already seen, in order to become a cognitive subject (i.e., a subject whose interest is objective knowledge), the individual human being must turn his attention away from his existence and become disinterested.[103] This requirement is contrary to the ethical demand that he be essentially interested in his own existence. The cognitive subject is not then the real subject. Indeed, if this were the case, an essential difference would be established between the plain man and the philosopher (or the scientist) which would confound existence at its very core.[104] It would follow that not every human being could become a real subject, since it seems clear enough that not every man has the talent and skill require to become a philosopher. This would contradict the ethical presupposition that "every human being must be assumed to be in essential possession of what essentially belongs to being a man." [105]

We have now completed our discussion of the three determinants which are involved in the task of *existing*. Neither thought by itself (not even subjective thought) nor passion by itself but only the reciprocal interplay of the two in the individual's inner existence, and subservient to his essential interest in his own existence, produce that achievement which Climacus terms "the *existing* individual."

In the *Symposium*, Plato characterizes Eros as a constant striving. Climacus finds this to be an apt description of the individual human being's mode of existence. "But what is existence? Existence is the child that is born of the infinite and the finite, the eternal and the temporal, and is therefore a constant striving." [106] The individual human being is finite, yet he is involved in a task which is infinite in the sense that it will never be completed so long as he remains in existence. Existence as a medium is a constant process of becoming. If a man takes this fact seriously and applies it to himself, he must realize that he cannot look forward to a time when he will no longer have to strive to be a human

---

[102] *Ibid.*, p. 281.

[103] On this point, Climacus is surely right. Recall, for instance, Einstein's statement to the effect that the little word "I" has no role to play in the exposition of scientific topics. Cf. Chapter II, p. 69. The same little word plays an absolutely indispensable role in existential tasks.

[104] *Post.*, pp. 203-204.

[105] *Ibid.*, p. 318. This most crucial presupposition is treated at greater length in the conclusion of this chapter.

[106] *Ibid.*, p. 85.

being. This is Climacus' complaint against the men of exalted wisdom who "have finished perhaps once for all the task in which the very point is that it should last for a whole life." [107] "It is only systematists and objective philosophers who have ceased to be human beings, and have become speculative philosophy in the abstract, an entity which belongs in the realm of pure thought." [108] The philosopher becomes philosophy in the sense that he adopts its ways of thinking and the mode of existence that goes with them.[109] He considers everything *sub specie aeterni*. He no longer says that he does such-and-such but that philosophy does.[110] But, of course, he never can abrogate his own existence (he makes the existential concession of drawing his salary once a quarter[111]). He cannot, therefore, truly become philosophy; instead he becomes absent-minded and forgets what it means to *exist*.

In light of the above, we can understand better Climacus' discussion of human existence. The characteristics which he has emphasized in his treatment are just those which differentiate the individual human being from speculative philosophy (or, if one prefers, the philosophical community). The individual human thinks subjectively; philosophy is objective. The individual has passion; philosophy is disinterested. The individual has inwardness; philosophy is public and externalized. Philosophy adheres to the intellectual principle that "no reality is thought or understood until its *esse* has been resolved into its *posse*." [112] Philosophy seeks to extract intelligibility from what is given. It proceeds from the concrete to the abstract, from the particular to the universal. The individual human being, on the other hand, adheres to the ethical principle that "no possibility is understood until each *posse* has really become an *esse*." [113] A man may claim that he has understood a certain possibility; but unless he has acted in such fashion as to actualize that possibility, he has not truly understood it.[114] By calling attention to these features wherein the

---

[107] *Ibid.*, p. 162. They are like the man who, given the task of entertaining himself for an entire day, manages miraculously to finish by noon. Cf. *Ibid.*, p. 147.

[108] *Ibid.*, p. 85.

[109] One might rather say, to use Climacus' own phrase, that the philosopher becomes "what might be called the contemplative energy of philosophy itself." *Ibid.*, p. 54.

[110] Cf. *ibid.*, p. 50.

[111] *Ibid.*, p. 172.

[112] *Ibid.*, pp. 288-89.

[113] *Ibid.*

[114] Cf. above p. 90 and *Post.*, p. 304, *n*.

individual human being differs from philosophy, Climacus is in effect reminding his reader that he should not confuse himself with the philosophical community and its standpoint.

No man, for example, should forget the fact that his own intellect has definite limitations.[115] This is the basis of Climacus' criticism of the world-historical veiwpoint. By continually viewing human affairs from this perspective, an individual may easily be lured into forgetfulness of his condition as a single man with limited powers of comprehension.[116] While it may be the case that, from the divine standpoint, *"die Weltgeschichte ist das Weltgericht,"* [117] yet no human being should claim this standpoint as his own. If he does, he forgets the infinite qualitative difference that stands between the human mode of existence and the divine.[118] No matter how committed philosophy is to the ultimate unity and intelligibility of all phenomena (we are referring here to the Hegelian conception of philosophy), this commitment cannot suffice to shield the individual human mind against unknowings.

Does Climacus, then, by opposing the (in his opinion) excessive rationalism of Hegelian philosophy fall into the posture of irrationalism? Hardly. In the first place, he emphasizes very much one particular use of human reason: subjective thought. Secondly, he straightforwardly acknowledges the validity of abstract thought.[119] Abstract thought is valid so long as the thinker remains responsive to the ethical imperative.[120] If he can fulfill that obligation and still has time and energy to undertake the additional labor of abstract thought, then "not another word, except

---

[115] "Every man, the wisest and the simplest, (the comparative produces misunderstanding, as in the case when a clever pate compares himself with a simple man, instead of understanding that the same task is for each one severally and not for the two in comparison) can qualitatively distinguish just as essentially between what he understands and what he does not understand (of course his laborious conclusion will be the fruit of his utmost effort, and two thousand years lie between Socrates and Hamann, the two upholders of this distinction),..." *Ibid.,* p. 495.

[116] "What wonder that we admire the historical spectator who is so lofty as to forget that he, too, is a particular man, an individual existing human being. He stares at the historical spectacle until he is lost in it; he dies and leaves the scene, and nothing remains of him; or rather, he himself remains like a ticket in the hands of the usher, an indication that the spectator has gone." *Ibid.,* p. 142.

[117] *Ibid.,* p. 126. The line is taken from Schiller's poem, "Resignation."

[118] Cf. *ibid.,* pp. 195, 369, 439.

[119] Cf. *ibid.,* pp. 85, 135, 294. Cf. also Ralph McInerny, "Kierkegaard and Speculative Thought," *The New Scholasticism,* XL (1966), pp. 23-35.

[120] Cf. above p. 79.

a word of admiration for the distinguished, and a word of inspiration and encouragement for the aspiring." [121] Even though it is disinterested in existence, abstract thought (by which Climacus understands, for example, mathematics, history, and some kinds of philosophy) yet retains a relationship to existence. It acknowledges existence in the very act of abstracting from it.[122] Pure thought, on the other hand, attempts to dissolve any relationship to existence.[123] Even Hegel could not erase all traces of existence.[124]

In summation, we can say that Climacus is attempting to persuade his reader to take seriously as a task that very given which he may have come to regard (under the influence of philosophical habits of thought) as trivial; namely, his own existence.[125] He does this by calling attention to basic truths about human existence,[126] and to a way of thinking about them that involves appropriating them.[127] Existing as a human being is

[121] *Post.*, p. 136.

[122] "I can abstract from myself; but the fact that I abstract from myself means precisely that I exist." *Ibid.*, p. 196. Cf. also pp. 272-74, 278-79, 295.

[123] "It would be an altogether different thing if pure thought would accept the responsibility of explaining its own relation to the ethical, and to the ethically existing individual. But this it never does, nor does it even pretend; for in that case it would have to make terms with an entirely different dialectic, namely, the Greek or existential dialectic." *Ibid.*, p. 274.

[124] Climacus criticizes Hegel for publishing his *Logic* with a date of publication, notes, etc. All of these are indicators of existence and becoming, which are supposedly not to be found within the realm of pure thought. "But as it now is, the *Logic* with its collection of notes makes as droll an impression on the mind as if a man were to show a letter purporting to have come from heaven, but having a blotter enclosed which only too clearly reveals its mundane origin." *Ibid.*, p. 297.

[125] "Existing is ordinarily regarded as no very complex matter, much less an art, since we all exist; but abstract thinking takes rank as an accomplishment." *Ibid.*, p. 273. If Climacus is to be successful in his attempt, he must cut the ties which bind author and reader together. He gave considerable thought to the hazards of the author-reader relationship. Cf. *Ibid.*, pp. 3-6, 225-66, 545-50. How he deals with these will be taken up in Chapter VI.

[126] These truths concern the "simply human" (*Post., p.* 77) or the "universally human" (*ibid.*, pp. 320-21) and are before us at all times. The idea that what it is most important for us to know is before us at all times and is consequently easily missed is found in Wittgenstein, too. Compare the passage from his *Philosophical Investigations* (on the page after our title-page) with *Post.*, pp. 116-17.

[127] Wittgenstein, too, calls attention to a style of thinking. "I am in a sense making propaganda for one style of thinking as opposed to another.... Much of what we are doing is a question of changing the style of thinking." Ludwig Wittgenstein, *Lectures and Conversations on Aesthetics, Psychology, and Religious Belief,* ed. Cyril Barrett (Oxford, 1966), p. 28.

then more a matter of *how* a man thinks than *what* he thinks.[128] Climacus maintains that the requirements of a truly human existence are such that every man can meet them. Yes, there are differences between men. This one has a talent for abstract thought; that one, the knack of using words prettily; still another has an eye for color. Such differences, however, are insignificant in the face of this universal ideal. Climacus says:

> To wish to live as a particular human being (which is what everyone undoubtedly is), relying upon a difference, is the weakness of cowardice; to will to live as a particular human being (which everyone undoubtedly is) in the same sense as is open to every other human being, in the ethical victory over life and all its illusions.[129]

This ideal is equally difficult for the talented and the simple:

> ...the secret of it is that it is equally difficult for the most eminent talent, since the task is not comparative: a task for a simple man in comparison with a distinguished talent, but rather a task for the distinguished talent in comparison with himself...[130]

Some tasks permit comparisons. In science, for example, one man's theory may explain a given phenomenon more adequately than another's. But the task of existing involves each man essentially with himself alone. "The difficulty is proportioned to each individual separately, absolutely requiring his absolute exertion, but no more." [131] With these points in mind, then, let us consider next what Climacus says about human existence and truth.

C. HUMAN EXISTENCE AND TRUTH

Perhaps no single claim in the *Postscript* has occasioned as much controversy, polemic, and misunderstanding as the claim that subjectivity is the truth. In order to understand both this claim and the definition of truth that goes with it correctly, it is imperative to understand, first, what Climacus means by "subjectivity"; and, secondly, the context in which the claim is proposed. It will be our interpretation that the claim cannot be construed as a denial that there is such a thing as objective truth. The very fact that Climacus distinguishes between subjective and objective truth should of itself prevent such a misreading. In addition, we noted in the previous section that Climacus has nowhere taken the

---

[128] Cf. *Post.*, pp. 85, 116.
[129] *Ibid.*, p. 319. Cf. also p. 318.
[130] *Ibid.*, pp. 419-20.
[131] *Ibid.*, p. 385. The difficulties involved in *existing* are not subject to a "comparative dialectic."

position that objective thought is invalid.[132] Nor is this important claim meant to sanction the introduction of an individual's personal beliefs and opinions into situations where they are not relevant, as in science or mathematics.[133] Nor yet does Climacus mean to defend the subjectivist position that whatever a man really believes to be true is true (for him).

The claim that subjectivity is the truth is better understood as a very general description of the direction in which the individual human being should proceed in order to come into possession of the truth which has to do with him as an individual human being. It describes, we shall maintain, his *mode of access* to the truth. It defines a view of truth which lies between that of Plato and Hegel, on the one hand (if they are interpreted as affirming the principle that objectivity is the truth), and that of Christianity, on the other (if it is interpreted as affirming the principle that subjectivity is untruth).

First, then, what does "subjectivity" mean? *Webster's New World Dictionary* defines "subjectivity" as "the tendency to consider all things only in light of one's own personality; concern with only one's own thoughts and feelings."[134] If this is what Climacus means by the term, then the claim that subjectivity is the truth would ratify every manner of idiosyncrasy and eccentricity in human affairs.[135] This is not, however,

---

[132] Cf. above pp. 95-96.

[133] "It must always be remembered that I speak of the religious, in which sphere objective thinking, when it ranks as highest, is precisely irreligious. *But wherever objective thinking is within its rights,* its direct form of communications is also in order, precisely because it is not supposed to have anything to do with subjectivity." *Post.,* p. 70, *n.* (Italics mine.)

[134] *Webster's New World Dictionary of the American Language,* College Edition (Cleveland and New York, 1962), p. 1452.

[135] This seems to be the interpretation of Arthur E. Murphy. Cf. his article, "On Kierkegaard's Claim that 'Truth is Subjectivity,'" in Gill, *Essays,* pp. 94-101. Murphy says: "Given his definitions of 'subjectivity,' 'truth,' and 'faith,' it seems to follow, as he claims, that such a 'faith' *is* the truth, though why this self-centered passion should be identified as religious faith rather than sheer ego-centricity is so far hardly clear. And why it should be dignified as the highest truth attainable for an existing individual is a further question" (p. 96). Murphy is off to a bad start when he states (p. 94) that: "The point of Kierkegaard's discussion of 'truth,' I take it, is to offer a justification of faith, in his special sense of 'faith,' by showing that the believer is 'in the truth' subjectively in his groundless affirmation of what is rationally absurd,..." Oblivious to the nuances of Climacus' treatment, Murphy can hardly be expected to grasp the difference between faith *sensu laxiori* and *sensu strictissimo* (cf. *Post.,* p. 286). It is of course simply false to suggest that the author of the *Postscript* (who is, after all, not a Christian but is asking what it means to become one) is offering a justification

what Climacus means by this term. In proposing the task of becoming subjective, he is not urging a man to develop his idiosyncrasies [136] or to consider everything in light of his personality,[137] but rather to understand what it means to be a human being and consider things in this light. Subjectivity does not mean being concerned with *only* one's own thoughts and feeling; it means rather to have one's own existence as one's primary (though not exclusive) concern and to direct one's thoughts to understanding this fundamental fact and its many implications.[138] Subjectivity, then, is a steady mindfulness of what it means to be an individual human being.

What, then, does it mean to affirm that subjectivity is the truth? Truth is often defined as a correspondence between being and thought. Which of these two poles, thought or being, is taken as primary depends upon the underlying epistemology. Thus if being is taken as the reference point, then we have the realist definition of truth as the correspondence of thought with being. If, on the other hand, thought is taken as the reference point, then we have the idealist definition of truth as the

---

of faith, *sensu strictissimo*. The fact that Murphy simply does not understand what subjectivity means is clear from the following remarks: "That what Kierkegaard has to tell us about faith fits the facts of his own subjectivity is clear enough. Rarely has a man been more persuasive in projecting his private ailments as 'existential' profundities. His relations to his father and to Regina Olsen take on ontological significance, as the commentators love to tell us, and his fears and frustrations are dignified as the embodiment of the highest truth attainable to man—the truth of subjectivity" (p. 98).

[136] Cf. above pp. 76-77.

[137] "I am well aware that every human being is more or less one-sided, and I do not regard it as a fault.... So far are we human beings from realizing the ideal, that the second rank, the powerful one-sidedness is pretty much the highest ever attained; but it must never be forgotten that it is only the second rank." *Post.*, p. 312.

[138] There is an interesting passage relating to this point in the *Phaedrus*. It occurs as Socrates and Phaedrus pass by a famous spot. This prompts Phaedrus to ask Socrates his opinion about the current thinking on some of the Greek myths. Socrates sidesteps: "I myself have certainly no time for the business: and I'll tell you why, my friend: I can't as yet 'know myself,' as the inscription at Delphi enjoins; and so long as that ignorance remains it seems to me ridiculous to inquire into extraneous matters. Consequently I don't bother about such things, but accept the current beliefs, and direct my inquiries, as I have just said, rather to myself, ..." Plato, *Phaedrus*, 229^{b}4-230^{a}2; trans. R. Hackforth, *The Collected Dialogues of Plato*, Bollingen Series, ed. Edith Hamilton and Huntington Cairns (New York, 1961), p. 478. Subjectivity means being able to distinguish between extraneous matters and essential ones, and not allowing the former to interfere with the latter.

correspondence of being with thought.[139] In either case, however, the term "thought" refers to objective thought: and "the term 'being,'... must therefore be understood (from the systematic standpoint) much more abstractly, presumably as the abstract reflection of, or the abstract prototype for, what being is as concrete empirical being."[140] That is, both definitions aim to define the truth which science, history, philosophy, and other forms of objective thought pursue.

What of the existing individual, though? In so far as he engages in objective tasks, the definition of truth as the correspondence of thought with being is appropriate. It tells him what to aim for. "For an existing spirit *qua* existing spirit, the question of truth will again exist. The abstract answer has significance only for the abstraction into which an existing spirit is transformed when he abstracts from himself *qua* existing individual."[141] Climacus' point might be put this way. The abstract definition of truth is adequate for philosophy and other forms of objectivity. It is adequate for the individual human being in so far as he is engaged in philosophical reflection. Since, however, the individual cannot become philosophy, the abstract definition is not totally adequate. It is adequate for the individual in so far as he abstracts from his existence, but it is not adequate for the individual in so far as he is interested in his existence. Within the context, then, of these carefully drawn distinctions, we are ready for a closer investigation of the claim that subjectivity is the truth and the definition of truth which goes with that claim.

We may begin with the following text:

It is therefore an existing spirit who is now conceived as raising the question of truth, presumably in order that he may exist in it; but in any case the question is raised by someone who is conscious of being a particular existing human being.[142]

We discussed in the previous sections the elements of such a consciousness. Thought here will be subjective thought, and the being which it must interpenetrate is the thinker's own existence which is in constant process of becoming. In this context, the attempt to define truth as a correspondence between thought and being will not suffice. Such a definition does not tell a man *what* he, as an existing individual, should be aiming for nor does it tell him *how* to proceed. The claim that subjectivity is the truth must be read as an indicator of *how* the

---

[139] *Post.*, p. 169.
[140] *Ibid.*, p. 170.
[141] *Ibid.*
[142] *Ibid.*

individual human being should proceed in order to reach the truth concerning his existence. He has only two choices. He may proceed by way of objective thought (thus focussing his thought on something outside of himself) or by way of subjective reflection.[143] Quite clearly, the principle that subjectivity is the truth affirms that the latter is the proper way for the individual to proceed.

For objective thought, as we have seen, truth is a matter of correspondence. "For a subjective reflection," Climacus claims, "the truth becomes a matter of appropriation, of inwardness, of subjectivity, and thought must probe more and more deeply into the subject and his subjectivity."[144] Why is this? In the realm of objectivity, it is *what* an individual thinks that is important. In science, for example, this *"what"* may be a theory proposed to explain a particular phenomenon. Whether a given scientist's theory is accepted or not will depend upon many factors; the evidence for it; its compatibility with previously accepted theories; its ability to bring new data to light. However, whether the theory occurred to him after long years of concentrated effort or only a few months, whether he invested a great deal of himself in his work or very little, none of this matters. In short, the nature of the scientist's relationship to *what* he thinks is unimportant when scientific truth is at stake.[145] *"When the question of truth is raised subjectively, reflection is directed subjectively to the nature of the individual's relationship;..."* [146] Since the content of a subjective reflection is always a universal which pertains to human existence,[147] and since everyone knows what these are,[148] the important issue here is appropriation. The subjective thinker's task is to relate himself to the universally human with the passion of the infinite. That is, he must not content himself with a moment of striving now and again. The only way to arrive at the truth here is to concentrate one's entire energy on the task. To embrace one's existence with a transient passion, a fleeting interest, is to fail to relate to it properly and is not the way to acquire the truth. How, then, will an individual human being gain access to the truth? He must relate himself to his own existence with infinite passion. "But the passion

---

[143] Climacus is quick to point out that a man cannot proceed simultaneously in both directions. *Ibid.*, pp. 171-73.

[144] *Ibid.*, p. 171.

[145] Cf. *ibid.*, pp. 178, 181.

[146] *Ibid.*, p. 178.

[147] Cf. above pp. 78-80.

[148] Cf. above p. 78.

of the infinite is precisely subjectivity, and thus subjectivity becomes the truth."[149] The claim that subjectivity is the truth, therefore, describes the individual human being's mode of access to the truth.

Is this, however, all that is meant by the claim? If it is, then Climacus has stated it poorly. He ought rather to have said: subjectivity is *the way* to the truth. To answer this objection, let us recall that "the development of the subject consists precisely in his active interpenetration of himself by reflection concerning his own existence, so that he really thinks what he thinks through making a reality of it."[150] Now as the individual probes his subjectivity, he will undoubtedly arrive at an opinion of his existence. He will discover what he really thinks about himself as an individual human being. (It is, of course, impossible for someone who has not taken the pains to become a human being to have a significant opinion about this matter.) When, by probing his own thoughts, he extracts what he really thinks about himself as a human being, it will be true that he thinks what he thinks about his existence. This is a trivial sense of "true," however. The important question is: What about the truth or untruth of what the individual really thinks about his own existence? Presumably this judgment will itself be either true or false. The principle that subjectivity is the truth means that the opinion of his own existence which the individual arrives at through the process of subjective reflection will be the truth.[151]

It may seem that this principle simply opens the flood-gates and allows each man to set his own valuation on his existence. To see that this is not the case, Climacus refers us to Socrates:

In spite of the fact that Socrates studied with all diligence to acquire a knowledge of human nature and to understand himself, and in spite of the fame accorded him through the centuries as one who beyond all other men had an insight into the human heart, he has himself admitted that the reason for his shrinking from reflection upon the nature of such beings as Pegasus and the Gorgons was that he, the life-long student of human nature, had not yet been able to make up his mind whether he was a stranger monster than a Typhon, or a creature of a gentler and simpler sort, partaking of something divine.[152]

After years of reflection on this question, Socrates still does not know

---

[149] *Post.*, p. 181.

[150] *Ibid.*, p. 151. Cf. above p. 86.

[151] The principle that subjectivity is the truth is simply a condensed way of putting the thoughts developed by Climacus himself at greater length in "A" of the thought-project of the *Fragments*. Cf. *Frag.*, pp. 11-16.

[152] *Frag.*, p. 46.

what to think of himself. He is uncertain. This is "...the Socratic wisdom, whose everlasting merit it was to have become aware of the essential significance of existence, of the fact that the knower is an existing individual. For this reason, Socrates was in the truth by virtue of his ignorance,..." [153] His ignorance is really an achievement, not the lack of one. It was his way of maintaining a steady consciousness of himself as an existing individual, even though that meant foregoing interesting questions about Gorgons and Pegasuses and contenting himself with the accepted opinion.

But more than two thousand years stand between Socrates and the nineteenth century. Is it still possible for an individual to find himself in the grips of Socratic Ignorance? [154] "It may be a genial observation that the world and the human race have grown older; but is not everyone still born in infancy?" [155] Climacus does not deny that great contributions have been made to the various branches of learning since Socrates' time. But:

Spiritual development is self-activity: the spiritually developed individual takes his development with him when he dies. If an individual of a subsequent generation is to reach the same development, he will have to attain it by means of his own activity, and he cannot be permitted to omit anything.[156]

Like Socrates before him, then, the individual of any later generation has the task of finding out what he thinks about his own existence. Through the centuries, many different opinions have been rendered about the significance of human existence. These range from the view that human existence is of no greater moment than the existence of a blade of grass to the view that it has eternal significance. Even if an individual has been taught to treat one or another of these views with respect (even to the point of labelling it the *Truth*), his task as an existing individual is to find out whether this "official answer" (the one he has been taught to treat respectfully) really is *his own*. He must discover whether his answer is spoken with his own voice or that of one he admires. He must discover—and this is a discovery which no one else can make for him—whether that answer is his answer or whether he

---

[153] *Post.*, p. 183.

[154] Climacus says: "I have heard people, stupid enough to run their heads against a stone wall, say that it is impossible to remain at the standpoint of Socratic ignorance." *Post.*, p. 228.

[155] *Ibid.*, p. 311.

[156] *Ibid.*, p. 309. Cf. also p. 221: "A direct relationship between one spiritual being and another, with respect to the essential truth, is unthinkable."

has become one well-rehearsed in speaking certain lines. He must probe his own subjectivity.

In light of these remarks about the meaning of the principle that subjectivity is the truth, we are ready to consider Climacus' definition (or "conceptual determination," as he refers to it) of the truth:

When subjectivity is the truth, the conceptual determination of the truth must include an expression for the antithesis to objectivity, a momento of the fork in the road where the way swings off; this expression will at the same time serve as an indication of the tension of the subjective inwardness. Here is such a definition of truth: *An objective uncertainty, held fast in an appropriation-process of the most passionate inwardness is the truth,* the highest truth attainable for an *existing individual.*[157]

First of all, it is important to observe that Climacus has introduced his definition with a qualification: "When subjectivity is the truth,..." The significance of this should not be overlooked. Climacus realizes that his definition of truth does not apply in all circumstances. It does not apply where objective thought is within its rights: i.e., in science, mathematics, or history. There truth will consist in a proper relationship between thought and being, and the conceptual determination will contain an

---

[157] *Ibid.,* p. 182. Allison has proposed an interesting interpretation of this definition. He argues that given such a definition of truth, Christianity becomes indistinguishable from nonsense. Cf. Allison, *Nonsense,* pp. 439-59. He traces this misologism to the definition of truth. "The starting point of his trouble, the decisive passage which gives rise to the misologistic consequences is the assertion: 'When subjectivity is the truth, the conceptual determination of the truth must include an expression for the antithesis to objectivity.' The key words here are 'conceptual determination' for they make clear that Climacus' misologism is a direct consequence of the 'principle of subjectivity'! But to conceptualize is to objectify, and, as we have seen, to speak objectively about inwardness (and Christianity, it will be remembered, is the highest form of inwardness) is stupidity. Thus unless we are to view Kierkegaard as guilty of the very stupidity which he went to such great lengths to condemn, we must view the whole 'argument' as a jest, an expression of the author's artistry, the intent of which is not to 'prove' the superiority of Christianity..., but rather to help us realize existentially what it means to become a Christian,..." *Ibid.,* pp. 459-60. While it is true that the author of the *Postscript* is a humorist, Allison goes a bit too far in interpreting the definition of truth as part of a jest. He quite correctly points out that a subjective author faces a dilemma. In Chapter VI, we shall propose our own interpretation of how Climacus resolved it. Whether Climacus' views entail the position that Christianity and nonsense are indistinguishable is debatable. On this, cf. Rudolph J. Gerber, "Kierkegaard, Reason and Faith," *Thought,* XLIV (1969), pp. 29-52. In *The Anti-Christianity of Kierkegaard* (The Hague, 1965), Herbert Garelick, in agreement with Allison, argues that this misologism vitiates Climacus' conception of Christianity.

expression for the antithesis to subjectivity. As was stated earlier in this section, the relationship between the thought and the thinker plays no significant role in determining objective truth. When subjectivity is the truth, however, the relationship between thought and thinker is all important. The proper relationship here is one of appropriation, and Climacus' definition points this out.

Perhaps the most perplexing element of the definition is the phrase "an objective uncertainty." Why does Climacus specify the thought involved in this definition of truth as "an objective uncertainty"? It is important to keep in mind here the nature of subjective thought. It is not thought about the world or some aspect of it, as scientific thought is; it is not about the human past, as historical thought is; it is not about concepts and ideas, as some philosophical thought is. It is thought about what it means to be an individual human being, thought directed to securing an understanding of this fundamental fact about any thinker. Now as we have recently seen, one of the culminating points of such thought will be the individual's own thoughts about his existence as a human being. Obviously, since the thoughts are supposed to be *his* thoughts, he cannot look to the realm of objective knowledge for confirmation or contradiction. For whatever his thoughts about his own existence are (and let us not forget that after seventy years Socrates still does not know what to think of himself as a human being, yet he keeps his ignorance front-and-center at all times; moreover, if it should turn out that death is not the end, Socrates plans to continue searching for an answer [158]), he will undoubtedly find that they fall somewhere within the spectrum of human thinking on this question. That is, there will be those who have expressed thoughts about their existence similar to the ones he has of his own. But there will be others who have expressed conflicting thoughts. Thus, from the objective point of view, he will have no certainty, no assurances.[159] The issue of paramount importance now becomes the relationship between the thinker and this objective uncertainty, for nothing more remains to be said about the relationship of his thought to reality. He may *either* hold fast to this uncertainty, exploring its implications for his own existence and shaping

---

[150] Cf. above p. 103.

[159] "At a point where the way swings off (and where this is cannot be specified objectively, since it is a matter of subjectivity), there objective knowledge is placed in abeyance. Thus the subject merely has, objectively, the uncertainty; ..." *Post.*, p. 182.

his existence in light of those; [160] *or* he may let it go and concentrate on something else. The *existing* individual will surely opt for the former alternative.

Climacus' definition of truth must be understood in context. It is *not* an all-embracing definition of truth, but functions within the claim that subjectivity is the truth. Just as a good definition of objective truth will seek to articulate what all such truth has in common, so Climacus' definition of subjective truth attempts to specify what all such truth has in common: appropriation. It is a reminder that, in those situations where we stand as individual human beings, truth will be a function, not so much of *what* we think or say, but *how* we relate ourselves to it.[161]

It is clear, then, that Climacus' definition of truth grows out of the larger claim that subjectivity is the truth. The meaning of that claim is clarified even further as Climacus considers other possibilities. "Can any expression for the truth be found which has a still higher degree of inwardness?" Climacus asks. "Aye, there is such an expression, provided the principle that subjectivity or inwardness is the truth begins by positing the opposite principle: that subjectivity is untruth." [162] Now there are two ways to understand this "opposite principle." First, there is the sense in which speculative philosophy might propose it:

Speculative philosophy also says that subjectivity is untruth, but says it in order to stimulate a movement in precisely the opposite direction, namely, in the direction that objectivity is the truth.[163]

From an objective point of view, it is the task of the individual to divest himself of his subjectivity, to abstract from his own existence. But this will not result in a still higher degree of inwardness.

Climacus understands something else by this "opposite principle":

---

[160] How does Socrates deal with the problem of immortality? "He puts the question objectively in a problematic manner: *if* there is an immortality.... On this 'if' he risks his entire life, he has the courage to meet death, and he has with the passion of the infinite so determined the pattern of his life that it must be found acceptable—*if* there is an immortality." *Ibid.,* p. 180.

[161] "Thus, to make use of an erotic relationship, if a loving maiden were to long for the wedding day on account of the assured certainty that it would give her; if she desired to install herself as wife in a legal security, exchanging maidenly longing for wifely yawning, her lover would have the right to complain of her unfaithfulness, and that although she loved no one else; because she had lost the Idea constitutive of the inwardnes of love, and did not really love him...; loving another is accidental." *Ibid.,* p. 68, *n.*

[162] *Ibid.,* p. 185.

[163] *Ibid.*

This second determination of ours, however, places a hindrance in its own way while proposing to begin, which has the effect of making the inwardness far more intensive. Socratically speaking, subjectivity is untruth if it refuses to understand that subjectivity is truth, but, for example, desires to become objective.[164]

From the Socratic point of view, if an individual attempts to forget the fact that he is an existing individual in order to master Hebrew, he is headed in the wrong direction. His mode of existence will be an existence loosely so called. "Here, on the other hand, subjectivity in beginning upon the task of becoming the truth through a subjectifying process, is in the difficulty that it is already untruth." [165] What would this mean?

It would mean that subjectivity is the way to the truth, but that in coming into existence the individual comes into untruth.[166] His every effort results in his being further and further away from the truth. Subjectivity is his path; yet what he really thinks about his own existence, in so far as he has been able to uncover it, is *wrong*. Or, if he is like Socrates unable to reach a definite opinion, that is also *wrong*. As existing, he is sealed off from the truth and hence could not recognize it even if he came across it. The principle that subjectivity is untruth charges the individual with the task of existing—of becoming a subject—and yet claims that even if he has taken up the task in earnestness, he yet fails to exist. Such a principle would certainly intensify subjectivity. It says that the individual is to find out what he really thinks, but adds that what he really thinks is wrong. But how can the individual unthink what he really thinks about his existence?

Climacus does not himself affirm this "opposite principle." His thesis is that subjectivity is the truth. But the meaning of his thesis is thrown into clearer relief by considering the dialectical consequence of this "opposite principle." Climacus' thesis means that each individual human has the task of becoming a subject; and that he is born in such a condition that he can, in truth, become one. It affirms, with the Socratic doctrine of recollection, that:

...the knower is essentially *integer,* and that with respect to the knowledge of the eternal truth he is confronted with no other difficulty than the circumstance that he exists; which difficulty, however, is so essential and decisive for him that

---

[164] *Ibid.*

[165] *Ibid.,* pp. 185-86.

[166] It is Climacus' understanding that Christianity takes this view. Cf. *Frag.,* pp. 10-27.

it means that existing, the process of transformation in and by existing, is the truth:...[167]

It means that to take possession of that truth he must take possession of himself. It affirms, in sum, that the truth awaits the individual who undertakes the task of becoming subjective.

D. CONCLUSION

Having presented Climacus' views on human existence, we shall here offer some reflections on their significance. James Collins, for instance, asserts that the importance of the *Postscript* "...lies in its...*preliminary sketch of a new theory of existence,* as religiously orientated." [168] In the next chapter, we shall point to other differences between our interpretation and that of Collins. Here we intend to indicate why Collins' assertion is mistaken and in so doing bring out what we take to be the importance of the *Postscript*'s analysis of human existence.

Has Climacus presented his reader with any *new insights* into human existence? There are three reasons for saying "No" to this question. In the first place, the claim that men have *forgotten* what it means to exist clearly implies that they once knew (and in some sense still know) what it means. The very fact that Climacus chose this way of characterizing the situation he was dealing with seems to suggest that he did not believe that there was a great need for innovation. Because it has failed to recognize the centrality of the forgetting-claim, most Kierkegaard-scholarship has consistently missed this important implication.

Secondly, our own results in this chapter dispute Collins' claim. For we have not found anything in Climacus' treatment of human existence which could reasonably be termed novel. Indeed, and this is the third reason, Climacus himself admits that "..., I say only what every school-boy knows, though he may not be able to express himself quite so clearly." [169] Elsewhere he writes:

What I here write must be viewed as *elementary reading* for the primer class, not in the speculative sense, but in the simple sense. Every child knows it, if not precisely with the same *background of experience;* everyone understands it, if not precisely with the same *sharpness of definition;* everyone is able to understand it.[170]

---

[167] *Post.,* p. 184.
[168] Collins, *Mind,* p. 98. (Italics mine.)
[169] *Post.,* p. 53.
[170] *Ibid.,* p. 350. (Italics mine.)

And at the very end of the *Postscript,* Climacus states:

My attempt is *eo ipso* without importance and only for my own diversion—as must be the case when a learner in the art of existence, who thus cannot want to teach others (and far be from me the vain and empty thought of wanting to be such a teacher!), propounds something which one might in a way expect of a learner who essentially knows neither more nor less than what pretty much every man knows,...[171]

Even the editor of the *Postscript* would have to reject Collins' interpretation. Speaking *in propria persona,* Kierkegaard renders his opinion of the pseudonymous works:

...their importance...absolutely does not consist in making any new proposal, any unheard-of discovery, or forming a new party, or wanting to go further, but, precisely on the contrary, consists in wanting to have no importance, in wanting (at a distance which is the remoteness of double reflection) to read solo the original text of the individual human existence-relationship, the old text, well known, handed down from the fathers—to read it through yet once more, if possible in a more heartfelt way.[172]

We may conclude from this that the importance of Climacus' treatment of existence does not stem from its novelty or originality.

Nor does Climacus offer his reader anything as formal as a theory of existence. The simple presence of the word "unscientific" in its title should suffice to discourage such an interpretation. Climacus is quite explicit on this point:

If the concept of existence is really to be stressed, this cannot be given a direct expression as a paragraph in a system;... An actual emphasis on existence must be expressed in an essential form; in view of the elusiveness of existence, such a form will have to be an indirect form, namely, the absence of a system.[173]

Climacus is not attempting to replace one theory about existence with another. And for a good reason. For a theory is something other than

---

[171] *Ibid.,* p. 550.

[172] *Declaration,* p. 554. Swenson's rendering (*Something,* p. 94) is better: "Whatever actual significance the pseudonyms may come to have in the world is absolutely not to be found in the making of any new proposal, or in exploiting any unheard of discovery, or in beginning any new movement, or in taking up any advanced position. Their significance lies in the precise opposite, in the renunciation of all claim to significance, and in the mere attempt to read through again, *solo,* at a distance of double reflection, the scriptures of our human, individual existential relations, the old and well-known scriptures handed down to us from the fathers; if possible, reading them through again with increased inwardness."

[173] *Post.,* p. 111.

the individual himself.[174] But as we have seen, Climacus would like his reader (who is presumedly already interested in the philosophical issues of the times and will therefore have been exposed to systems and theories) to set aside his zeal for objective thought and *wissenschaft* in order to come to some understanding of himself as an existing individual. Given this purpose, a theory might simply prove to be an added distraction, especially if it is the reader's misfortune that he knows too much already. Of course, if one thinks of a theory as nothing more than a collection of thoughts on a particular topic, then it is true to say that Climacus has a theory of existence.

Since Climacus' treatment of human existence is rooted in a protest, we grasp its true significance only when we understand what injustices it aims to expose. As we observed at the beginning of this chapter, the protest stems from Climacus' conviction that speculative philosophy ignores the indivdual human being. For he maintains that "...existence has only individual human beings." [175] Speculative philosophy may study the concept of existence, yet "A particular existing human being is surely not an Idea, and his existence is surely something quite different from the conceptual existence of the Idea." [176] Still we have seen that Climacus is less concerned to expose the epistemological limits of abstract thought (that it cannot capture the individual *qua* existing) than to unmask its "ethical" consequence. Abstract thought requires the individual to abstract from his own existence; but it is precisely this which Ethics would emphasize. Without denying that abstract thought is both valid and valuable, Climacus opposes the idea that it is an unmitigated good.

A slightly different aspect of Climacus' protest was pointed out at the beginning of the second chapter. There we noticed that Climacus displays a kind of irritable sensitivity to certain locutions such as "Speculative philosophy doubts everything." These provoke him to ask: "Is speculative philosophy a human being?" "Is mediation then a man?" [177] Such a response may sound peevish, but the point is an important one. It may be that in some respects philosophy resembles the individual human being. "But the difficulty is that no human being is speculative philosophy;..." [178] As an existing individual, the philosopher has a mode of existence which is sharply different from that of speculative

---

[174] Cf. Michael Polanyi, *Personal Knowledge* (London, 1955), p. 4.

[175] *Post.*, p. 310.

[176] *Ibid.*, p. 293.

[177] *Ibid.*, p. 177.

[178] *Ibid.*, p. 184, *n.*

philosophy, and he is therefore subject to the claims which that mode of existence makes upon him.[179] In the *Postscript*, Climacus emphasizes the differences between philosophy and the individual human being in order to persuade the reader to give these claims their due.

These two aspects of Climacus treatment of human existence are as closely related as the inequities which elicit the protest. It is by ignoring the individual human being that the differences between philosophy and the individual are obscured. But the tendency to identify philosophy and the individual human is symptomatic of a more important species of myopia. This nearsighted condition reveals itself if we raise this question: Are the requirements of a truly human existence such that every man can, in principle, meet them? There is a view with an honorable history which has it that not every man is capable of meeting these requirements. To understand what such a view amounts to, we shall consider three propositions.

(1) *Thinking is an essential ingredient of a truly human existence.* It is a commonplace observation that the ability to reason (and all that goes with it) is what distinguishes man from the brute.[180] Some philosophers have argued that reason is the highest of human faculties.[181] None would deny thought a role in human existence.

(2) *The kind of thinking that is essential for a truly human existence is abstract thinking.* For it is not sufficient simply that a man think. He must, some have held, think in a certain way and about certain things.

---

[179] *Ibid.*

[180] A concise presentation of this thought is found in Aristotle, *De Anima*, Book II, Chapter 3 (414ª29-414ᵇ14). In this passage, Aristotle classifies all living things hierarchically. Man is at the summit in virtue of his ability to reason and calculate. Cf. Book III, Chapters 3 and 10. Susanne K. Langer has recently proposed an interesting variation on this theme. She claims that what distinguishes man from the brute is his ability to symbolize. Cf. *Philosophy in a New Key* (New York, 1962), Chapter 1.

[181] A clear statement of this position can be found in Plato's *Republic*, 441ª4-441ª6: "And it will be the business of reason to rule with wisdom and forethought on behalf of the entire soul;..." *The Republic of Plato*, trans. and intro. Francis MacDonald Cornford (New York and London, 1964), p. 140. (Subsequent English citations of the *Republic* are from Cornford's translation.) According to Plato, the individual human soul is just, is in its rightful condition when the reasoning part rules. "Justice is produced in the soul, like health in the body, by establishing the elements in their natural relations of control and subordination,..." *Republic*, p. 143. Cf. also p. 226, where intelligence is said to be the highest state of mind. In attributing this and other views to Plato, we are aware of the difficulties involved in interpreting his works.

Plato, for example, calls the kind of thinking which is involved "intelligence" and "knowledge." He calls the reality to be thought about the "idea." [182] Other philosophers would specify both the type of thinking and its object differently.

(3) *Not all men are either endowed by nature or can develop the ability to think abstractly.* This is especially clear in the *Republic.* Plato uses the Allegory of the Three Metals partly to make this point, partly (it seems) to soften its impact.[183] The philosopher-king is the only one who has the ability to undertake the dialectical journey which culminates in the apprehension of Goodness Itself. The apprehension of this Ultimate is absolutely essential for a truly human existence. But one may not choose to become a philosopher-king. One is born into this condition; one has it *by nature.*[184]

These three propositions entail a fourth.

(4) *Not all men are able to meet the requirements of a truly human existence.* Plato, for example, seems committed to this proposition. For he ordains it that the philosopher-king is to use his natural ability, not for his own personal benefit, but for the good of the entire commonwealth.[185] The philosopher-king must return from the apprehension of Goodness Itself to the world of becoming and belief, and bring his knowledge to bear on that world for the good of all. The return, it is clear, will be painful; even reluctant.[186]

However later generations of philosophers have described this man of supreme ability and insight, he still seems to dwell in a world apart and no more eager than Plato's philosopher-king to return to this world which William James so aptly described as "...multitudinous beyond imagination, tangled, muddy, painful and perplexed."[187] The alternative to this return is to remain in the realm of abstract thought and to interpret

---

[182] "Intelligence" is a translation of "νόησις" and "knowledge" a translation of "ἐπιστήμη." What Plato means by these is described at great length, first metaphorically (504ᵈ6-521ᵇ11), then more literally (521ᶜ1-535ᵃ2). "Idea" is a translation of "εἶδος."

[183] Plato, *Republic,* 414ᵈ1-421ᶜ6.

[184] "... ἐννοῶ γὰρ καὶ αὐτὸς εἰπόντος σοῦ, ὅτι πρῶτον μὲν ἡμῶν φύεται ἕκαστος οὐ πάνυ ὅμοιος ἑκάστῳ, ἀλλὰ διαφέρων τὴν φύσιν, ἄλλος ἐπ' ἄλλον ἔργου πράξει." *Platonis Opera,* ed. John Burnet (Oxford, 1956), IV, 370ᵃ7-370ᵇ1. Cf, also 370ᶜ3-5: " Ἐκ δὴ τούτων πλείω τε ἕκαστα γίγνεται καὶ κάλλιον καὶ ῥᾷον, ὅταν εἷς ἓν κατὰ φύσιν καὶ ἐν καιρῷ, σχολὴν τῶν ἄλλων, ἄγων πράττῃ."

[185] Plato, *Republic,* 419ᵃ1-421ᶜ6.

[186] *Ibid.,* 519ᵇ7-521ᵇ11.

[187] William James, *Pragmatism* (Cleveland and New York, 1955), p. 27.

what is required for a truly human existence accordingly. But this has the result of placing a truly human existence beyond the possibility of at least some human beings.[188]

Climacus clearly believes that this view has been maintained, though he does not identify it with any particular philosopher. He refers to it, generically, as a view of human existence which would establish a "differential dialectic." [189] It is a view to which he is *irrevocably* opposed. And the significance of his thinking about human existence must finally be seen and appreciated in the context of his opposition to this "differential" view.

That Climacus is opposed to (4) is clear from the following texts:

Every human being must be assumed in essential possession of what essentially belongs to being a man.[190]
But every essential existential task puts all humans on a level with respect to it, the difficulty being precisely proportioned to the capacity of the individual.[191]
Ethics concentrates upon the individual, and ethically it is the task of every individual to become an entire man; just as it is the ethical presupposition that every man is born in such a condition that he can become one.[192]

Clearly, then, and consciously, Climacus holds that every human being is, in principle, capable of becoming an entire man.

Still Climacus does not reject (1). Thinking does play an essential role in a truly human existence. What he does reject is that conjunction of (2) and (3) which would stipulate the kind of thinking which is essential in such a way as to place it beyond the capacity of some individuals. He would doubtless agree with the thought that "there can be no reason in existence unless every man may be assumed to have as much understanding as he needs, if he will honestly labor." [193] Instead of (2), then, Climacus would affirm (2'): *The kind of thinking that is essential for a truly human existence is subjective thinking.* Instead of (3), he would affirm (3'): *All men have the ability to think subjectively.*

---

[188] This same conclusion can be reached by emphasizing, instead of the ability to think abstractly, the ability to poetize. Some of the other pseudonymous works, notably *Either-Or,* protest this viewpoint.
[189] Climacus makes this point again and again in the *Postscript.* Cf. for example pp. 80, 201, 269, 318, 337, 383; 492, *n.;* and 502.
[190] *Ibid.,* p. 318.
[191] *Ibid.,* p. 342.
[192] *Ibid.,* p. 309.
[193] *Adler,* pp. 8-9.

Notice that (1), (2') and (3') do not together entail the conclusion that every human being is, in principle, capable of becoming an entire man.[194] They are however compatible with what Climacus calls "the ethical presupposition."

The argument presented above might just as easily have been formulated using the concept of knowledge or truth in place of the concept of abstract thinking. Climacus' objections would still remain. The *Postscript* can be characterized as an attempt to formulate conceptions of thought, knowledge, and truth which are compatible with what Climacus would call the ethical demand on every man that he *exist* and the ethical presupposition that he is born in such a condition that he can meet this demand. Or looking at it the other way round, Climacus presents in the *Postscript* a conception of existence which squares with the ethical demand and presupposition. To do this, he found it necessary to draw out the implications of the then current philosophical views on thought, knowledge, and truth and criticize them. Thus his protestations.

If we had to characterize Climacus' treatment of human existence, we would say that Climacus thinks about human existence in *the basic human posture*—a posture which is available to every man. Climacus does not deny that there are differences between men, but he does not believe that they make a significant difference when it comes to the task of existing as a human being. For this is a task which is proportioned to the capacity of each man and demands his best but no more. If one individual has been gifted with more brain than another, he has an added task. For he must keep that special talent from intruding; he must hold it in check. Every difference, every "plus" is relativized by the absolute task; for there is in every human being that basic core which Climacus calls "the existing individual." The *Postscript* may help a man to become conscious of that core, if he has lost sight of it. When this core is reached, all the differences fade from sight; and there remains "...merely this vanishing little distinction, that *the simple man knows the essential,* while the wise man little by little learns *to know that he knows it,* or learns *to know that he does not know it.* But what they both know is the same."[195]

---

[194] In order for that conclusion to follow, (1) would have to be strengthened considerably. That is, we would have to have something like: (1*) Thinking *and only thinking* plays an essential role in a truly human existence. Climacus, as our exposition has shown, could certainly not assert such a proposition.

[195] *Post.,* p. 143.

Climacus' treatment of human existence is not an original one. This does not mean that it is not valuable. For that which is always before us tends to lose its significance and its stature by that very fact. It is always more enjoyable to think about other things. As Climacus says, "...thinking about the highfalutin is very much more attractive and glorious." [196] What is so much before us as our own existence? What makes Climacus' treatment of this most pervasive phenomenon important is its willingness to think again about the basics (what every schoolboy knows) and to do so with a *background of experience* and a *sharpness of definition* (which perhaps not every schoolboy has).

[196] *Ibid.,* p. 117.

CHAPTER IV

A GLANCE AT TWO CONTEMPORARY EFFORTS IN KIERKEGAARDIAN SCHOLARSHIP

It may seem that the main difference between this study and others is the trifling one that we have insisted upon attributing the *Postscript* (and the views on human existence found there) to Climacus rather than to Kierkegaard. In this chapter, we shall indicate that there are substantive differences as well.

As in science the fruitfulness of an hypothesis is judged not only by how adequately it explains existing data but also by its ability to bring new data to light, so also the fruitfulness of a philosophical interpretation may be judged not only by how adequately it covers the familiar terrain but also by its ability to open up previously uncharted territory. There are numerous studies of Kierkegaard's concept of existence, yet very few of these exhibit more than a superficial awareness of the forgetting-claim.[1] None of them has yet provided a satisfactory elucidation of it. Yet we have shown that this claim lies at the very heart of the treatment of existence in the *Postscript*. Our efforts, in the next two chapters, to elucidate the forgetting-claim and its implications have no parallel in the secondary literature. This fact alone, we believe, is some indication of the fertility of the approach we have taken. If then we are to make comparisons between our study and others, the basis of the comparison will have to be the material of our previous chapter. While many works might have been selected for comparison, we have singled out the following two well-known and well-received studies: George Price's *The Narrow Pass,* and James Collins' *The Mind of Kierkegaard.* Both of these devote substantial space to the *Postscript's* analysis of existence. We have chosen them because each is paradigmatic of a kind of mistake that can be and often is committed in interpreting Kierkegaard. Price

---

[1] Diem is a reputable Kierkegaardian scholar, yet his best known work has but a single reference to this claim. Cf. Hermann Diem, *Kierkegaard's Dialectic of Existence,* trans. Harold Knight (London and Edinburgh, 1959), p. 53.

makes the mistake of *psychologizing* the account of existence in the *Postscript,* while Collins' mistake is to *metaphysicize* it.

Price approaches the problem of interpreting Kierkegaard's works with admirable clarity. He begins by giving his reader a sampling of the many divergent interpretations which have been offered of Kierkegaard's works, and moves quickly from this to the conclusion that there is an obvious need for a new and less ambiguous principle of interpretation.[2] After a quick survey of the entire authorship, Price admits that at first glance it appears to be disorderly and confused.[3] Since the main obstacles to interpretation seem to be the pseudonymous works, Price launches into a discussion of the explanation Kierkegaard himself gives of the pseudonyms and the entire authorship.[4] He concludes that this explanation, particularly that of the authorship itself, will not stand up against the many criticisms made of it, the most serious of which Price then reviews.[5]

This sets the stage for Price to state his own views which are in obvious sympathy with what we earlier termed the holistic approach.[6] While he does not completely reject Kierkegaard's own explanation, he is not completely satisfied with it:

We see then that the authorship has the unity of a pattern imposed upon it from the beginning. The works are not a scattered collection but an organized arrangement in which no work is out of place. In addition there is also the unity of intention which lies behind the pattern, determining the precise order of the works, the manner in which they complement each other, and above all, the precise religious impact the whole production would achieve. The presence of these two 'unities', while not solving all our problems, at least makes them no harder, and they suggest where we might yet find a third 'unity', for when we examine the works in the light of them, we see that every work is cut out to fit the pattern of the authorship like the stones of a steeple.[7]

Price educes this third unity by means of a somewhat curious inspection of the individual works. Certainly his summary of the *Postscript* is odd. He states:

It was a vast work which gathered together the pseudonymous productions into a whole. His views of philosophy and theology are concentrated and given their final form; the issues raised by human existence, the problem of truth in its various

---

[2] Price, *Pass,* p. 11.
[3] *Ibid.,* p. 14.
[4] *Ibid.,* pp. 14-22.
[5] *Ibid.,* pp. 18-22.
[6] Cf. Chapter I, p. 6.
[7] Price, *Pass,* p. 26.

aspects, the illusiveness of God, the nature of reality and of the historical continuum of society and, above all, the meaning of Christianity, are—as far as he understood them—definitively stated.[8]

It would have been helpful if Price had documented his claims so that we might understand where precisely the *Postscript*—in his view—takes up the issue of "the illusiveness of God" or "the nature of reality and of of the historical continuum of society." [9] Moreover, Climacus might himself insist that the problem of the meaning of Christianity is quite different from *his* problem: How does one become a Christian? But then, Price's view of Climacus is, if possible, even more peculiar than his view of the *Postscript*. He states:

The urbane Climacus, who has no committed religious belief, takes the whole field of human concern, defines the ways that lead nowhere, exposes the claims without substance, and, always at the reader's right hand, leads him deviously but carefully towards God.[10]

This is rather a lot to claim on behalf of an author who has said that "a direct relationship between one spiritual being and another, with respect to the essential truth, is unthinkable"; [11] who thinks of himself as a learner in the art of existence "who thus cannot want to teach others"; [12] who is so far from embracing the whole field of human concern as to claim that his work has to do solely with himself;[13] who, finally, adds that anyone who would appeal to him as an authority has *eo ipso* misunderstood him.[14] Price rounds off his description of the *Postscript* with these words:

But all this wide-ranging discussion is fundamentally an analysis of human consciousness, of the way it emerges, thinks, reaches its views, works day by day, gropes for God and seeks *self-authenticity*. It is the final elaboration of his doctrine of man, the gathering together of all the preceding analyses and results.[15]

There is a "gathering together" in the *Postscript,* although it has nothing

---

[8] *Ibid.,* p. 30.
[9] Probably what Price is thinking of are the discussions in the *Postscript* about world-history. If this is true, then he has missed the point which is this: Is a thinker's primary obligation to think about world-history, or about himself?
[10] Price, *Pass,* p. 30.
[11] *Post.,* p. 221.
[12] *Ibid.,* p. 550.
[13] *Ibid.,* p. 545.
[14] *Ibid.,* p. 546.
[15] Price, *Pass,* pp. 30-31. (Italics mine.)

whatever to do with the elaboration of a doctrine of man. Climacus shows how the other pseudonymus works, taken in conjunction with his own, may be seen as an attempt to delineate the decisively Christian categories and to distinguish them from both aesthetic and philosophical categories.[16] This was necessitated, in Climacus' judgment, by the existence of a widespread confusion which would reduce faith to the status of a relative moment,[17] and thereby subjugate Christianity to philosophy. In his eagerness to find a third unity in the authorship, Price has failed to do justice to those proposed by Kierkegaard himself—thus missing this very basic point about the *Postscript*. Moreover in his characterization of the *Postscript* as "an analysis of human consciousness, of the way it emerges,...gropes for God and seeks self-authenticity," Price discloses a tendency to "psychologize" what the *Postscript* says about human existence. We shall see more of this unfortunate tendency as we proceed.

A doctrine of man, then, is the third unity which Price finds in the authorship. It is:

The unity of a fundamental theme, that is, of a certain understanding of man, of which all the works are an elaboration, but for which the pseudonymous are used for the purpose of specific analysis. All Kierkegaard's ideas, even the apparently contradictory ones, have their fitting place in this theme and we shall see that his views of sin, of faith, of reason, of ethics, of subjectivity and paradox fall naturally into place, making together a powerful and consistent statement of human self-understanding.[18]

It was, we may recall, the supposed inadequacy of Kierkegaard's own explanation of his authorship that gave rise to Price's search for this third unity. Although Price would claim that he has deduced this unity from the works rather than imposed it upon them, there is reason to doubt whether this is in fact the case. At least as far as the *Postscript* is concerned, the explanations of both Kierkegaard and Climacus as to the nature and purpose of the works are more accurate and therefore preferable. Hence from our point of view, Price's claim that a new principle of interpretation is needed is suspicious, as is the collateral claim that there is a doctrine of man in the pseudonymous works which may be used as such a principle.[19]

---

[16] Cf. *Post.,* pp. 225-56. Cf. also pp. 323-29.

[17] *Ibid.,* p. 216. Cf. Chapter I, pp. 11-13.

[18] Price, *Pass,* p. 32.

[19] If Price and others were to subject the *criticisms* of Kierkegaard's own explanations to the same scrutiny that his explanations themselves are subjected, they might find, as for example Martin has, that Kierkegaard's own views stand up quite well.

For, and this is our second conflict with Price in the matter of interpreting Kierkegaard, if one abides by Kierkegaard's plea to treat the pseudonymous works as authored by their various pseudonyms and not by Kierkegaard himself, one cannot assume that these works are homogeneous in their point of view. Price, however, goes along with the traditional practice of assuming that one can safely disregard this request. In fleshing out the doctrine of man from the pseudonymous works, Price quotes from all of them as though he were quoting Kierkegaard. He concludes his preliminary search of the pseudonymous works by saying:

Now, these brief intimations of the themes of the individual works from 1843 to 1849 show how they are all related together and also how the pseudonymous works serve a special purpose. They are his analysis of man, of the human condition to which Christianity is the only answer.[20]

Now it may be true that for Anti-Climacus, the pseudonymous author of *The Sickness Unto Death,* Christianity is the only answer to the human condition. But this is most certainly not the thinking of Johannes Climacus:

The fact that faith and the Christian-religious mode of existence have humor as the precedent stage, shows besides what a tremendous existential compass is possible outside Christianity;... It is possible both to enjoy life and give it significance and content outside of Christianity, as is indeed evident, since the most famous poets and artists, the most eminent of thinkers, even devout men, have lived outside of Christianity.[21]

And as our own analysis has demonstrated, Socrates is one of the archetypes Climacus is thinking of when he speaks of "the existing individual." What is true from Anti-Climacus' point of view is not, therefore, true from Climacus' point of view. This is a most compelling reason for not attempting, as Price has, to lump these works together under a common thematic.

Having shown how Price's method of interpretation differs from our own, let us turn to his treatment of the concept of existence. Price devotes an entire chapter—Chapter VI—to "The Meaning of Existence." In order to compare our results with those of Price, however, it is necessary to take cognizance of some earlier developments in his book. Price begins his analysis of Kierkegaard's concept of man as follows:

[20] Price, *Pass,* p. 31.
[21] *Post.,* pp. 259-60. Cf. also p. 248.

Our first task is to grasp quickly the basis of Kierkegaard's concept of man, and there is no better starting-point than his well-known formula, brief, bare of detail, but going straight to the heart of the matter:
'Man is a synthesis of the soulish and the bodily. But a synthesis is unthinkable if the two are not united in a third factor. This third factor is spirit'.[22]

This passage, and the trichotomy which it presents, occurs in *The Concept of Dread*. This work especially, along with *The Sickness Unto Death*, is the foundation upon which Price has built the first stage of his analysis of Kierkegaard's concept of man. These two works are *psychological* in a different and much stronger sense than is the *Postscript*. In them, the self is considered as a psychological reality, and concepts like *spirit, dread, freedom,* and *despair* play prominent roles. But as we have already seen, these concepts play very little part in the *Postscript's* analysis of human existence.[23] True, Climacus also talks of man as a synthesis. We would suggest, however, that it would be dangerous to assume that because Climacus and Vigilius Haufniensis (the pseudonymous author of *The Concept of Dread*) both speak of man as a synthesis, they therefore share a common approach to human existence. No matter how accurately the following passage reflects the analysis in *Dread*, it would surely be a foreign body in the type of analysis which is typical of the *Postscript:*

What is this self of mine? he asks. In the most abstract and yet the most concrete sense, it is freedom. And what is freedom?... *Freedom is the will.*
Kierkegaard sees the self as a highly individualized pattern which has emerged from a synthesis of 'the soulish and the bodily' and the spirit or will—a unique reality that cannot be explained in terms of any single factor or of any one range of experience. *And the decisive factor in this emergence is the will.*[24]

Prefiguring his discussion in Chapter VI, Price states that *"Existence* has different levels of meaning for Kierkegaard, but the most fundamental —and the one from which all the others arise—is 'that which stands out or emerges': *human reality,* the reality of the individual human self..."[25] While this word has other meanings, Price's claim is that it "was designed to cover with precise relevance something odd in the universe—a living self, the breathing, dreaming, toiling, self-creating, suffering reality of an individual human being."[26]

---

[22] Price, *Pass,* p. 36.
[23] The *Postscript* contains only one reference to the above trichotomy. Cf. p. 307.
[24] *Ibid.,* pp. 37-38.
[25] *Ibid.,* p. 41.
[26] *Ibid.*

This leads Price to a discussion of what he calls "The Existential Imperative":

We have frequently mentioned the 'process of becoming'. What starts this process, and why? Cannot a man simply remain a nobody, a non-self? No, says Kierkegaard. He is driven to be somebody by a compulsion within him which he cannot deny. His most fundamental endowment is an imperative to be himself: to be not this man or that, but to be his own particular self.[27]

This "compulsion" which cannot be denied may be a factor in the analysis given in *Dread,* but one would be hard pressed to find such thoughts in the *Postscript.* Given the degree to which Price stresses psychological categories in this early chapter,[28] and given his policy of ignoring the pseudonymous points of view, one is skeptical of what will happen when Price turns to an analysis of a very different kind of work—the *Postscript.*

Since the majority of the references for Part II (which includes Chapter VI) are to the *Postscript,* it seems fair to assume that Price believes his analysis there to be based on the *Postscript.* Price claims that "*existence* has three meanings for Kierkegaard." [29] The first meaning is "the realm of the contingent" [30] and "here *existence* emphasizes the paradoxical nature of man's living experience—its freedom, guilt, grief, fear, despair, anxiety over death, 'the gaping chartless world of human existence.'" [31] Price is surely right in pointing to contingency as one of the elements in Climacus' analysis of what it means to exist as a human being. Climacus stresses the fact that existence is a constant process of becoming. The important thing, he holds, is for the individual human to understand his own existence in light of this basic truth. Here it must be recalled that this emphasis is aimed as a reminder at those who long to dwell "*sub specie aeterni*" where there is no becoming and, presumably, no fear, guilt, grief, and so on. His emphasis on becoming must be viewed in light of his claim that men have forgotten what it

---

[27] *Ibid.,* pp. 41-2.

[28] Especially interesting in this regard is a footnote in which Price claims that "as he [Kierkegaard] saw it, the most striking characteristic of the thrust towards self-fulfillment was the dread which threw it into action—the desperate anguish which fear of non-being creates in man and which, as a dread forever lurking in spirit, prompted those near-suicidal leaps to new levels of existence" (p. 79, *n.* 39).

[29] Price, *Pass,* p. 98.

[30] *Ibid.*

[31] *Ibid.*

means to *exist*. By ignoring this, Price creates the impression that the account of existence in the *Postscript* is not only more "psychological" than in fact it is; but also, that it is rather morbid.[32]

The second sense which Price detects is "the realm of human reality. Here *existence* has the proper linguistic usage of that which stands out or emerges—the singular human self. Not the abstract self, but the existing self of an actual individual." [33] Here again we must notice Price's tendency to force a psychological interpretation—a tendency that declares itself more fully when he reintroduces the notion of the existential imperative:

> We have already dealt with his attempt to represent the self formally as an unfinished synthesis of soulish and bodily, of the theoretical and the practical, whose emergent process lies below the level of conscious thought where the will plays a decisive part—and where the will again is subject to the demands of the *existential imperative*....
> The ordinary, actual man's thinking, feeling and intuitions are all subject to his will, to various choices which he makes about himself—which, again, are all subject to the dictates of the *existential imperative,* the primary factor in man, that drives him to seek self-fulfilment in terms of an ideal picture he has of himself or in terms of some other notion, so that when he thinks, or feels, or intuits, he will do so in accordance with it and in terms of what will serve it best.[34]

Without denying the point that Price is trying to make with these texts (that the author of the *Postscript* uses the concept of existence to attack certain philosophical practices), we must still lament the unnecessary intrusion of psychological categories into the analysis of human existence which Climacus gives. It is interesting that Price cites no texts to support his claim about "dictates of the *existential imperative*."

The third meaning cited by Price is "the realm of ideal selfhood. Here the word has the charismatic meaning of the self at its ultimate level of authenticity." [35] Price concludes:

> *Existence* is the realm of contingency in which every man must live and conduct his affairs; it is also his own personal reality, the unrepeatable, solitary reality of an individual man whose emergence is his own fearful responsibility; and finally it is his personal eschaton, the task which provides a human being with enough to do 'to suffice for his entire life.' [36]

[32] Of the six concepts mentioned by Price, only one—*freedom*—might be said to lack a negative connotation.
[33] Price, *Pass,* p. 103.
[34] *Ibid.*
[35] *Ibid.,* p. 111.
[36] *Ibid.*

As we have seen, Climacus does distinguish a loose and a strict sense of "exist"—an insight which Price verges on but never states. To *exist* (in the strict sense) means to become aware of oneself as an existing individual, to understand the basic features which characterize human existence and to apprehend one's own existence in light of this awareness. As we have seen, this is closely related to "subjective thinking"—to the task of becoming a subject. This task is the one that Climacus wants to urge his reader to undertake. It is this road—not the road of abstract or pure thinking—which an existing individual must follow if he is to exist in the sense which Climacus calls an art. But this task can be described, and is so described by Climacus, is considerably less dramatic terms than Price would lead one to think. He does not, for example, speak of a drive towards self-fulfillment. If we were to characterize the mistake which Price makes, we would put it this way: He "psychologizes" Climacus' account of existence.

Not only does this result in distortion, as we have seen, but it causes Price to miss altogether some important elements in Climacus' account. Claiming on the one hand that Kierkegaard did not deny the laws of thought and logic [37] or the possibility of science,[38] Price goes on to say:

What then can I know? Nothing, says Kierkegaard, nothing with any degree of real certainty: nothing about God, nothing about the world as it really is. The only thing known with certainty is myself, my own *existing* self, and even that is not, and never will be, fully 'transparent' to me. 'The only reality to which an existing individual may have a relation which is more than cognitive (*that is: more than "approximate"*) is his own reality, the fact that he exists; and this reality constitutes his absolute interest.' [39]

The text quoted by Price does not support the claim he has made. Indeed, his claim is mistaken, since Climacus surely does believe that the individual's existence can be fully transparent to him. This belief is at the heart of Climacus' critique of abstract thought. But Price does not see this. His "Kierkegaard" does not deny the laws of thought and logic, yet claims that nothing can be known "with any degree of real certainty."

In Chapter VIII, Price discusses "the subjective thinker":

After so much cut-throat skepticism, we might well ask, How then do we survive? For that we do survive requires no proof, and we certainly have no great difficulty

---

[37] *Ibid.,* p. 113
[38] *Ibid.*
[39] *Ibid.,* pp. 113-14.

in conducting our affairs, planning our lives and thinking through most of our problems.

Obviously we survive, says Kierkegaard. But we owe our success not to 'reason' but to the fact that we live our lives and solve our problems—even intellectual ones—by a process peculiar to ourselves as human beings. He calls this process 'subjective thinking'. He talks about it in three different ways:...[40]

These are, according to Price, "the form of ordinary thinking," [41] "the form of authentic philosophical thinking," [42] and "the form of religious thinking." [43] Actually, subjective thinking is introduced as an alternative to objective thinking—as the kind of thinking which is involved in the task of becoming a subject, of existing in the strict sense. By failing to engage with the distinctive concerns of the *Postscript,* by imposing on it a teeology which is not really there, Price misses the significance of Climacus' treatment of subjective thinking. Nowhere does Climacus propose subjective thinking as the form of authentic philosophical thinking. For Climacus is not primarily concerned to rescue philosophy from the speculative idealists, but, if possible, to rescue individual human beings from the clutches of philosophy.[44]

This very same failure reasserts itself when Price discusses inwardness:

Having destroyed all bridges between appearance and reality, known and unknown, man and God, Kierkegaard must now find a new one.

But where? *He has repudiated the Bible and the Church; he has discredited the reason,* and dismissed the presence in man of any faculty, aesthetic or otherwise, for penetrating the unknown; he has destroyed not only the bridges but all bridgeheads as well.

He starts from 'inwardness'—a word which has nothing to do with faith, intuition or a religion of the heart in preference to a religion of the head. *Inwardness is an attitude towards oneself*—an attitude of serious concern, of 'infinite passion'.[45]

The last paragraph is on target. But the two paragraphs which lead up to it are not. In the first paragraph, Price pictures "Kierkegaard" as a metaphysical solopsist—an interpretation which we have already argued is incorrect.[46] As to the second paragraph, it is surely a mistake to

---

[40] *Ibid.,* p. 115

[41] *Ibid.,* pp. 115-19.

[42] *Ibid.,* pp. 119-20.

[43] *Ibid.,* pp. 120-21.

[44] Cf. *Post.,* p. 152, *n.,* and our discussion in Chapter I, pp. 32-33. Mackey makes the same mistake. Cf. *Existential,* pp. 51 ff. It is significant that Mackey is able to cite but one text to support his contention that the *Postscript* contains the seeds of an existential philosophy. Cf. *ibid.,* p. 55.

[45] Price, *Pass,* p. 122. (Italics in the second paragraph are mine.)

[46] Cf. Chapter III, pp. 91-93.

portray Climacus as having repudiated the Bible and the Church; for he is no Christian, though he is asking what is involved in becoming one. Typically, no texts are cited to support this spurious set of claims.

Price goes on to observe that "Inwardness is not a mere 'brooding over one's own miserable self', nor a devouring of oneself with self-observation 'as though no other man had ever existed'." [47] This observation is not only important in itself, but serves to correct a somewhat morbid impression created by Price in the earlier sections of his account.[48] He does not, however, maintain this line for very long:

> Inwardness is the serious recognition that one's task begins with oneself, and that one's life's work is to emerge as *an individual*.
> But inwardness of this sort is not come by easily. Its drastic self-appraisal never comes except under extreme pressure—and, in life, this pressure is usually applied by despair.
>
> . . . .
>
> It is despair which forces a man to turn inwards: it is despair which compels a self-clarification a man would not otherwise make; and it is despair which gives inwardness its passion and desperate intent, for a man must defeat despair or perish.[49]

Three comments are relevant here. First, Price seems to have taken back with his left hand what he has earlier (the text above this last one) offered with his right. That is, if inwardness is precipitated by despair; and if "despair" and "brooding over one's miserable self" are synonymous, then inwardness would seem to have the connotation which Price previously denied. Secondly, Climacus nowhere suggests a correlation between inwardness and despair. Thirdly, existence itself—when it is interpenetrated with thought and taken as the individual's task—is the source of passion, not despair.[50]

In Chapter X, Price discusses Climacus' equation between truth and subjectivity. Once again, however, Price's failure to appreciate certain nuances in the *Fragments* and the *Postscript* leads to serious mistakes. For he attempts to interpret the dictum that subjectivity is the truth in light of the "Project of Thought" in the *Fragments*. But the view of truth which is developed there is the Christian view. And Climacus is not a Christian. To attribute the Christian view to Climacus, to interpret his claim that subjectivity is the truth as anything but an affirmation

---

[47] Price, *Pass*, p. 124.
[48] Cf. above pp. 122-23.
[49] Price, *Pass*, pp. 175-76.
[50] Cf. Chapter III, pp. 87-88.

of the Socratic view, is, therefore, categorically mistaken. As we shall see, this is exactly what Price does.

Price begins well enough:

Once again let us remind ourselves what the word 'subjective' does not mean for Kierkegaard. It is not an emotional or interested way of looking at things, or of studying something with such intense concern that one is carried mysteriously to the heart of it. It does not mean the distortion of reality by the introduction of a personal equation, nor the idealistic doctrine that reality is in a sense *idea*. Nor yet does it mean the grasping of the truth by intuition or some other sort of inner awareness. Subjectivity is another aspect of inwardness. We are back again with man as an unfinished synthesis.[51]

Climacus does use "subjectivity" and "inwardness" interchangeably. But Price's discussion of inwardness has not been strong enough that one can profit from it here. Price wisely warns against the tendency to equate subjectivity with emotional eccentricity, though the *caveat* against interpreting it as "the idealistic doctrine that reality is in a sense *idea*" seems gratuitous. Price says that subjectivity is not an interested way of looking at things. He is surely right if he means that Climacus would not endorse the notion that an individual is justified in preferring, say, the Ptolemaic conception of the universe to the Copernican *on the ground that it is more interesting or appealing to him*. But there is a sense in which subjectivity is an interested way of looking at things. "Existence constitutes the highest interest of the existing individual, and his interest in his existence constitutes his reality," Climacus has said.[53] What this means is that an individual human being might, like Socrates, forego his interest in speculating about the universe in the interest of understanding himself as an existing individual.

Price turns to the *Fragments,* and, after recounting Climacus' discussion of the "Platonic view of truth," asks:

But what if the predicament of the self is quite different from this Platonic view? What if the truth is not resident in man? [54]

Price has claimed that he is going to allow Kierkegaard to "explain it in his own way." [55] The author of the *Fragments*, having described the Platonic-Socratic view of Truth, continues in this fashion: "Now if

---

[51] Price, *Pass,* p. 126.
[52] *Post.,* pp. 248, 250-51.
[53] *Ibid.,* p. 279.
[54] Price, *Pass,* p. 127.
[55] *Ibid.,* p. 126.

things are to be otherwise,..." [56] The entire subsequent dialectical development is governed by this "if," and Climacus nowhere asserts that the situation described in opposition to the Socratic view actually obtains. The hypothetical carries through right to the end, the Moral:

The projected hypothesis indisputably makes an advance upon Socrates, which is apparent at every point. Whether it is therefore more true than the Socratic doctrine is an entirely different question, which cannot be decided in the same breath,...[57]

But Price's rendition of the *Fragments* leads one to think that Climacus *asserts* propositions which are in fact still governed by the initial "if." Thus he says:

It will avoid confusion if we now sum up the *conclusions* which Kierkegaard has reached:
God, as Unknown, can alone provide the condition for knowing Himself,...

. . . .

God comes as Teacher,...
He presents Himself as Paradox, as the absurd, which is 'that the eternal truth has come into being in time, that God has come into being, has been born, has grown up, and so forth, precisely like any other individual human being'. Faced with this Paradox, Faith transcends reason in belief...[58]

The author of the *Fragments* cannot be said to have *concluded* that the God has come as Teacher and presented Himself as Paradox. He has merely described the situation which would obtain *if* the Socratic view were not the right one. The presence of this "if" makes it difficult to summarize the *Fragments*, and Price's exposition confirms what Climacus himself has said:

It has never been a mystery to me why the pseudonymous authors have again and again asked to be excused from being reviewed. Since the contrasting form of the presentation makes it impossible to report the content in an abstract, *because the abstract takes away the feature of greatest importance and falsely transforms the book into a dogmatizing treatise,* the authors are fully justified in contenting themselves with a few actual readers,...[59]

Finally, then, we come to Price's exposition of the equation between truth and subjectivity:

---

[56] *Frag.,* p. 16.
[57] *Ibid.,* p. 139.
[58] Price, *Pass,* pp. 130-31. I have italicized the word "conclusions" in the first paragraph for emphasis.
[59] *Post.,* p. 252. (Italics mine.) Cf. also pp. 244-45.

Kierkegaard says that Lessing gives the clue to this peculiar situation: 'The pursuit is better than the quarry.' The struggle to achieve is the actual achievement. The struggle to believe, to hold passionately, is the act that contributes *existence*...or, as we might say, it is in the act of believing as the passion to *exist* directs itself towards the Paradox that the personality finds the factor which integrates it, and by this act, constantly repeated with increasing passion, the personality becomes— *Truth*.

In this latter sense alone do we find the meaning of the statement, *Truth is Subjectivity*. Truth, for Kierkegaard, is a mode of being, a quality of the person, *existence*.[60]

Price's exposition of the principle that truth is subjectivity is vitiated by its reference to the Paradox. For in his articulation of it in the *Postscript*, Climacus makes no reference to the Paradox of the thought-project in the *Fragments*. It means that it is by becoming subjective, with all that that entails, that a human being will truly exist as a human being. In so far as this involves the individual's interpenetrating his existence with thought in order to find out what he really thinks about himself *qua* existing human, the principle that subjectivity is the truth affirms that his judgement will be a correct one.

Again Price writes:

This is Kierkegaard's order: First, the man 'believes' the Paradox, and this act of will contributes *existence*: a new man is in *being*, and he is at the optimum level of self-authenticity. Secondly, he voluntarily accepts the God-Man's 'interpretation' of reality, which he then struggles to work into the substance of all his thinking, so that he finally interprets God and the world, society and its utensils, other people and himself, through the eyes of Christ. This is what Kierkegaard means by becoming the *Truth*.[61]

Now this may well be "Kierkegaard's" thinking; but it is not what is meant in the *Postscript* by the claim that subjectivity is the truth, unless this principle begins by positing "the opposite principle that subjectivity is untruth." [62] As we have already seen, however, Climacus analyzes and traces the consequences of the principle that subjectivity is untruth (which is the claim of Christianity), without himself positing it as a principle.[63] Let us remember that Climacus is attempting to see what is involved in becoming a Christian. Among other things, he shows that becoming a Christian will mean parting with his own view that subjectivity is the truth, that the task of becoming subjective is the task for

---

[60] Price, *Pass*, p. 131.
[61] *Ibid.*, pp. 132-33.
[62] *Post.*, p. 185.
[63] Cf. Chapter III, pp. 106-107.

human beings *qua* existing. He sees that becoming a Christian will mean coming to have an infinite interest in the reality of another human being.[64] This grates against the view that it is unethical to be interested in the reality of another human being.[65] Climacus points out these and other obstacles which have to be overcome if one is to become a Christian. Although Climacus sees these obstacles, he does not confuse this with overcoming them. Hence he affirms at the end of the *Postscript* that he is still a humorist and not a Christian. Price's account overlooks these important nuances.

Our discussion of Price's study has been long and critical, for we believe that it exhibits a number of unfortunate tendencies. At the level of interpretation, Price ignores Kierkegaard's own view of the authorship in order to seek a "third unity." He must therefore also ignore Kierkegaard's strictures about quoting from the pseudonymous works, for that would inhibit his search for a doctrine of man. Specifically, in dealing with the *Postscript*, Price misses important nuances which might not have been lost had he looked more closely at the explanations of this work given by Kierkegaard and Climacus. Finally, Price far too often gives in to a tendency to *psychologize* what the *Postscript* says about existence. This results in the distortion of some insights and the failure to grasp others. Such tendencies must finally take their toll.

We have claimed that Price's account suffers from its tendency to "psychologize" the concept of existence in the *Postscript*. The second study which we will consider—James Collin's *The Mind of Kierkegaard*— exhibits a different, though equally dangerous, tendency. It would be unfair not to mention the fact that this study was one of the first in American Kierkegaardian scholarship to insist upon dealing with Kierkegaard's ideas rather than his personal life. Further, Collins' work is greatly enhanced by the author's highly developed knowledge of and insight into the history of philosophy. He situates Kierkegaard's work within the twofold frame of "the proximate philosophical situation created by Kant, Hegel and other German thinkers, and the wider current of Christian philosophical thought, found in St. Augustine and St. Thomas Aquinas." [66] Yet it is precisely his prepossession with the thought of Aquinas that leads Collins, as we shall point out, to "metaphysicize" the concept of existence in the *Postscript*.

---

[64] *Post.*, p. 288.
[65] *Ibid.*, p. 287.
[66] Collins, *Mind*, p. ix.

Collins' general approach to the interpretation of Kierkegaard is sound.[67] His treatment of the pseudonymous works, like Price's, is flawed by the failure to honor Kierkegaard's strictures.[68] He insists on referring the *Postscript* to Kierkegaard himself rather than to Climacus.[69] We have already criticized Collins' basic claim that the *Postscript* offers the reader a new theory of existence, implying that the reason for Collins' mistake here is his failure to grasp the forgetting-claim as the analytical bedrock of the *Postscript*.[70] Collins seems to confirm our suspicion when he writes:

Kierkegaard did not analyze Hegelian philosophy for its own sake, but only as a principal cause of the watered-down version of moral life and Christianity to which his age was exposed. He traced the misunderstanding between true Christian existence and this philosophy to Hegel's *failure to grasp the meaning of existence,* in the human mode of inwardness.[71]

This slight rephrasing (from "forgetting what it means to *exist*" to "failure to grasp the meaning of existence") in an otherwise accurate account of Climacus' fundamental claim makes all the difference. Indeed, it is the difference between interpreting the *Postscript* as a metaphysical essay on the nature of human existence or as a special kind of reminder; between claiming that it offers a new theory of existence (in order to meet Hegel's failure) or realizing that it says what every schoolboy

---

[67] Collins states that Kierkegaard "...was neither a philosopher nor a theologian but belonged to the borderline category of the 'religious thinker'" (*Ibid.*, p. vii), and realizes that "The entire literary production of Kierkegaard is motivated by the intent of bringing men into a religious relationship with God" (*Ibid.*, p. ix).

[68] In his lengthy discussion of the pseudonyms (*Ibid.*, pp. 34-42), Collins states that Kierkegaard "...has the right to ask us not to identify any of their statements with his own definitive position" (*Ibid.*, p. 38). Strangely enough, Collins himself does not grant this right in practice. On his claim that the reader in turn has the right to know where Kierkegaard himself stands (*Ibid.*), cf. *Post.*, pp. 60-66, and especially p. 73.

[69] Aside from passing references to Climacus, the only extended reference to this pseudonymous author is found on p. 157, where Climacus is described as a pagan thinker; and on p. 291, where Collins asserts that "On most matters pertaining to the structure of existence and the refutation of Hegel, Johannes accurately represents the standpoint of Kierkegaard himself" (cf. *n.* 1). This claim is not supported by any argumentation. Oddly enough, if it is correct, then the reader does not have the "right" mentioned in the previous footnote.

[70] Cf. Chapter III, pp, 108-110.

[71] Collins, *Mind,* p. 119. (Italics mine.) The alteration of Climacus' claim is no accident. Cf. p. 131: "Hegel's *failure to understand* real change, is one with his *general failure to grasp the meaning of finite being.*" (Italics mine.)

already knows (in the hope of attracting attention to the forgetting). Collins is not completely ignorant of the forgetting-claim;[72] but his preoccupation with metaphysical questions seems to have prevented him from understanding how fundamental it is for an appreciation of Climacus' thought.

Collins precedes his treatment of the concept of existence with a chapter on Kierkegaard's attack upon Hegelianism. After reducing the contentions to three main theses, Collins states:

> Kierkegaard's common sense told him that all would be lost, if he were once lured into conducting the discussion on the idealistic terrain. He saw that, were the Speculative labyrinth entered even for a moment, the Ariadne thread connecting him with the real world would be snipped, beyond repair. Hence his analyses are directed at the presuppositions and the initial steps in the Hegelian dialectic.[73]

Collins' "Kierkegaard" approximates very closely the philosophical neophyte whose singleminded criticism of any philosophy takes the form: "Aha! Your presuppositions are false!" Climacus' encounter with the speculative philosophy of the nineteenth century is both more varied and more sophisticated than Collins' description would lead one to think. Where some might want the speculative philosopher to define "mediation," Climacus fights back with humor:

> There is constant talk of mediation and mediation; is mediation then a man, as Peter Deacon believes that *Imprimatur* is a man? How does a human being manage to become something of this kind? Is this dignity, this great *philosophicum,* the fruit of study, or does the magistrate give it away, like the office of deacon or grave-digger? [74]

But the serious issue is never far behind:

> Try merely to enter into these and other such plain questions of a plain man,... But it is important not to direct the polemic to the wrong point, and hence not to begin in a fantastic objective manner to discuss *pro* and *contra* whether there is a mediation or not, but to hold fast to what it means to be human being.[75]

It is because Socrates knew how to hold fast to what it means to be a human being that Climacus would like to see him in conversation with Hegel.[76] It is because an enthusiastic young man has not yet forgotten

---

[72] *Ibid.,* pp. 128, 152.
[73] *Ibid.,* p. 120.
[74] *Post.,* p. 177.
[75] *Ibid.*
[76] *Ibid.,* p. 291.

what it means to exist that he stands the best chance of refuting Hegel.[77]
Even when Climacus does engage with the Hegelian presuppositions, he
never forgets the fact that he is an existing individual.[78] The Climacus
of the *Postscript* advises his reader to make use of a "powerful formula
of incantation" [79] in order to get the philosopher transformed back into
his status as an existing individual. The "Kierkegaard" of Collins' treatment turns out to be a latent Thomist:

Had he known the texts, he would have agreed with Aquinas that the former
discipline [logic] is concerned with the universe of being, precisely in its logical status
as conceived by the mind, whereas metaphysics is directed primarily and properly
towards being in its physical reality and act of existing. As it was, Kierkegaard had
no acquaintance with a metaphysics which is clearly distinguished from logic; and
hence his positive contention was that the act of existence is beyond the reach of
every philosophical discipline.[80]

Although Collins devotes his fifth chapter to "The Meaning of Existence," and although his account is based primarily upon the *Postscript*,
his discussion is more wide-ranging than our own. This would be to the
good, except for the fact that three of his five sections deal with religious
existence.[81] This creates the impression that the *Postscript*'s account of
existence is religious in its orientation. Collins himself believes this to
be the case, so the impression is not accidental.[82] But as we have seen,
there is a developed body of thought in the *Postscript* about human
existence which could hardly be called religious.[83]

Collins states that "The two genuinely real modes of being are: that
of God and that of existing individuals." [84] His treatment of the latter
is sketchy. He says that "By existence, Kierkegaard means exclusively
a finite, temporal mode of being, which is essentially subject to becoming." [85] "What is peculiar to finite existents is that they *come to be*
what they are. Their being is the being of process; the law of reality

---

[77] *Ibid.*, p. 275.
[78] *Ibid.*, pp. 99-107. These are the pages to which Collins refers most frequently
in his account of Kierkegaard's attack.
[79] *Post.*, p. 324.
[80] Collins, *Mind*, p. 121.
[81] Thus Section 2 is "Existential Knowledge of God"; Section 4 is "Existence and
Religious Transcendence"; and Section 5 is "Faith and the Historicity of Existence."
[82] Collins, *Mind*, p. 98.
[83] The account of existence which we offered was, in Climacus' terms, "ethical."
More would need to be said before it could take in Religiousness A or B.
[84] Collins, *Mind*, p. 130.
[85] *Ibid.*, p. 147.

for them is to persevere in becoming, throughout time." [86] Although Collins strikes these and other basic notes in the *Postscript's* treatment of existence,[87] he never explicitly marks the distinction between the loose and the strict sense of "exist." The closest he comes is the following text:

Hegel, the methaphysician, and Goethe, the esthete, are so enamored of the notion of a "pure humanity," that they seem to forget the empirical and quite individual being that each one is. This places their thought in comical contradiction with their life, and forces the rest of us to face the one question left unasked and unanswered by the System. What does it mean for each one of us singly to be a human being, existing in an individual, finite way, and with a unique ethical and religious task to perform? [88]

For Climacus, to *exist* means to ask this question, to take up the task of becoming subjective, of interpenetrating one's own human existence with thought and existing in that understanding.

In an interesting footnote, Collins writes:

Because of his [Kierkegaard's] total preoccupation with the idealistic formulation of the problem of knowledge, he overlooked the alternative of a thoroughly finite and realistic way of grasping the order of existence through the *speculative* judgement of existence.[89]

For our part, we would suggest that Professor Collins' preoccupation with Thomistic metaphysics and epistemology has caused him to overlook the distinctive characteristics of Climacus' account of existence.

Climacus was not interested in a metaphysics based upon a speculative judgment of existence. Oddly enough, Collins seems well aware of this point when he writes:

The cognitive needs of man are wider than is the ability of the scientific method to satisfy them. Men cannot help asking questions about the meaning of existence, the nature of the human person, and the uses of freedom. These questions fall within the region of what Kierkegaard terms "subjective reflection" or "existential thinking." The most important human issues lie in this latter field, rather than in that of objective reflection.[90]

Two points should be made here. The questions cited here by Collins (What is the meaning of existence? What is the nature of the human

[86] *Ibid.*, p. 131.
[87] Collins mentions, at various points, freedom (p. 136), will (p. 127), limited cognition (p. 138; pp. 288-89), inwardness (pp. 141, 152), constant striving (p. 143), and infinite uncertainty (p. 153) as characteristic of human existence.
[88] *Ibid.*, p. 129.
[89] *Ibid.*, pp. 288-89, *n.* 21.
[90] *Ibid.*, p. 140.

person?) are not precisely the kinds of question which Climacus would steer his reader into asking. Such questions are "objective" and might conceivably be answered by abstract thought. The kind of question which Climacus wants his reader to ask is "subjective" in the sense that it is to have an essential reference to the asker's own particular existence:

The person of an abstract thinker is irrelevant to his thought. An existential thinker must be pictured as essentially thinking, but so that in presenting his thought he sketches himself.[91]

The question that Climacus is urging his reader to ask would have to be put something like this: "What does it mean for *me* to exist as a human being—a being with limited time, intellect, etc?" Considering the audience to whom the *Postscript* is addressed and the philosophical climate, it should be quite clear that such questions are easily avoided in favor of objective (that is to say, philosophical) reflections about the nature of man in general.

But, and this is our second point, Collins is unable to see this:

Historically considered, Kierkegaard was ripe for reception of a realistic metaphysics. Having repudiated the Hegelian postulate, he was unwilling to relapse into Kant's concealed skepticism. For him it was no sufficient proof of the unknowableness of existence that it finds no place in abstract thinking, and is denatured in the context of pure thought. He hoped to show that existence is indeed accessible to an ethico-religious dialectic, but he placed such knowledge beyond philosophical science. We cannot expect guidance from him in solving the question of existence *philosophically,* and that is why many existentialists have returned covertly to idealism.[92]

Climacus places existence and subjectivity (in the strict sense) beyond philosophical reflection for obvious reasons. The question of existence which he raises cannot be asked, much less answered, philosophically. A different kind of question about existence may will be susceptible of a philosophical treatment. But that is not to the point. More to the point is the claim (which is in some sense philosophical) that the task of becoming a subject is the highest for every human being, a claim which is at the very core of the *Postscript*. It is Climacus' view that human existence is not a differential affair.[93] Philosophy is a differential affair. The clear implication and the crucial consequence is that philosophy is not a

---

[91] *Post.,* p. 319.
[92] Collins, *Mind,* p. 125.
[93] Cf. Chapter III, pp. 111-14.

sine qua non for a human being. He can get along without it. What he cannot get along without is an understanding of himself as an existing individual, "subjective reflection." But this does not require more talent for thinking than the normal individual has.

We have shown that Climacus does not deny the validity of the sciences, of scholarship and learning all of which require abstract thought. But he would criticize anyone whose pursuit of these blinded him to ethical issues. In abstract thought, thought is pointed away from the thinker's own existence. But the task of becoming a subject requires that one pay close attention to his own existence.

Collins' account of Climacus' position on abstract and pure thought misses this important nuance:

> Kierkegaard admits that the greater part of our thinking is carried on in terms of objective, abstract reasoning. The natural, mathematical, and social sciences deal with objects through their essential natures, abstract relations, and inductively necessary natural laws. Such sciences give genuine knowledge within these methodic limits, but they are not competent beyond the sphere of essence and possibility. Scientific laws do not determine the condition of the individual as such, nor do scientifically constructed concepts give formal insight into existence and the actual order. The sort of scientific understanding that recognizes and acknowledges these limits upon its competence, is usually termed by Kierkegaard *abstract thought*.[94]

Climacus' discussion of abstract thought is somewhat more critical than Collins' account suggests and indeed has a rather different point to make.[95] It is not the epistemological dimension of abstract thought (that it cannot attain to actuality: a point we are unable to find in the pages of the *Postscript*) but the ethical dimension—that it requires abstraction from the thinker's own existence—that Climacus is concerned to bring to light.[96] Climacus is not concerned to draw attention to the cognitive limitations of abstract thought. What he desires to point out are the ethical dangers of any kind of abstract thinking. "Pure thought," he declares, is a "phantom," [97] "a fantastic medium." [98]

Collins is surely right in stating that "Kierkegaard is no enemy of abstract thinking for its own sake, but he protests rightly against any attempt to disguise the fact of abstractness and so to deny the limitations

---

[94] *Ibid.*, p. 122.

[95] *Post.*, pp. 267-82.

[96] Cf. *Post.*, pp. 267-68, for example.

[97] *Ibid.*, p. 281.

[98] *Ibid.*, p. 269.

of scientific thinking." [99] Again, however, this is not the best way of putting it. But the reason Collins has put the matter this way becomes clear as we read on:

Pure thought denies its original dependence upon a non-conceptual source, and claims to include existence and actuality within itself, in such an absolute way that they are generated in and by the dialectical movement of thought. Hence, there is a great chasm separating abstract from pure thought, one which Kierkegaard feels called upon to emphasize rather than bridge.

Readers trained in the tradition of realistic philosophy would add that there is a third position, which Kierkegaard has overlooked. While admitting the restricted scope of abstract scientific thought and joining in opposition to absolute idealism, Thomistic realism would yet propose a view of metaphysics in which the formal object is being as existent, rather than a "pure" concept of being, correlative to a concept of nonbeing. A nonidealistic metaphysics is based upon an original judgment of existence, which gives some knowledge about the act of concrete existent being. An existentially oriented metaphysics does not pretend to be able to give a complete conceptual formulation about the existent subject, but returns to it again and again, as to an independent and inexhaustible source... It deals by means of concepts and judgments with that which is more than, and other than, concepts and judgments. *It is the perfection of human scientific thinking.*

Such an alternative did not present itself to Kierkegaard,...[100]

It seems clear that the "chasm" to which Collins refers is his own creation, one for which he believes Thomistic metaphysics to be the remedy. For his part, Climacus is quite clear in his insistence that neither abstract nor pure thought can perform the vital service and function which he has assigned to "subjective thought." (Collins' own bias is only too evident when he claims, gratuitously, that an existentially oriented metaphysics is the "perfection" of human scientific thinking.)

We turn then to Collins' treatment of subjectivity and truth. He states, and quite rightly, that Climacus "sensed a great danger in the empiricist stress upon objectivity and the discipline of experience." What danger?

There is a point beyond which we should not rely exclusively upon the scientific method or what Kierkegaard called "abstract thought" and "objective reflection." The movement of this method is away from the personal, interested subject, in the direction of impersonal laws and statements of determined fact. If one's life is completely governed by the requirements of such research, the significance of the individual man is liable to be reduced to nothing more than that of a manipulator of scientific instruments, a point of departure in the exploration of the material world.[101]

[99] Collins, *Mind*, p. 123.
[100] *Ibid.*, pp. 123-24. Italics are mine for emphasis except for the word "human."
[101] *Ibid.*, p. 139.

This is well-said. What Collins does not appear to recognize is that this argument applies (*mutatis mutandis*) to philosophical reflection as well, no matter how securely grounded in the judgment of existence and no matter how often it returns to it as a source. The danger in all objective reflection is that it can too easily become a snare, a diversion of attention from the thinker's own existence and its tasks (which, after all, are sufficient to last one's whole life). But Collins fairly glances off this important point:

When man is studied by means of objective reflection, he is treated in terms of the same laws, traits, and determining conditions that prevail in the rest of nature. This is reasonable enough, until it is declared to be the *only* valid way of regarding man, a claim which has been made by naturalism in every form.[102]

Unfortunately, this is not a claim that Climacus was concerned to dispute. The *Postscript* was written, let us recall, in 1846; not, as the above passage would imply, in 1946! Philosophical, not empirical, science is the focus of Climacus' concern. Once again, Professor Collins' own preoccupations have found their way into his interpretation.[103] We continue with Collins:

Kierkegaard realized that such a claim involves an overthrow of human values and a destruction of the right order upon which morality and religion build. The rule of prudence is destroyed, when exclusive rights are given to the method and the categories of the natural sciences.
For this reason, Kierkegaard seeks to delimit the scientific method in the case of man, and so to make room for another kind of truth.[104]

Collins provides no textual references for this interpretation, nor could he. By imposing a naturalist critique on the *Postscript*, he has missed the real significance of the equation between truth and subjectivity, though he once again takes the opportunity to criticize Climacus' views from his Thomistic frame of reference.[105]

[102] *Ibid.*, pp. 139-40.

[103] We are sympathetic to the idea of *extending* Climacus' view of Truth and his critique of philosophical science to the claims of naturalism. We shall do so in the next chapter, although not along the lines suggested by Collins.

[104] Collins, *Mind*, p. 140.

[105] *Ibid.*, p. 142. "What is missing from Kierkegaard, is a treatment of existential truth along speculative and metaphysical lines. He has not supplied a metaphysical analysis of truth and existence, and this failure has forced later thinkers in the existentialist line to choose between an idealistic and a naturalistic metaphysics.... It would be misleading to accept his teaching as a rounded, theoretical study of truth" (p. 142). Climacus would be the first to agree with this last statement!

Let us finally observe how Collins, by ignoring the fact that the *Postscript* reflects the point of view of a humorist, manages to create a problem where none exists. As a humorist, Climacus is committed to the Socratic view that no human being can penetrate the ethical reality of another and that it is unethical to try.[106] He does not deny that other human beings exist. Now according to Collins:

Kierkegaard is dissatisfied with this limitation, declaring that it is characteristic only of existential thinkers in the ethical sphere. Religiously existential thinkers can gain some insight into the actuality of other selves in their own right, whereas Christian faith impels a man to regard the actual state of others as of equal importance with one's own.[107]

First, we would suggest that Climacus has not indicated any dissatisfaction with the Socratic view. Secondly, Collins' contrast ("insight into the actuality of other selves" vs. "regard[ing] the actual state of others as of equal importance with one's own") is askew. Thirdly, Climacus is aware that faith, in the strict sense, requires the individual to develop an infinite interest in the reality of another human being— the Teacher, Jesus Christ. But this is a *paradox*; and once the individual has made his peace with it and with the Teacher, the Socratic principle is once again reinstated. He must regard his fellow human beings as important, true; but his faith does not give him the ability to apprehend the inwardness of his fellow humans. If Collins does not claim this, he at least has explained himself poorly.

In any event, Climacus makes no amendment to the Socratic position, as Collins goes on to suggest:

This amendment of the "Socratic" position is by no means satisfactory. Kierkegaard has stumbled upon a real difficulty, which philosophers do not often face as honestly as he does. He puts it this way: I can know myself as I actually am, but how can I know others as they actually are, since I must approach them by means of abstract thinking?[108]

One desires to know where the author of the *Postscript* has "put it this way." Climacus does not believe *that he can* know others as they actually are (in the strict sense). Collins appears to be assuming that Christian faith requires that one be able to know the inwardness of other human beings. This assumption misfires twice. First, it is not the view of Christian faith taken by the author of the *Postscript*. Secondly,

---

[106] *Post.*, p. 287.
[107] Collins, *Mind*, p. 154.
[108] *Ibid.*, pp. 154-55.

since Climacus is not a Christian, he does not have to amend his Socratic position in order to bring it in line with the Christian faith and its requirements. Collins continues:

An answer to this question would place one at the very heart of the existentialist conception, but Kierkegaard only supplies a few hints. In the first place, he does not clarify what he means by self-knowledge transpiring "in the medium of actuality." The point is assumed rather than explained.[109]

But why is an explanation needed? Where can a thinker come to an understanding of himself as existing? In the realm of abstract thought? In order to enter this realm, he must abstract from his own existence.

Even in knowing oneself, concepts, along with a certain amount of reasoning, are usually employed. There is no mention of an intuition of self or even of a feeling of self, in moments of activity. The epistemological aspects of the problem do not interest Kierkegaard. His argument is, rather, that an ethically serious thinker always relates his thoughts about himself to some plan of action and self-development. They are existential thoughts, in that they always retain this orientation to a free plan about one's personal existence and moral condition. But if this accounts sufficiently for existential thinking, then the latter does not differ *in the cognitive order* from other sorts of thinking. *Only the use and personal reference of the thinking are different.* The conclusion is inescapable that *only a non-cognitive shift of attitude* is needed to convert abstract thinking...into existential thinking.[110]

"Only"?! (One might also say that lying does not differ *in the grammatical order* from telling the truth. Only the use and the personal references of the saying are different! But what a difference.) Collins apparently thinks that this "non-cognitive shift" is easily accomplished. But Climacus speaks about "the weight of objectivity"[111] and the difficulty of changing one's matrix of thought from world-history to one's own existence.[112] Obviously, subjective thinking requires the use of concepts. In this respect, it will not differ from abstract thinking. Climacus would scarcely deny that subjective thinking is a kind of thinking. But apparently he thinks of it as a much more significant achievement than Collins does.

Finally, Collins offers his criticism:

But he [Kierkegaard] has no basic philosophical explanation of the existential way of knowing the other—whether a thing or another self—precisely as another

---

[109] *Ibid.*, p. 155.
[110] *Ibid.* (Italics, except for *"in the cognitive order,"* added for emphasis.)
[111] *Post.*, p. 62.
[112] *Ibid.*, p. 116.

subject, *in quantum aliud*. Despite his own intentions, this weakness has led to theoretical solipsism and practical egoism, on the part of later existentialists.[113]

Our analysis in Chapter III indicates that it would only be by misunderstanding what is said in the *Postscript* about human existence that one could be led either to solipsism or egoism.

Our criticisms of Collins have been numerous and perhaps a bit harsh. We believe that his preoccupation with Thomistic metaphysics has caused him to misinterpret important aspects of the view of human existence offered in the *Postscript* and to miss others. We do not question, it should be clear, Collins' right to his own preferences philosophically. Clearly he finds Aquinas' thought more satisfactory than Kierkegaard's. But we hold with Bradley Dewey that although the scholar has the right to interpret and criticize, he must earn this right by diligent research, and the restraint of laudatory or pejorative inclinations when selecting, analyzing, and interpreting the material from primary sources.[114] We suspect that Collins' tendency to "metaphysicize" the *Postscript's* account of human existence stems from the framework of his analysis.

In conclusion, then, we believe that we have demonstrated the fact that our treatment of Climacus' concept of existence differs in important respects from that of Price and that of Collins. The differences are not merely technical but substantive as well. It does seem, however, that there is a close relationship between many of the inadequacies in both accounts and the fact that neither of them takes Climacus' authorship of the *Postscript* at all seriously. But just as grievous as their mistakes is their almost total silence about what we regard as the analytical bedrock of the *Postscript*—the claim that men have forgotten what it means to *exist*. To that claim itself and to Climacus' advice about how forgettings may be dealt with, we turn now in the next two chapters.

---

[113] Collins, *Mind,* p. 156.
[114] Cf. Chapter I, p. 4.

CHAPTER V

FORGETTING

A. INTRODUCTION

Our objective in this chapter is to analyze the claim that men have forgotten what it means to *exist*.[1] In Chapter III, we explained that Climacus distinguishes between a loose and a strict sense of the predicate "exist" and that the forgetting-claim is to be understood as referring to the strict sense.[2] The individual who is conscious of what it means to *exist* will be constantly seeking to understand himself as a particular existing human being. "In all his thinking he therefore has to think the fact that he is an existing individual." [3] Climacus states:

Two ways, in general, are open for an existing individual: *Either* he can do his utmost to forget that he is an existing individual, by which he becomes a comic figure, since existence has the remarkable trait of compelling an existing individual to exist whether he wills it or not.... *Or* he can concentrate his entire energy upon the fact that he is an existing individual.[4]

How does an individual forget? Is Climacus claiming, for example, that a man can forget the fact that he has limited time? Not exactly. Climacus is well aware that everyone "knows" this to be true. The real task, he says, is to become *"executively aware"* of this proposition (and others pertaining to human existence)—to let it saturate one's thinking and one's own existence. The speculative philosopher finds his tasks elsewhere:

---

[1] The forgetting-claim is stated in various ways. Sometimes, Climacus terms the individual who has forgotten what it means to *exist* "absent-minded" (*Post.*, p. 108) or "fantastic" (*Ibid.*, p. 107). Our analysis of existence was based primarily on pp. 67-322. The forgetting-claim occurs many times in those pages. Cf. pp. 85, 107-111, *passim;* 130; 142; 148-151, *passim;* 162-63; 169; 172; 176; 178; 183-85, *passim;* 196; 203; 216; 223; 255; 283-84; and 307. Given the pervasiveness of this claim and its analytical centrality, it is all the more remarkable that it has gone so long unnoticed and uninvestigated.

[2] Cf. Chapter III, pp. 74-75.

[3] *Post.*, p. 314.

[4] *Ibid.*, p. 109.

But for the speculating philosopher the question of his personal eternal happiness cannot arise; precisely because his task consists in getting more and more away from himself so as to become objective, thus vanishing from himself and *becoming what might be called the contemplative energy of philosophy itself.*[5]

As Climacus sees it, two things happen when an individual engages in philosophical (or scientific) reflection. First, he must take his attention away from himself; he must abstract *from* his own existence. Secondly, in doing so, he becomes objective. That is, he becomes part of a community of thinkers devoted to the task of objective reflection. He acquires, in a sense, a new mode of existence:

It is only systematists and objective philosophers who have ceased to be human beings, and have become speculative philosophy in the abstract, an entity which belongs to the realm of pure being.[6]

Climacus' point could be put this way. When an individual becomes a philosopher or a scientist, he becomes a member of a community; and he assumes the community's mode of existence. He learns to look at things through the eyes of the community and to speak with its voice. But if an individual becomes so accustomed to the community's mode of existence that he begins to think of its properties as his own; if he loses sight of the fact that his own existence is characterized by a sharply different set of properties, then he has begun to forget what it means to *exist* as a human being.

It follows, then, that to indulge in any form of objective reflection would involve a temporary forgetting. But as long as the individual's pursuit of philosophical (or scientific) knowledge is ethically responsible,[7] the forgetting is not serious. It does become serious when the individual pursues objectve knowledge with such single-mindedness that he, in effect, seals himself off from ethical scrutiny and from existence as his medium. It is this more permanent type of forgetting that Climacus would expose.

Climacus cannot, however, reveal these more grievous forgettings except in a generic way. He could not, in other words, say of a particular human being that he had forgotten what it means to exist. For this would be inconsistent with his position that the reality of one individual cannot be apprehended by another. Instead, we find Climacus using phrases

[5] *Ibid.*, p. 109. (Italics mine.)
[6] *Ibid.*, p. 85.
[7] Cf. Chapter III, pp. 95-96.

such as "the individual who...has forgotten what it means to exist." [8]
For ultimately, Climacus' purpose is to expose and describe the phenomenon of forgetting in such detail that his reader will be able to
determine whether or not he himself stands on the verge of such a
fate. He alone has the necessary access to his own thought and
existence.

To call attention to the phenomenon of forgetting, Climacus must
be content to describe its symptoms:

> The existing individual who forgets that he is an existing individual, will become
> more and more absent-minded; and as people sometimes embody the fruits of their
> leisure moments in books, so we may venture to expect as the fruit of his
> absent-mindedness the expected existential system—...[9]

The claim that an existential system is possible would be, as we shall
shortly see, one manifestation of a possible forgetting. Another symptom
might be that an individual starts to use "...the strange mode of speech
which assumes that a human being becomes speculative philosophy in the
abstract,..." [10]

We believe that the forgetting-claim is not only an important part
of Climacus' thought but that it also is a contribution to philosophy.
If we are to substantiate this opinion, it will be necessary for us to
produce specimens of this phenomenon other than those which Climacus
calls attention to. For if there are none, then this claim is simply a
tour-de-force, designed to combat a particular philosophical excess but
without enduring value. In the next section, we show how the forgetting-
claim is to be understood in reference to Hegelian philosophy. In the
third section, we shall illustrate the forgetting-claim with examples from
popular scientific literature.

B. FORGETTING IN HEGEL

The relationship between Kierkegaard and Hegel has been the topic of
a great deal of research.[11] Although our study has no new light to shed

---

[8] Cf. for example *Post.,* p. 107: "If the logical thinker is at the same time human
enough not to forget that he is an existing individual,..."

[9] *Ibid.,* pp. 109-10.

[10] *Ibid.,* p. 109. Recall that it was a similar text that also directed attention
to this "strange" manner of speech which served as our point of departure in
Chapter II.

[11] The essential leads on this topic are furnished by Thulstrup. Cf. *Commentary,*
pp. 177-80. Cf. also Collins, *Mind,* pp. 99-107.

(since we are deliberately abstaining from mentioning Kierkegaard), we may point out for the record that Climacus shows respect for Hegel:

> The frivolity with which systematists concede that Hegel has perhaps not been successful in introducing movement everywhere in logic, about as when a huckster thinks that a couple of oranges more or less is nothing to worry about when the purchase is a large one—this farcical complaisance is naturally an expression of contempt for Hegel, which not even his most violent antagonist has permitted himself.... Let admirers of Hegel keep to themselves the privilege of making him out to be a bungler; an opponent will always know how to hold him in honor, as one who has willed something great, though without having achieved it.[12]

Climacus himself is such an opponent. As he sees it, the issue which stands between himself and Hegel (and even more, the Danish Hegelians[13]) is whether or not an existential system is possible.[14] For the claim that an existential system is possible harbors, in his view, a forgetting. Why is this?

In the first place, Climacus would argue that "System and finality correspond to one another,..." [15] An incomplete system is not a system but only the promise of one. But, as we have seen, existence is precisely the opposite of finality.[16] The individual who concentrates his entire energy upon the fact that he is an existing individual, the individual who undertakes the task of becoming subjective, can have no result. Since his existence is a constant becoming, his task will always be unfinished:

> It may be seen, from a purely abstract point of view, that system and existence are incapable of being thought together; because in order to think existence, systematic thought must think it as abrogated, and hence as not existing.[17]

Hence the proposed system cannot include the individual human being. But if it does not, then how could it possibly be an *existential* system? For "...existence has only individual human beings." [18]

It might seem that the past, since it is complete, could be encompassed in a system. Climacus writes:

---

[12] *Post.*, p. 99, *n.*

[13] Cf. T. H. Croxall, intro., *Johannes Climacus or, De Omnibus Dubitandum Est* by Søren Kierkegaard (London, 1958), pp. 46-54.

[14] It may be argued that Hegel's is a system of reason. But since he devotes himself to overcoming the distinction between the rational and the real, such a system would be a system of existence.

[15] *Post.*, p. 107.

[16] *Ibid.*

[17] *Ibid.*

[18] *Ibid.*, p. 310.

Whenever a particular existence has been relegated to the past, it is complete, has acquired finality, and is in so far subject to a systematic apprehension. Quite right —but for whom is it so subject? [19]

Can an individual human being arrive at a complete understanding of the past? This, of course, is the goal of the community of thinkers who study history, and of the individual *qua* member of that community. An individual speaking with the voice of the community might say:

It is indeed this desire for rational insight, for cognition, and not merely for a collection of various facts, which ought to be presupposed as a subjective aspiration in the study of the sciences. For even though one were not approaching world history with the thought and knowledge of Reason, at least one ought to have the firm and invincible faith that there is Reason in history and to believe that the world of intelligence and self-conscious willing is not abandoned to mere chance, but must manifest itself in the light of the rational Idea. Actually, however, I do not have to demand such a belief in advance. What I have said here provisionally... must...be taken as a summary view of the whole. It is not a presupposition of study; it is a *result* which happens to be known to myself because I already know the whole. Therefore, only the study of world history can show that it has proceeded rationally, that it represents the rationally necessary course of the World Spirit,...[20]

But from whose point of view, we might ask, does history appear as a "rationally necessary course"? From whose point of view does history manifest itself as a succession of intelligible necessities? Will history look this way to the individual human being who is conscious of being a particular human being and therefore conscious of his own limited range of perception and powers of explanation? From his point of view, history may seem to disclose as much unintelligibility as intelligibility, as much chance as necessity. His knowledge of history and the past may contain undotted *i*'s and uncrossed *t*'s, as well as events of which he can only say: "I do not know why that happened."

Naturally, the point of view of the historian—especially the philosopher of history—is different. His goal is to understand the past and to seek explanation. He cannot be satisfied with an undotted *i*. But this point of view is not his own personal point of view. It belongs to the community of historians, the result of years of work and hard study by many minds. It would be a forgetting if an individual thought that the community's properties were his own, if he so identified himself with the community

---

[19] *Ibid.,* p. 108.

[20] Georg Wilhelm Friedrich Hegel, *Reason in History,* trans. Robert S. Hartman (New York, 1953), p. 12.

that he lost sight of the fact that his own existence is characterized by a different set of properties.

Climacus would not deny, then, that the past can be apprehended systematically by the community of historians. But the individual who joins this community to uncover the secrets of history remains an existing individual whose first task is to understand himself. Ironically, Climacus points out, if a man is too successful in his endeavors to understand history, he may find that he has no self to understand:

All understanding comes after the fact. Now while the existing individual undoubtedly comes after the proceding six thousand years, if we assume that he spends his life in arriving at a systematic understanding of these, the strangely ironic consequence would follow that he could have no understanding of himself, because he has no existence and thus nothing which required to be understood afterwards.[21]

Such a man has thus "vanish[ed] from himself and becom[e] what might be called the contemplative energy of [history] itself." [22] The individual who concentrates his entire energy upon existing must treat with suspicion the suggestion that he can both engage in historical studies and at the same time understand himself. For although "Hegel is utterly and absolutely right in asserting that viewed eternally, *sub specie aeterni,* in the language of abstraction, in pure thought and pure being, there is no *either-or,*" [23] this is not true in the medium of existence and becoming. There the absolute qualitative disjunction applies.[24] The individual must make decisions, among them the decision whether or not to undertake historical (or philosophical) reflection.[25] But existence cannot be postponed so that the individual can first give himself to world history and then return—who knows how many years later—to himself. Thus Climacus asserts:

Anyone who is himself an existing individual cannot gain this finality outside existence which corresponds to the eternity into which the past has entered. If a thinker is so absent-minded as to forget that he is an existing individual, still, absent-mindedness and speculation are not precisely the same thing. On the contrary, the fact that the thinker is an existing individual signifies that existence imposes its own requirements upon him.[26]

---

[21] *Post.*, p. 108.
[22] *Ibid.*, p. 109. Cf. above p. 143.
[23] *Ibid.*, p. 270.
[24] *Ibid.*, pp. 272, 313. Cf. Chapter III, pp. 87-88.
[25] *Ibid.*, pp. 271-72.
[26] *Ibid.*, p. 108.

The crucial question, then, regarding any proposed existential system is the following:

> ..., let us then ask quite simply,...(and if the superlative wisdom can explain everything, but cannot answer a simple question, it is clear that the world is out of joint): "Who is to write or complete such a system?" Surely a human being; unless we propose again to begin using the strange mode of speech which assumes that a human being becomes speculative philosophy in the abstract,...[27]

If an individual human being claimed possession of an existential system, would this not indicate that he regarded his own existence as already finished and complete? If so, then he has forgotten what it means to exist, much like the man who, given the task of entertaining himself for the entire day, manages to finish at noon.[28]

If there is to be an existential system, then, it will have to be formulated and articulated by some one individual human being:

> Or if the speculative thought which brings the systems to light is the joint effort of different thinkers: in what last concluding thought does this fellowship finally realize itself, how does it reach the light of day? Surely through some human being? And how are the individual participants related to the joint effort, what are the categories which mediate between the individual and world-process, and who is it again who strings them all together on the systematic thread? Is he a human being, or is he speculative philosophy in the abstract?[29]

Some individual must be the means by which the community's results are written down on paper. "But if he is a human being, then he is an existing individual." [30] And the choice is his: either to concentrate his entire energy upon the fact that he exists or to do all in his power to forget this fact.

Climacus' claim then is weaker than might be thought. He does not state that there is no existential system, but rather that no human being can, *qua* existing, possess or formulate such a system:

> An existential system cannot be formulated. Does this mean that no such system exists? By no means, nor is this implied in our assertion. Reality itself is a system —for God; but it cannot be a system for an existing spirit.[31]

To claim possession of a system of existence is tantamount to aspiring to be God, thus forgetting the absolute qualitative difference between

[27] *Ibid.*, pp. 108-109.
[28] *Ibid.*, p. 147.
[29] *Ibid.*, p. 109.
[30] *Ibid.*
[31] *Ibid.*, p. 107.

being God and being an existing individual human being.[32] This is the point at issue between Climacus and the systematic thinkers:

But who is this systematic thinker? Aye, it is he who is outside of existence and yet in existence, who is in his eternity forever complete, and yet includes existence within himself—it is God.... Such a thinker would either have to be God, or a fantastic *quodlibet*.[33]

An individual human being, mindful of what it means to exist, cannot claim to possess a system of existence. To make such a claim is to forget the basic human posture and to attempt to assume a supra-human one instead. Metaphorically:

If a dancer could leap very high, we would admire him. But if he tried to give the impression that he could fly, let laughter single him out for suitable punishment; even thought it might be true that he could leap as high as any dancer had ever done. Leaping is the accomplishment of being essentially earthly, one who respects the earth's gravitational force, since the leaping is only momentary. But flying carries a suggestion of being emancipated from telluric conditions, a privilege reserved for winged creatures, and perhaps also shared by the inhabitants of the moon—and there perhaps the System will first find its true readers.[34]

The dancer stands for the human being in his earthly condition. The leap symbolizes the moment of thought, of abstracting from that condition in order to pursue science. Climacus observes elsewhere that the most difficult leap of all is the one which brings the man back to the very spot from which he made the leap.[35] Similarly, the most difficult kind of thought is that which always returns the thinker to his own existence. This is the situation of the abstract thinker who does not forget that he is an existing individual. Pure thought, on the other hand, is like flying and "carries a suggestion of being emancipated from telluric conditions." [36] Such a thinker has attempted to desert existence. Yet one who speaks as though he could fly, who beats his arms madly at his sides and invites others to follow, is really extending an invitation to his hearer to become absent-minded and forgetful of the fact that a human being is a telluric creature. The philosopher who claims to have a system has perhaps leaped higher than any other human being, but he cannot fly. Claiming to have a system is one symptom of the hazardous condition

[32] *Ibid.*, p. 195. Cf. also Collins, *Mind*, p. 288, note 21.
[33] *Post.*, p. 108.
[34] *Ibid.*, pp. 112-13.
[35] *Ibid.*, p. 327.
[36] *Ibid.*, p. 113. Cf. also pp. 278-79.

which Climacus calls "forgetting." He would remind his reader that flying is not for humans and that the attempt is an important sign of disrespect for the basic human posture. Better, he says, the solo dance of Socrates.[37]

C. FORGETTING IN SCIENCE

In the second chapter, we listed several features of the scientific community's mode of existence which differentiate it from that of the individual human being. In his work, *Physicist and Christian*, William G. Pollard has said:

Education in science is a gradual process of incorporation into a community. *This process, to be effective, must expose the student to the spirit of the community so that the becomes infected by it.* He must, of course, master a large body of factual material and instrumental skills. But much more than this, he must somehow come to share the characteristic viewpoint and attitude of science toward phenomena.[38]

The metaphor is an interesting one. The student must be "infected" by the "spirit of the community." It must take possession of him. He must internalize its attitudes, taking on the community's properties for the sake of doing scientific work. He must learn to see phenomena through the community's eyes:

The scientist really has to believe in his bones that the world must be made in a certain way, in spite of overwhelming evidence to the contrary, in order to find the strength and courage necessary to keep going. *The faith on which such confidence rests is clearly a gift which others may catch as they would an infection,* but which cannot in any way be mechanically taught as one might teach a subject or a technique.[39]

There is, however, a risk involved in exposing oneself to such an infection; namely, that the spirit of the community may take such total possession of him that he loses sight of the fact that his own mode of existence as an individual is different in important respects from that of the community's.

If he masters the community's attitudes and is a successful worker, an individual may qualify as one of the spokesmen for the community:

Scientific knowledge is not created solely by the piecemeal mining of discrete facts by uniformly accurate and reliable scientific investigators. The process of criticism and evaluation, of analysis and synthesis, are essential to the whole system. It is

[37] *Ibid.,* p. 82.
[38] Pollard, *Physicist,* p. 7. (Italics mine.)
[39] *Ibid.,* p. 16. (Italics mine.)

impossible for each one of us to be continually aware of all that is going on around us, so that we can immediately decide the significance of every new paper that is published. *The job of making such judgment must therefore be delegated to the best and the wisest amongst us, who speak, not with their personal voices, but on behalf of the whole community of Science....* It is impossible for the consensus —public knowledge—to be voiced at all, unless it is channelled through the minds of selected persons, and restated in their words for all to hear.[40]

Although each segment of the community will have its acknowledged spokesmen, each scientist—as he learns to say "we"—learns to speak with the voice of the community. That, at any rate, must be his goal. He is trying to shape and articulate the mind of the community. There is, though, the danger that he becomes so used to speaking with the voice of the community that he forgets that he has a voice of his own, the voice of one existing individual. In order to understand what a forgetting is, one must learn to recognize the symptoms of this danger.

Generally, a forgetting is signalled by the fact that an individual speaks or writes in a fashion that suggests that he considers the community's properties to be his own. Recalling the four tables which we presented in the second chapter, we could say that when an author, for example, delivers an utterance which is more appropriate to the community's column than to the existing individual's, this is symptomatic of a forgetting. It should be clear, at this point, that one could hardly expect to find such utterances in the literature of the scientific community—i.e., in a journal of theoretical physics. In such forms of communication, the pronoun "I" is contraband. We will look instead to works containing the reflections of scientists and to those devoted to the popularization of scientific knowledge. Although these may have some "scientific" content, they will frequently contain an "extra-scientific" subject matter in the form of the writer's own personal views.[41] The latter will prove to be the habitat of the phenomenon we are seeking.

The first set of differences we educed in Chapter II had to do with the fact that the community has a timeless mode of existence, whereas the individual's mode of existence is rooted in time. The legendary story is told of a woman who, in breathless tones, confronted the astronomer who had just concluded a lecture about the Sun. "Did you say

---

[40] Ziman, *Knowledge*, pp. 136-37. (Italics mine.)

[41] A sentence such as the following signals the presence of such subject matter: "It should not be necessary to emphasise that this pamphlet is in no sense a pontifical utterance in the name of science." C. H. Waddington, *The Scientific Attitude*, 2nd ed. (London and Aylesbury, 1948), p. x.

that the Sun will burn up in fifty thousands years," she asked, "or fifty million?" "Fifty million," was the reply. "Oh," said the woman, "I feel much better now." This, of course, is an exaggerated example of someone who has apparently forgotten that for an individual human being there is not much difference between fifty million and fifty thousand years.

A slightly more serious species of this sort of forgetting is recounted by Fred Hoyle:

My difficulty with consciousness is that it forces on one a concept that lies outside physics, the concept of the present, the present moment of time. According to physics, the events that constitute the physical world form a four-dimensional continuum, *and physics does not permit us to attach any more significance to one moment of time than another.*[42]

Needless to point out, physics is here at odds with the individual human being who will surely accord special significance to some moments—his birthday, his wedding anniversary, etc. "This sharp difference," Hoyle continues, "between physical theory and subjective experience has led some physicists to suggest that subjective experience is illusory, that there is no such thing as the present." [43] One who would take such a position would have forgotten what it means to *exist.* He would have lost sight of one important characteristic of *his* kind of being—that to exist as a human being is to have a past, a present, and a future. The fact that the community of physicists takes a different view of time (and one which is perfectly legitimate in its own place) is simply evidence that its mode of being is different from that of the existing individual.

As we indicated in the second chapter, the scientific community takes a relaxed view of time. In the following passage, in which George Lundberg pauses to heed a possible objection to his proposal that the scientific method be applied to social problems, this relaxation is the basis of a response which may well signal a forgetting:

I know that the method I propose is scoffed at in some quarters on the ground that, while it may be the solution for the long run, life is a short run. *Whose life?* Human life in its collective aspect stretches backward at least a million years and may reach much farther into the future."[44]

---

[42] Fred Hoyle, *Man in the Universe* (New York and London, 1966), p. 32. (Italics mine.)

[43] *Ibid.*

[44] George Lundberg, *Can Science Save Us?*, 2nd ed. (New York, London, and Toronto, 1961), p. 16. (Italics mine.)

The objection Lundberg voices here is one that might be expected from someone conscious of what it means to exist as a being with limited time. Lundberg's reply is the one which might be expected from a man who is voicing a proposal in the name of a community which expects an indefinite future. The scientific community has all the time in the world (cf. Table 1, Row E [45]). As Julian Huxley writes:

Granted that man does not destroy himself by some nuclear idiocy, then, according to geophysicists, he has at least as much time before him as he had behind him, all the way back to the amoeba and beyond.[46]

The community cannot be cowed by the objection that life is a short run. Then why should Lundberg's remark be counted as an instance of a forgetting?

Lundberg's treatise is not, in fact, a scientific communication. It is not an attempt to "diminish the unknown" (to use Sarton's phrase [47]) but is rather written with a view to disarming certain biasses which Lundberg believes to be unfounded. He is attempting to persuade his reader of the value of the social sciences. Certainly *that* is no forgetting. Yet Lundberg is presumably also an individual human being and as such might be expected to have some understanding of what it means to exist as a being who feels the pinch of time. The fact that he overrides the imagined speech of such an individual without the slightest recognition of its validity may, *in these circumstances,* suggest that he has so accustomed himself to one of the community's properties that he has begun to think of it as his own. That *would* be a forgetting.

It may be objected that we have missed Lundberg's point, that his proposal that scientific methods be brought to bear on social problems stems from his concern for the future of the species *man,* not for the immediate future of this or that particular man. Certainly it is true that the eye of the scientific community (here that segment of it designated as "sociology") is fixed on the species, not the individual. But as he would himself admit, Lundberg is not here proposing a scientific theory about man.[48] He is making a recommendation to men, to his readers, all of whom are individual human beings. He is writing as an individual human being who is also a scientist. But then his words

---

[45] Chapter II, p. 46.

[46] Julian Huxley, *The Human Crisis* (Seattle, 1963), p. 19. (Italics mine.) Hereafter cited as: Huxley, *Crisis.*

[47] Cf. Chapter II, p. 44.

[48] Lundberg, *op. cit.,* pp. 30-41.

might be expected to manifest some awareness of the individual's condition as a being with limited time. "Can we not agree," Climacus would ask, "to be human beings? "

Furthermore, it would seem to follow that if his proposal were adopted, Lundberg would have to allow that future generations of man would have an important advantage over the present and past generations. For if there is any essential relationship between the ability of the individual human being to realize a truly human existence and the solution to social problems (war, for example), these later generations would surely have an advantage—if his proposal is adopted. This establishes a "differential dialectic" with respect to history—contravening the ethical presupposition that every man is in possession of what essentially belongs to being a man.[49] No doubt, later generations of social scientists will have an advantage over this one in terms of an understanding of man as a social entity. But existing as an individual human being is a different task from existing as a member of a scientific community. Lundberg seems—by implication—to be on the verge of forgetting this. Science progresses; man evolves. But, as Climacus would say, isn't every individual still born in infancy?[50] What is the relationship between scientific progress and the ability of the individual human being to *exist*? Are we to think of the individual as essentially the same kind of being as the scientific community? Lundberg's proposal (and its implications) raises these issues. Climacus would remind us that no matter how strong the ties are which bind an individual to the scientific community, the bonds which fasten him to his own existence are stronger still. They do not even lose their grip when, absent-mindedly, he fails to acknowledge them.

We conclude our exhibit of forgettings in connection with the differences mentioned in Table 1 with the following specimen. The following are the words of an eminent biologist, Albert Szent-Györgyi:

Is science not more than just a method of thinking, tools, or a collection of data and books? Is science not a living society? I think it is. To me, science, in the first place, is a society of men, which knows *no limits in time and space*. I am living in such a *community,* in which Lavoisier and Newton are my daily companions; an Indian or Chinese scientist is closer to me than my own milkman.[51]

[49] Cf. Chapter III, p. 113.
[50] *Post.*, p. 311.
[51] Albert Szent-Györgyi, "Lost in the Twentieth Century," in *The Excitement and Fascination of Science*, ed. J. Murray Luck (Palo Alto, 1965), p. 474. (Italics mine.)

Clearly this is the voice of one human being. Yet it is a strange one. For it almost seems as though he believes that he has himself appropriated the community's property of being timeless as though it were his own. It almost seems as if, looking back to Table 1, Szent-Györgyi belongs under the scientific community's column of Row A rather than the individual's. But has he really forgotten that he is a temporal creature of limited temporal assets?

He alone can provide the answer to this question. Yet in an interview which he gave to the editors of *International Science and Technology*, we find an ominous saying. When asked about his plans for the future (it should be added that he was seventy-three years old at this time), he replied: "Well, my plans for *my next fifty years of research* are to find out how living systems are generated." [52] One would not wish to gainsay the possibility that a man might live to be one hundred and twenty-three. It is possible. It is even possible that he might still be active in scientific research. But his words do have the aroma of the fantastic. Certainly, they would fit better under the community's column of Row D than they would under the individual's. The community visualizes an indefinite future for itself and hence is perfectly confident in planning its future using the larger temporal units like the decade and the century. The words of Szent-Györgyi would be in character if he were speaking on behalf of the scientific community. But he is speaking on his own behalf. Perhaps because he has so habituated himself to the community's attitudes towards time, he has forgotten that his own future is both limited and speckled with uncertainty.

In the third section of Chapter II, we discussed the cognitive faculties of the scientific community, noting that they were very different from those of any single human. Some of the more calamitous forgettings occur when an individual speaks or writes as though the community's faculties were his own personal property.

The scientific community has a range of perception which can take in all events. Human beings are not thus gifted. Yet it would seem that Einstein believes otherwise. He writes:

The more a man is imbued with the ordered regularity of all events, the firmer becomes the conviction that there is no room left by the side of this ordered regularity for causes of a different nature.[53]

---

[52] Robert Colborn, ed., *The Way of the Scientist* (New York, 1962), p. 126. (Italics mine.)
[53] Einstein, *Years*, p. 32. (Italics mine.)

Would it not be *strange* for an individual man to say: "Having taken all events in survey and observed their ordered regularity, I am firmly convinced that there is no room for causes of a different nature"? If we look back to Row A of Table 2,[54] we would have to conclude that a man who said this would appear to believe that the property listed under the scientific community's column is more truly descriptive of his mode of existence than the corresponding one listed under the individual's column.

The scientific community regards every phenomenon as explicable all the way. Hence the term "mystery" is conspicuously absent from the community's vocabulary. An eminent biologist, Leo Szilard, appears to contravene this point when he states that he finds the mysteries of biology more intriguing than those of physics.[55] We say "appears," because it is clear that what he means by "mystery" is "the not-yet-explained":

No, I think what I brought into biology...was not any skills acquired in physics, but rather *an attitude,* the conviction which few biologists had at the time, *that mysteries can be solved. If secrets exist, they must be explicable.* You see, this is something which modern biologists brought into biology, something which classical biologists did not have. They were often astonished, but they never felt it was their duty to explain. *They lacked the faith that things are explainable*—and it is this faith, you know, which leads to major advances in biology.[56]

The faith that things are explainable is characteristic of the scientific community's attitude toward events and phenomena. But the community has a very sound basis for this faith. It has unlimited time and "...the best brains of all countries and all times" [57] required to divest nature of her secrets. If an individual human being thought that his own cognitive faculties were similarly protected against the inexplicable and the mysterious, he would have forgotten what it means to exist as a being with limited cognitive powers.

How might such a forgetting declare itself? Consider the following passage from an article written by a scientist:

It goes almost without saying that the scientist cannot accept most religious legends as fact. All the traditional religions are based on myths and legends that have a high degree of content of miraculous or unnatural events.... The scientist cannot

---

[54] Chapter II, p. 55.
[55] Colborn, *op. cit.,* p. 26.
[56] *Ibid.,* p. 28. (Italics mine.)
[57] Einstein, *Years,* p. 109.

believe that these miracles or unnatural events really occurred; there is no verifiable evidence, and they do not fit into the pattern of knowledge we now have of the physical world.[58]

Although the scientific community is by nature forbidden to honor any account which records a gap or a cleft in the natural order, it must also be remembered that no single individual human being is the community. The individual scientist remains an existing individual whose powers of understanding come to an end somewhere. He remains the kind of being whose empirical intuitions will allow of gaps in the perception of phenomena, and who can be stumped and baffled by what he sees. If a scientist's manner of speaking begins to resemble that of the kind of being described in Rows B and C under the scientific community's column in Table 2 of Chapter II, this may be a sign that he has forgotten what it means to exist as an individual human being.

MacPherson, it would seem, has appropriated the community's properties as his own. Thus adorned, he believes himself to be in a position to state that certain things ("miracles") cannot have occurred. This forms the basis of his rejection of traditional religion. Let us ask, however, how Lazarus' resurrection, for example, would have looked to the eye of an individual human being. The following is one answer:

To the eye of someone present, the sight of Lazarus waking up...would be a non-plus, an instance of the baffling. But what Kant and...[MacPherson] profess to know is that the baffling cannot happen. Nobody can be baffled by anything. Baffling elements are of course conventionally out of place in a finished piece of science, yet it would mean a strange forgetting of someone's identity if he imagined that the same convention protected his own head against such embarrassments.[59]

MacPherson would seem to be very close to such a forgetting.

There is another forgetting in MacPherson's allusion to "the pattern of knowledge we now have of the physical world." In the second chapter, we explained that the scientific community—with its unlimited range of perception and its vast cognitive powers—has developed a view of nature as a continuous succession of events in which there are no gaps, no leaps, and no dark patches. There is "...a conviction that all that happens in nature is subject to inexorable laws." [60] But the vision

[58] H. G. MacPherson, "What Would a Scientific Religion be Like?" *Saturday Review*, August 2, 1969, p. 44.

[59] H. A. Nielsen, "Bultmann's Philosophical Troubles," *Dialogue*, VIII (1970), p. 644.

[60] Einstein, *Years*, p. 131.

of nature which this conviction gives rise to is not the property of any individual scientist, as Pollard reminds us:

In the three centuries since Newton, the human communal enterprise which we designate as physics has been engaged in constructing an ever more detailed, comprehensive, and extended image of the physical structure of the natural world. What has been achieved is an already beautifully unified and coherent conceptual scheme which certainly stands as one of the most exalted achievements of human intelligence and imagination man has ever made. *This achievement cannot, however, be attributed to any one person or sequence of isolated individual investigators.* Quite clearly, this achievement has been possible only because there came into existence *a community of men,* charged with high hopes and an unshakeable belief in the fertility of their enterprise, *empowered by an indomitable spirit,* and filled with vitality and dynamism has carried the enterprise forward with unbroken success and achievement. Without this community, physics as we know it now would be unthinkable.[61]

Clearly the scientist must be "empowered by an indomitable spirit" if he is to withstand the years of toil and disappointment which will inevitably dot his career. All manner of mischief can result, if this "indomitable spirit" *overpowers* the individual scientist so that he begins to think—as seemingly MacPherson has—that the community's vision is one that he can claim for himself.

Huxley alludes to the community's vision when he states:

As a result of the new knowledge gained during the hundred years since Darwin's *Origin of the Species,* and especially during the last half-century, it has become possible to get a reasonably comprehensive and reasonably accurate picture of the present and past workings of physical and biological nature, of human nature and human history.[62]

But since this picture belongs to the scientific community and to its mode of existence, an individual must be careful when he would make use of it. Consider, for example, the following vivid rendition of this picture:

Professor Dorn recently worked out an interesting calculation in order to make clear *the significance which can properly be claimed for the life and history of mankind* in the context of the overall history of the earth. Let us assume, he says, that the earth is 2,850 million years old. If we consider this as a day of twenty-four hours, from midnight to midnight, then the end of the 'stellar age,' i.e. the awakening of organic life on our planet does not occur until 10.51 p.m., the appearance of man only at twenty-two seconds before midnight, and the whole of what is called 'world history', including all the establishments of states, the

---

[61] Pollard, *Physicist,* p. 39. (Italics mine.)
[62] Huxley, *Crisis,* pp. 3-4.

wars between nations, the ideological struggles, the conflicts of the faiths and the foundations of religions, takes place in the last three-tenths of a second.[63]

The reader can almost hear the tick of the cosmic clock. This scenario can be useful in acquainting the lay reader with the latest findings of the scientific community about the history of man and his earth. It gives one a sense for the temporal magnitudes involved. (Presumably such a picture would have a very diminished role to play in the scientific community proper.)

But there is another use to which such a picture can be put, as we discover in the author's subsequent development:

In these circumstances, is it not incredibly preposterous for us human beings to assert that only these last instants in the development of mammals are 'history' and that everything which preceded them was merely 'a natural process'? That it has been only in these last moments of cosmic time, in which human history has taken place, that the Creator of the universe has come down to earth to speak and to act...? [64]

As we have already seen, from the scientific community's point of view no one moment of the space-time continuum can be singled out and accorded any special significance. From the point of view of the existing individual, on the other hand, a moment can have decisive significance. Continuing with the author's application of this picture, we read:

Does not the assertion of a 'supernatural dignity,' raising man above the whole of nature, appear positively grotesque if we consider not merely how short the time is during which mankind has been alive...but also the infintesimally small space which human existence occupies in relation to the immeasurable dimensions of the cosmos...? And now Man, *this tiny ephemera,* appearing for a few moments on a speck of dust in the cosmos and vanishing again, thinks that he is the crown of creation, the centre around which everything revolves, and that the Creator of all the galaxies has come down to raise him above all the stars! [65]

Here the community's vision is being used to suggest that any human being who takes his own existence as a matter of ultimate seriousness is guilty of cosmic myopia.

If the individual human being looks at his own existence through the eyes of the scientific community, he would have to conclude that it cannot

    [63] Karl Heim, *Christian Faith and Natural Science* (New York, 1953), pp. 11-12. (Italics mine.)
    [64] *Ibid.,* p. 12.
    [65] *Ibid.* (Italics mine.)

be of much significance in the cosmic view. At the same time, he would be in the process of forgetting what it means to exist as an individual human being equipped with a pair of eyes of his own. By no means is this a criticism of the community's picture nor an attempt to deny its validity. But the scientific community is a different kind of existent. When an individual puts on someone else's spectacles, it is to be expected that he will see things differently. If he forgets to take them off, he is the victim of a remarkable species of absent-mindedness.

The species of forgettings which we have been discussing in the last six pages have one common trait. They occur when an individual speaks as though he had appropriated some feature of the scientific community's cognitive apparatus (its unlimited range of perception or its vast powers of explanation or its comprehensive and unified vision) as his own. Precisely because of the communal nature of science, this is an easy temptation to succumb to. One author puts it this way:

Scientists today interact with each other so much that they begin to think of themselves as *cells in a collective mind,* thinking and criticizing and creating together. If one drops out, another takes his place. What is done is done by many at once and indeed is done by all.[66]

What belongs to all—to the entire community—does not belong to any one scientist. If he treats the community's property as his own, then he is guilty of larceny—though not the kind that can be prosecuted in court. The scientists acknowledges his dependence on the community every time he writes "we." [67] But he must not forget how to say "I." If he does, he will never be able to distinguish between the community's property and his own.

The fact that the scientific community refuses to acknowledge mysteries has led some writers to the conclusion that science is guilty of pride. Thus:

The optimism of science is boundless.... A famous biologist has said, "This century will go down in history as the century when life ceased to be a mystery. ... Life is only chemistry. It is complicated, yes. But *we* no longer have any reason to believe that it is beyond human understanding." There is of course no trace of humility in this statement, but it is absurd for gods to be humble. Humility belongs to men.[68]

[66] George Platt, *The Excitement of Science* (Boston and Cambridge, 1962), p. 173. (Italics mine.)

[67] Ziman, *Knowledge,* p. 9.

[68] Rousas John Rushdoony, *The Mythology of Science* (Nutley, 1967), p. 7. (Italics under "we" are mine.)

We may presume (notice the pronoun—"*we*") that the biologist here quoted is speaking on behalf of the scientific community. That community is neither a god nor a man, but is rather a cognitive entity committed by its nature to the pursuit of total understanding. It seems a mistake to expect a statement of humility from such a being, or from someone speaking on its behalf. One may expect such a statement from the individual scientist. "Most scientists," says John Ziman, "are humble, practical men who have learnt from experience the limitations of their arts, and know that they know very little."[69] When an individual scientist begins to speak as though he knew more than a little—as Mac-Pherson, for example, who professes to know that certain things cannot have happened—then the proper complaint to lodge is not that he is lacking in humility but that he is suffering from a severe case of absent-mindedness.

Another, though much more complicated, species of forgetting can be found in some popular scientific literature. In the kind we are thinking of, the author assumes that his reader (a layman) is in possession of a false (i.e. non-scientific) set of beliefs. His goal is to get the reader to replace these with the truth. To this end, the author calls upon the reader to accept or believe certain things.

There is, of course, a significant difference between a scientific theory and its popularized counterpart. The theory addresses itself to the scientific community—to those who have the necessary training and skill both to understand the language of the theory and to appraise it. The popularization is written for the lay reader who has neither the time nor, presumably, the ability to read the technical scientific literature in which the theory has its natural home. Furthermore, the theory in its scientific form aims to shape the mind of the scientific community. Its popularized counterpart presents for general consumption what has already been incorporated into the consensus of the community. The differences between a scientific theory and its popularized counterpart stem from the differences between the scientific community as an exclusively cognitive being and the individual human being whose mode of existence is a varied one. We shall keep these differences in mind as we consider, first, several passages from Robert Ardrey's *African Genesis*.

In this book, Ardrey is attempting to acquaint the lay reader with recent advances in the scientific community's understanding of the origins of man. He writes:

---

[69] Ziman, *Knowledge*, p. 74.

Man is a fraction of the animal world. Our history is an afterthought, no more, tacked to an infinite calendar. *We are not so unique as we should like to believe.* And if man in a time of need seeks deeper knowledge concerning himself, then he must explore those animal horizons from which we have made our *quick little march.*[70]

Notice, first, that Ardrey assumes that his reader holds to a belief about man which is in conflict with scientific opinion. The danger inherent in such an assumption is that of treating the individual human being as if he were a scientific community in miniature. Secondly, Ardrey speaks of millions of years as a "quick little march." It is appropriate for the scientific community, or one who speaks in its name, to take this point of view. But the individual who concentrates his entire energy upon existing will become conscious of the limitations of time and must regard even a mere one hundred years as a very long time.

    Ardrey continues:

In the past thirty years a revolution has been taking place in the natural sciences. It is a revolution in our understanding of animal behaviour, and of our link to the animal world. In sum, therefore, the revolution concerns that most absorbing of human entertainments, man's understanding of man. Yet not even science, as a whole, is aware of the philosophical reappraisal which must proceed from its specialists' doings.[71]

Important changes have taken place in recent times in the scientific community's understanding of man, Ardrey claims, and these must have an effect upon any philosophical understanding of man. Neither of these claims is troublesome. Ardrey proceeds:

Assumptions concerning the nature of man...are being eroded by the tiny streams set loose from obscure scientific springs. And few of us, scientists or laymen, know.[72]

The implication of this last sentence is somewhat more troublesome. It suggests that the changes in the scientific community's view of man have consequences, not only for the scientific and philosophical communities, but also for the lay reader. This impression is confirmed as we read further:

---

[70] Robert Ardrey, *African Genesis* (New York, 1961), p. 11. (Italics mine). Hereafter cited as: Ardrey, *Genesis.*

[71] *Ibid.,* pp. 11-12.

[72] *Ibid.,* p. 12.

...the work of the revolution has been accomplished by such extreme specialists that it has been recorded only in such inaccessible pages as those of the *American Journal of Anthropology* or the *Biological Symposia*. Such heralds gain few hearers in the modern market-place.[73]

Ardrey seems to think that what has been recorded in these "inaccessible pages" has significance, not only for the scientific community, but for the lay reader as well. His book is an attempt to construct a tributary between these "obscure scientific springs" and the lay reader.

There is little doubt that Ardrey himself has been influenced by these springs:

When in 1930 I emerged from a respectable American university as a respectably well-educated young man, no hint had reached me that private property was other than a human institution evolved by the human brain.[74]

Any convictions which I may have held concerning such human tendencies as tyranny, aristocracy, or keeping up with the Joneses had been formed without knowledge of the ways of *my animal ancestry*.[75]

(A curious result ensues if we reword the opening clause of the last passage to read "My convictions concerning..." Notice then the difference between the sense of the possessive pronoun "my" in its two occurrences. In referring to "my convictions," Ardrey is referring to the opinions of one existing individual. Presumably—hopefully—when he refers to "my animal ancestry," Ardrey is speaking of himself—not as an existing individual—but as a member of the species *man*. At the risk of being cumbersome, we might say that Ardrey is speaking from both sides of his mouth. He speaks now with the voice of one man ("my convictions"), now with the voice of the scientific community ("my animal ancestry"). When a person speaks thus in one and the same sentence, it may be that he does not distinguish between these two voices. But this can be a symptom of that species of confusion which Climacus would call absent-mindedness.) Just as clearly, Ardrey believes that his reader must come to grips with this revolution:

All readers, lay or professional, confronted by a new interpretation of man's origin and nature, must be obliged continually to ask the question: Why should I believe this? [76]

---

[73] *Ibid.*
[74] *Ibid.*
[75] *Ibid.*, p. 13. (Italics mine.)
[76] *Ibid.*, p. 17. (Italics mine.)

This raises two questions. First, what is the relationship between a scientific theory and its popularized counterpart? Second, what kind of understanding or acceptance of a scientific theory is possible for the layman? These are not simple questions, although it is rare for a popularizer to give any consideration to them.[77] But if the layman has any *obligation* in connection with scientific knowledge, such questions will have to be answered before the precise nature of that obligation can be understood. Without some clarity about these questions, it is easy for a reader to be browbeaten into accepting an obligation which he cannot possibly fulfill. More important for our purposes in this chapter is the fact that Ardrey's challenge betokens a possible forgetting.

Let us consider, then, the first question. A scientific theory is an attempt to increase the community's understanding of a particular phenomenon or set of phenomena. It must be phrased in the language of the community and it must be presented through one of the acceptable channels. As a rule, the theory will be intelligible only to those who have the necessary background and training to appreciate the problems which it attempts to solve. Certainly without a great deal of training, the lay reader would be unable to "understand" the theory as it is presented to the community. Nor, as we saw in Chapter II, is it always possible to translate from the language of the community into the language of everyday life.[78] But no matter. For in Carnap's words, the scientist "... possesses that kind of understanding which alone is essential in the field of knowledge and science." [79]

It has often been argued that scientific understanding is not significantly different from that of everyday life. Here is one articulation of that viewpoint:

Scientific investigation is not, as many people seem to suppose, some kind of modern black art....

. . . .

The method of scientific investigation is nothing but the necessary mode of working of the human mind. It is simply the mode at which all phenomena are reasoned about, rendered precise and exact. There is no more difference, but there is just the same kind of difference, between the mental operations of a man of science and those of an ordinary person, as there is between the operations and methods of a baker or of a butcher weighing out his goods on common scales,

[77] Cf. Stephen Toulmin, *The Philosophy of Science* (New York, 1960) pp. 11-16, where Toulmin discusses the hazards of popularizations.

[78] Cf. Chapter II, p. 49.

[79] *Ibid.*

and the operations of a chemist in performing a difficult and complex analysis by means of his balance and finely-graduated weights.[80]

One wonders whether Huxley hasn't overstated the case in his desire to remove the veil of mystery from "the scientific method." To be sure, if one fixes on the "mental operations" and remains at a high mesa of generality, one can produce the illusion that there is no tremendous difference between what a scientist must do in order to understand and what we laymen do. He makes deductions; we make deductions. He uses induction; we use induction.[81]

But this ignores more than its brings to light. It overlooks the amount of training and hard work that precedes any particular deduction that a scientist might make. It overlooks the fact that while most human beings can easily learn how to weigh a slab of beef, a good many of us could not master all the skills which prove to be necessary to do quantitative analysis on a chemical compound. In sum, what such accounts ignore is the *form of life* (to use Wittgenstein's phrase) in which the "mental operations" of the scientist are imbedded. As we have argued, there are significant differences between the scientific community's form of life, or mode of existence, and the individual human being's.

We would say, then, that the relationship between a scientific theory and its popularized counterpart is tenuous at best. A theory is an essential moment in the life of the ongoing scientific community—a *sine qua non*. For the community is an exclusively cognitive entity which exists solely for the purpose of producing knowledge. In line with its mode of being, it has developed over the years a sense of "understand" which connects with theories, hypotheses, and evidence. The community has unlimited time and many other features (which the individual does not have) which enable it to pursue a complete understanding of any phenomenon that attracts its attention. But the individual is not through and through a cognitive entity. He has many other concerns.[82] Ardrey's

---

[80] T. H. Huxley, "We Are All Scientists," in *A Treasury of Science*, ed. Harlow Shapley, Samuel Rapport and Helen Wright (New York and London, 1943), pp. 14-15. Cf. also Einstein, *Years*, pp. 59, 95. Huxley's remarks demonstrate the aptness of Wittgenstein's remark: "It could very well be imagined that someone knows his was about a city perfectly,... and yet would be quite incompetent to draw a map of the city." Cf. *Zettel*, ed. G. E. M. Anscombe and G. H. von Wright, trans. G. E. M. Anscombe (Oxford, 1967), # 121. Huxley's "map" of scientific investigation seems misleading.

[81] Huxley, *op. cit.*, pp. 15-20.

[82] "The intellect is not all of man or even the primary part. We have dreams and

assumption that the lay reader has an *obligation* in connection with a scientific theory blurs over these differences. He assumes that there is a close relationship between the scientific theory itself and its popularized counterpart and that with the aid of this counterpart, the lay reader can eventually be brought to an understanding of the theory itself.[83] In sum, the assumption appears to be that, with the aid of the popularized account, the lay reader can become a kind of scientific community in miniature.

But, turning now to the second question, what kind of belief or acceptance of a scientific theory is possible for the lay reader? Let us focus our attention on another work of popular scientific literature, Jacob Bronowski's *The Identity of Man*. His fundamental assumption, Bronowski says, is that man is a part of nature.[84] Having discussed some of the "heresies" which science has injected into Western culture, he writes:

The scene, then, is set for the last act in the smoothing out: we sense that there is no break in the continuity of nature. At one end of her range, the star has been linked with the stone; and at the other end, man has been put among the animals. What now remains is between these ends to make a single chain of *Animal, Vegetable or Mineral,* along which nature becomes one with her creatures. An unbroken line runs from the stone to the cactus and on to the camel, and there is no supernatural leap in it. No special act of creation, no spark of life was needed to turn dead matter into living things.[85]

We are familiar with this scene, with the being whose vision of the natural world has no leaps. It is the scientific community. If a human being were to claim possession of this vision, we would have to issue a reminder to the effect that no individual is witness to more than an iota of the totality of events that is called "Nature." Nor will his survey of this small portion be characterized by the same smoothness as that which typifies the community's vision.

Having appropriated this vision for himself, however, Bronowski is able to imagine that it may prove troublesome for his reader. He writes:

desires and fears; we want to love and laugh and enjoy... Science, which is the intellect of mankind, is not all the life of mankind." George Platt, *The Excitement of Science* (Boston and Cambridge, 1962), p. 173.

[83] Cf. Ardrey, *Genesis,* p. 17.

[84] Jacob Bronowski, *The Identity of Man* (Garden City, 1966), p. 2. Hereafter cited as: Bronowski, *Identity.*

[85] *Ibid.,* p. 4.

What is it that troubles us in the assertion that living things are made from the
same atoms as dead, and ruled by the same laws? We may pretend that our
difficulties are intellectual, and that we are merely puzzled how this could come
about. But our uneasiness lies deeper.[86]

Bronowski imagines that this assertion will prove troubling to his reader.
(He may be right. But should a lay reader be troubled by this assertion?
Not necessarily, we would say. But let us not forget that science is an
enormously prestigious discipline, so that those who speak on behalf
of the community will be given a serious hearing. If such a speaker
claims that what he is saying should trouble the reader, it is understandable
that one might begin to squirm—even when one is not sure why!)
Let someone who is conscious of what it means to exist as an individual
human being raise a question or two. In the spirit of the *Postscript,* he
may inquire: "Who is it that makes this assertion? Whose voice are
we hearing?" It seems to be the community's voice, yet the language
is not that of the community. At the very least, it is not the language
found in its journals. Moreover, is there any reason to believe that a
layman should *understand* this popularized counterpart? [87] What would
"understand" mean in connection with the popularized counterparts of
scientific assertions? Suppose a lay reader understood the above assertion
to mean that the scientific community finds it possible to explain the
behavior of both living and non-living things with the same set of laws.
Should he be troubled by the idea that the law of gravity, for example,
applies to both himself and his house?

Bronowski continues:

This is where the fulcrum of our fears lies: that man as a species, and we as
thinking men, will be shown to be no more than a machinery of atoms.[88]

What do such fears amount to? Why should it bother any individual to
learn that, in the opinion of the scientific community, man is like a
rock in that both are constellations of atoms? Since it is the community's
aim to understand nature and to produce increasingly comprehensive
and unified theories,[89] what other result is possible? Suppose an individual
"understood" Bronowski's assertions and could stare at them without a
quiver of fear. Is such an individual missing the point?

[86] *Ibid.*, p. 6. (Italics mine.)
[87] If Wittgenstein is right, one must resist the temptation to think that if one
understands each word of a sentence, the sentence as a whole must make sense.
Cf. *PI*, #508-525.
[88] Bronowski, *Identity*, p. 7.
[89] Cf. Chapter II, p. 48.

Bronowski writes:

We have to accept the subtle but closely woven evidence that man is not different in kind from other forms of life; that living matter is not different in kind from dead matter; and therefore that a man is an assembly of atoms that obeys natural laws of the same kind that a star does.[90]

In Chapter II, we discussed very briefly the process of communication within the scientific community.[91] We noted that it may take the community some time to make up its mind about a theory. Generally speaking, a theory is considered to have attained acceptability when it is referred to in a review article written by an acknowledged spokesman for the community. The theory is then installed in the community's textbooks. In short, we know roughly what it means for the scientific community to accept a theory based on evidence. It is not clear what this would involve on the part of a lay reader, however. Since he does not possess "that kind of understanding which alone is essential in the field of knowledge and science,"[92] he presumably lacks the capacity to render a "yes or no" verdict. We would suggest, then, that it is a paralogism to hold, as Bronowski does, that a lay reader must make a response to a scientific theory.

We conclude our treatment of Bronowski's work with the following passage:

The atoms in the brain as much as those in the body constitute a mechanism, which ticks with the same ordered regularity, and abides by similar laws, as any other interlocking constellation of atoms. Men have uneasily pushed this thought out of their heads because they wanted to avoid the conflict with their rooted conviction that man is a free agent who follows only the promptings of his own will. But we cannot hide this contradiction forever.[93]

But where is this supposed contradiction? If the lay reader cannot understand (in the appropriate sense) a scientific theory, how can it be in conflict with whatever views (if any) he happens to have? Suppose an individual said to himself:

I accept—for what it's worth—the view of nature taken by those competent to make a pronouncement. They have said, so I hear, that the atoms in my brain and in my body obey the very same laws as the atoms in any rock. Is my thinking in conflict with theirs? Do I have any thoughts, given the little reading I do, about this?

[90] Bronowski, *Identity*, p. 8. (Italics mine.)
[91] Cf. Chapter II, pp. 60-61.
[92] *Ibid.*, p. 49.
[93] Bronowski, *Identity*, p. 8.

Suppose this individual could not locate any point of friction between his views and those of the community, in so far as he is able to understand them? Would such an individual be guilty of pushing thoughts out of his head?

Both Ardrey and Bronowski charge their lay reader with the obligation of accepting or believing a scientific theory, but in neither case is it clear what this involves. Acceptance, for a lay reader, might mean his willingness to acknowledge the superior insight and knowledge of the scientific community. But if this is what they are asking for, then it is not easy to understand why they believe their request will be troublesome. On the other hand, the layman cannot be expected to render the kind of verdict that a member of the scientific community can pronounce.

More important in the context of this chapter is the fact that a forgetting is concealed in the demands that Ardrey and Bronowski place upon the reader. In order to spot the forgetting, we must recall that terms like "understand," "accept," and "believe" have a definite sense within the scientific community. The community has an exclusively cognitive mode of existence. To expect a layman to make the same kind of response as this community is to forget that his mode of existence is unlike the community's in important respects. In demanding that the layman *"accept"* or *"believe"* a scientific theory, Ardrey and Bronowski speak to him as if he were a budding scientific community unto himself, thus forgetting what it means to exist as an individual human being.

A related species of forgetting occurs when an author, instead of imputing the scientific community's exclusively cognitive mode of existence to his reader, appropriates this mode of existence for himself. "It goes without saying," we have quoted H. G. MacPherson as having written, "that the scientist cannot accept most religious literature as fact." [94] This indicates that he would read the Bible, for example, through the eyes of the scientific community. Now the community, as an exclusively cognitive entity, can give one and only one sort of reading to any document which comes before its eyes. It must either blend in with the community's knowledge and vision or be rejected. No other kind of response is possible. But the individual human has a different mode of existence, which makes it possible for him to rejoice when he is sent an announcement of the birth of a child; to accept or to decline an invitation to a wedding; to send a letter expressing his sympathy when he hears of the death of a friend; to pledge his support to someone

[94] Cf. p. 156.

in time of need. All of these responses fall within the ambience of his mode of existence and all involve his faculty of understanding. But:

..., a human being can forget his native ability to get the point of countless sentences put together for purposes other than tidying up the sensorium. These include sentences used to fire a shot across his bow, to rattle or silence him rather than abide his question, and set him off balance by reviling or exalting him for no discernible reason. Such uses of language abound in the Bible,...[95]

If an individual begins to think that he has but one kind of response to any sentence—either it fits into the pattern of knowledge which the scientific community has of the world or it does not—this might be a symptom that he has so identified himself with the scientific community that he has forgotten what it means to exist as an individual.

We have been discussing that species of forgetting which takes place when an individual appropriates the community's features and begins to regard himself as a cognitive and exclusively cognitive entity. Einstein writes:

...I believe with Schopenhauer that one of the strongest motives that lead men to art and science is escape from everyday life with its painful crudity and hopeless dreariness, from the fetters of one's own ever shifting desires. A finely tempered nature longs to escape from personal life into the world of objective perception and thought;...[96]

Escape is necessary from time to time. To seek permanent release from one's own existence, however, is a formula for forgetting what it means to exist. Judging from the following passage in his "Autobiographical Notes," one would have to conclude that Einstein has successfully escaped from his own existence and achieved that insulation from the demands of everyday life which is characteristic of the community:

"Is this supposed to be an obituary?" the astonished reader will likely ask. I would like to reply: essentially yes. For the essential in being a man of my type lies precisely in *what* he thinks and *how* he thinks, not in what he does or suffers. Consequently, the obituary can limit itself in the main to the communicating of thoughts which have played a considerable role in my endeavors.[97]

If a man refers to his autobiography as an "obituary," and if that obituary "limits itself" to his thoughts, such a man would seem to regard

---

[95] H. A. Nielsen, "Bultmann's Philosophical Troubles," *Dialogue*, VIII (1970), p. 644.

[96] Einstein, *Essays*, p. 2.

[97] Albert Einstein, "Autobiographical Notes," trans. Paul Arthur Schilpp, in *Albert Einstein: Philosopher-Scientist*, ed. Paul Arthur Schilpp (New York, 1959). I, p. 33.

himself as a cognitive entity through and through. But Climacus would remind us that even if a man were to occupy himself his whole life through with science, he cannot become science. He must exist in different categories. Should a man's autobiography evidence little or no sense for these "different categories" (inwardness, action, suffering), then he has perhaps forgotten what it means to exist as an individual human being.

The final difference between the scientific community and the individual mentioned in Chapter II concerned the fact that the community's mode of existence was essentially public, whereas the individual's is both public and private. In light of this distinction, consider the following passage from Charles Darwin's autobiography:

My chief enjoyment and sole employment throughout life has been scientific work; and the excitement from such work makes me for the time *forget*, or drives away, my daily discomfort. *I have therefore nothing to record during the rest of my life except the publication of my several books.*[98]

That the scientific community would attach to the name "Darwin" no other significance than "the author of several important scientific works" is quite understandable. That Darwin is himself content with this view of himself as a public entity suggests that he has forgotten more than simply his "daily discomfort."

D. CONCLUSION

We could continue to catalogue various specimens of the phenomenon which Climacus calls "forgetting what it means to exist." But we believe that we have accomplished what we set out to do in this chapter: first, to expand on the forgetting-claim so that its significance can be grasped; second, to show that the claim has viability outside of the confines of Climacus' application of it. At the same time, we believe that our project in Chapter II has been vindicated. Without some such background as was offered there, the elucidation of the forgetting-claim would have been much more difficult.

The reader will no doubt have noticed that in pointing out particular species of forgetting, our phraseology has been tentative. We have deliberately avoided claiming categorically that this or that thinker has been guilty of forgetting what it means to exist. We have dealt with

[98] Nora Barlow, ed., *The Autobiography of Charles Darwin* (London, 1958), pp. 115-16. (Italics mine.)

symptoms. This is inevitable, as we certainly cannot claim the kind of vision which would permit categorical statements about the inwardness (or lack of it) of another human being.

If, however, there is reason to suspect that an individual may perhaps be the victim of a forgetting, there is a limited role that one can play to help bring this forgetting to his attention. In the next chapter, we shall investigate what Climacus says about the art which might fittingly be called the art of reminding.

THE ART OF REMINDING

A. INTRODUCTION

In this chapter, we ask the question: How can a forgetting be spoken to? Metaphorically, this is the situation:

When a man has his mouth so full of food that he is prevented from eating, and is like to starve in consequence, does giving him food consist in stuffing still more of it in his mouth, or does it consist in taking some of it away, so that he can begin to eat? [1]

Similarly, Climacus would suggest, a man can have *too much knowledge* and, as a consequence, forget what it means to *exist*. But how is this point to be communicated?

Imagine a man seated at a banquet table, systematically stuffing himself full, sampling every one of the delicacies. Suppose Climacus wandered into the banquet hall and, noting the situation, began to proclaim at the top of his voice the dangers of being a glutton. What effect is his speech likely to have on the man? Is it not likely that his thoughts will take some such turn as this: "Who is this noisy intruder? If he doesn't enjoy a fine feast, what business brings him here? I wish he would just leave and quit trying to spoil the fun." Now the man's attention is centered on Climacus; he has been provoked. Is it likely that he will get up and leave the table? Is it not more likely that he wil nudge the fellow sitting next to him and say, "Pass me some more *hors d'œuvres*." Such a tactic, then, would quite possibly be counter-productive.

Instead, then, let us suppose that Climacus takes a more subtle approach. He takes a seat next to the man, strikes up a conservation with him. After a few moments, he looks him squarely in the eye and asks: "Don't you think you've eaten enough already?" What would

[1] *Post.*, p. 245, *n.*

the result of this maneuver be? Might not the man be insulted and reply with a question of his own: "How does it happen, my good man, that you reckon yourself an expert on matters pertaining to my eating habits and my digestive system?" Again the man is agitated and perhaps a bit defensive. He is certainly not in a mood which is conducive to the result which Climacus had in mind.

Suppose Climacus adopted a very blunt and direct tactic. He goes right up to the place where the man is sitting and begins removing the food from in front of him. Now a wrestling match is in the offing. Even if Climacus were to overpower the man and take all the food from him, what is to prevent the man from finding himself another seat and beginning all over again?

This, then, is the situation:

And so also, when a man has much knowledge, and his knowledge has little or no significance for him, does a rational communication consist in giving him more knowledge, even supposing that he is loud in his insistence that this is what he needs, or does it not rather consist in taking some of it away? [2]

But how is one to *subtract* knowledge? If Climacus were to write an essay devoted to the proposition that there is too much knowledge, his essay becomes one addition to that already too great a quantity. Climacus realizes this:

If communicated in the form of knowledge, the recipient is led to adopt the misunderstanding that it is knowledge that he is to receive, and then we are again in the sphere of knowledge. [3]

In short, a direct approach to this situation seems to produce the very opposite result to the one hoped for. What is wanted is a communication which will prompt the recipient to take a close look at *his* situation, which will induce him to raise the pertinent questions *for himself*. An 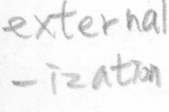 aggressive attack, either on the individual himself or the activity in which he is engaged (metaphorically, eating; literally, knowing), will very possibly put him on the defensive. It will certainly lure his attention away from himself and focus it either on the attack or the person attacking. What, then, is to be done?

Let us take the liberty of citing several passages from *The Point of View*. There Kierkegaard discusses the problem of dealing with an illusion. The illusion he is concerned with is a specific one—the idea,

[2] *Ibid.*
[3] *Ibid.*, p. 223.

widespread in his day, that everyone is a Christian. What he says, however, is applicable to the "illusion" that Climacus found himself struggling with—the idea that what the age demands and needs is *more* knowledge. "No," says Kierkegaard, "an illusion can never be destroyed directly, and only by indirect means can it be radically removed." [4] Referring back to our metaphor, we noted that the direct approach to the man who was eating too much (and under the misguided notion that he needed even more) tends to be counter-productive. Kierkegaard counsels:

First and foremost, no impatience. If he [the person who would remove an illusion] becomes impatient, he will rush headlong against it and accomplish nothing. A direct attack only strengthens a person in his illusion, and at the same time embitters him. There is nothing that requires such gentle handling as an illusion, if one wishes to dispel it. If anything prompts the prospective captive to set his will in opposition, all is lost. [5]

A direct attack will aggravate a man, make him obstinate. This is bad enough. But there is still another unfortunate consequence of a direct attack; for "...it implies moreover the presumption of requiring a man to make to another person, or in his presence, an admission which he can make most profitably *to himself privately*." [6] The very purpose of communication in this situation is to get the man to admit that he is overindulging himself. It is not easy to make such a confession in the presence of someone else, especially if that person is applying the pressure. It is much easier if he is alone. Kierkegaard writes:

This is what is achieved by the indirect method, which...*arranges everything dialectically* for the prospective captive, *and then shyly withdraws...*, so as not to witness the admission which he makes to himself alone... [7]

According to Kierkegaard, then, success in dealing with an illusion requires the use of the *indirect* method.

Climacus, too, believes that the indirect method offers the greatest promise of success in dealing with a forgetting. Hence in the next section, we shall discuss Climacus' position on communication generally and his views about the nature and the role of the indirect method specifically. In the third section, we put these results together with the important

[4] *POV*, p. 24.
[5] *Ibid.*, p. 25.
[6] *Ibid.* (Italics mine.)
[7] *Ibid.*, pp. 25-26. (Italics mine.)

hints found in the *Postscript* about what we have called the art of reminding. In the final section, we shall reflect on the *Postscript* itself in light of Climacus' views on communication.

B. COMMUNICATION AND THE INDIRECT METHOD

Just as there is a distinction between essential and accidental knowledge,[8] so there is a similar distinction between essential and accidental communication. An essential communication would be one containing essential knowledge—knowledge "essentially related to existence." [9] "Only ethical and ethico-religious knowledge has an essential relationship to the existence of the knower." [10] Scientific, historical and mathematical knowledge do not have this essential relationship to the knower's existence. When objective knowledge is the *desideratum,* a direct method of communication is called for. Climacus never denies this: "...wherever objective thinking is within its rights, its direct form of communication is also in order, precisely because it is not supposed to have anything to do with subjectivity." [11]

Climacus is generally skeptical about the need for communication in the area of subjectivity:

Communication assumes that the subject who exists in the isolation of his inwardness, and who desires through this inwardness to express the life of eternity, where sociality and fellowship is unthinkable, because the existential category of movement, and with it also all *essential communication,* is here unthinkable, *since everyone must be assumed essentially to possess all,* nevertheless wishes to impart himself; and hence desires at one and the same time to have his thinking in the inwardness of his subjective existence, and yet also to put himself into communication with others.[12]

Climacus' position can easily be misunderstood unless it is seen as a consequence of the claim that subjectivity is the truth. That claim means that each individual is able to acquire a knowledge of what it means to *exist* by turning his powers of reflection towards himself. It means that the knowledge which he needs in order to exist (essential knowledge) is already within him. His task is to bring that knowledge out. He stands in need of no teacher and no teaching. "For the study

[8] Cf. *Post.,* pp. 176-77.
[9] *Post.,* p. 177.
[10] *Ibid.*
[11] *Ibid.,* p. 70, *n.*
[12] *Ibid.,* p. 68, *n.* (Italics mine.)

of the ethical, every man is assigned to himself." [13] He does not require an "essential communication" from any other existing individual:

The very maximum of what one human being can do for another in relation to that wherein each man has to do solely with himself, is to inspire him with concern and unrest.[14]

The highest degree of resignation that a human being can reach is to acknowledge the given independence in every man, and after the measure of his ability do all that can in truth be done to help someone preserve it.[15]

Climacus' reservations, then, about the need for communication between existing individuals does not apply to every kind of communication or knowledge. If a man wants to know whether or not to carry his umbrella, he should consult the newspaper's weather report. If he wants to know whether it is a good time to invest in the stock market, he should get in touch with a broker. But neither of these involves "essential knowledge." It is with such distinctions in mind that Climacus makes this claim:

As soon as the truth, the essential truth, may be assumed to be known by everyone, the objective becomes appropriation, and here only an indirect form is applicable.[16]

If, then, there is to be communication between two existing individuals with respect to essential knowledge, the method will have to be *indirect*.[17] For the direct method—the communication of a result—assumes a state of finality which the existing individual never can arrive at, if he is conscious of what it means to *exist*:

---

[13] *Ibid.*, p. 127.
[14] *Ibid.*, p. 346.
[15] *Ibid.*, p. 232.
[16] *Ibid.*, p. 217.
[17] The theory of indirect communication is widely held to be one of "Kierkegaard's" most important contributions to philosophy. Cf. Eduard Geismar, *Lectures on the Religious Thought of Søren Kierkegaard* (Minneapolis, 1937), pp. 23-42; F. J. Billeskov-Jansen, "The Literary Art of Søren Kierkegaard," in Johnson and Thulstrup, *Critique*, pp. 11-21; H. Reidar Thomte, *Kierkegaard's Pilosophy of Religion* (Princeton, 1949), pp. 190-203. Worth consulting also are the journal entries VIII² B 79-89. Cf. *Søren Kierkegaard's Journals and Papers*, trans. and ed. Howard V. Hong and Edna H. Hong (Bloomington and London, 1967), I, #648-#657 (pp. 267-308). Once again, we must state that our discussion is centered on the views of *Climacus* concerning the indirect method and not on those of Kierkegaard. It should become progressively apparent that on this topic there is very close and substantial agreement between them.

For if inwardness is the truth, results are only rubbish with which we should not trouble each other. The communication of results is an unnatural form of intercourse between man and man, in so far as every man is a spiritual being, for whom the truth consists in nothing else than the self-activity of personal appropriation, which the communication of a result tends to prevent.[18]

If an individual is concentrating his entire energy upon the task of becoming subjective, what results can he have? The task is still not finished, for he is in a constant process of becoming. He can ill afford a "time out" so as to describe his achievements thus far, for existence is a "continuous meanwhile." Those results are like yesterday's supper. Presumedly, other existing individuals are engaged in a constant striving, in "the self-activity of personal appropriation." If this is so, then anything which would come between an individual and his task (e.g. someone else's "results") is a distraction.

If there is to be communication between existing individuals in the area of "essential knowledge," it will have to take an indirect form:

The difference between subjective and objective thinking must express itself also in the form of communication suitable to each. That is to say, the subjective thinker will from the beginning have his attention called to the requirement that this form should embody artistically as much of reflection as he himself has when existing in his thought.[19]

The "how" of an existing individual's communication must reflect the "what"; the form must reflect the content. The content of his thought is always, in some sense, his own existence. This sort of communication is so difficult that Climacus speaks of it as an *art*. He is aware that these stringent demands will be thought extreme by some, yet he refuses to weaken them:

To demand of a thinker that he should contradict his entire thought and view of life in the form which he gives to his communication; to offer him the consolation that he will in this way succeed in accomplishing something; to persuade him that no one will bother his head about such a pecadillo, aye, that no one will even notice it in these objective times, since so extreme a consistency is accounted a trifling thing, to which no systematic hireling pays attention,—all this is good advice, and quite cheap to boot.[20]

In a series of *reductios,* Climacus attempts to show that an indirect form is the only appropriate one for an existing individual. Suppose, for

---

[18] *Post.,* pp. 216-17.

[19] *Ibid.,* p. 68.

[20] *Ibid.,* pp. 69-70.

example, a man conceived the thought that no man should have any disciple. Such a thought would belong to the realm of essential knowledge and truth. Suppose, however, that this individual attempts to communicate this thought directly; i.e., he simply asserts, whenever he comes in contact with another human, that "No man should have any disciple." Or he writes an article devoted to this proposition. What would the result be?

Why then he would be understood; and he would soon have applications from at least ten candidates, offering to preach this doctrine, in return merely for a free shave once a week. That is to say, he would have experienced the peculiar good fortune of obtaining disciples to accept and disseminate this doctrine of not having any disciples.[21]

There was, Climacus would say, nothing wrong with this individual's thought. But the failure to express this thought in an appropriate form may lead to a result which is contrary to the thought itself. Thus Climacus says:

The form of the communication must be distinguished from its expression. When the thought has found its suitable expression in the word, which is realized by means of a first reflection, there follows a second reflection, concerned with the relation between the communication and the author of it, and reflecting the author's own existential relationship to the Idea.[22]

Just as there was need for a double reflection in connection with subjective thinking, so there is the need for a double reflection in connection with the communication of it. In the first reflection, the thought is put into words. But this is not sufficient. It must be followed by a second reflection in which the individual thinker apprehends his own relationship to his thought and reflects it. In the example we have been considering, the failure to follow through with the second moment of reflection is what caused the misfire. The indirect method of communication enters in with this second reflection.

To illustrate further the kind of confusion that results when the second reflection is omitted, Climacus gives another example. Suppose, he says, an individual conceives the thought that inwardness is the truth. If he proceeds to communicate this thought directly, what happens? Climacus writes:

[21] *Ibid.,* p. 70.
[22] *Ibid.,* p. 71.

Suppose him to display great zeal and enthusiasm for the propogation of this truth, since if people could only be made to listen to it they would of course be saved; suppose he announced it on all possible occasions, and succeeded in moving not only those who perspire easily, but also the hard-boiled temperaments; what then? Why then, there would doubtless be found a few laborers, who had hitherto stood idle in the market-place, and only after hearing this call went to work in the vineyard —engaging themselves to proclaim this doctrine to all. And then what? Then he would have contradicted himself still further, as he had contradicted himself from the beginning; for the zeal and enthusiasm which he had directed toward the end of getting it said and heard, was in itself a misunderstanding. The matter of prime importance was, of course, that he should be understood; the inwardness of the understanding would consist precisely in each individual coming to understand it by himself. Now he had succeeded in obtaining town criers of inwardness, and a town crier of inwardness is quite a remarkable species of animal.[23]

Again direct communication yields disastrous results.

The moral which Climacus would have us draw from these examples is that if there is to be communication between existing individuals about essential knowledge, the method will have to be indirect. He says:

Wherever the subjective is of importance in knowledge, and where appropriation constitutes the crux of the matter, the process of communication is *a work of art, and doubly reflected*. Its very first form is precisely the subtle principle that the personalities must be held devoutly apart from one another, and not permitted to fuse or coagulate into objectivity.[24]

Suppose, then, that an individual conceives the thought that no man ought to have any disciples. His second reflection might go like this:

My thought is that no man ought to have any disciples. I believe this is true. Now why do I wish to communicate this thought to others? Do I believe that they are ignorant of this truth, so that perhaps *they need a teacher*? But then do I really think that no man should have disciples? Perhaps I ought to delay any communications until I iron out my own thinking on this.

The thoughts may not flow as readily as we have imagined. But in any case, a second reflection would ensure that an individual had arrived at some clarity about the "why" of his intended communication. It is not enough, however, that he have thought through his own relationship to this communication. For "...artistry would always demand...an awareness of the form of communication in relation to the recipient's possible misunderstanding." [25] In terms of our example, he must be

[23] *Ibid.*, pp. 71-72.
[24] *Ibid.*, p. 73. (Italics mine.)
[25] *Ibid.*, p. 70.

aware of the fact that if he communicates himself directly, it is very possible that he will wind up having a disciple or two of his own. But the idea was for the recipient to understand this thought in his own existence, which would prevent him from being any man's disciple.

If an individual is to communicate with another about the essential truth, he must understand both his own relationship to his thought and have a sense for the situation of the recipient. "The personalities must be held devoutly apart, and not permitted to fuse or coagulate," says Climacus. For "the secret of all communication consists precisely in emancipating the recipient." [26] Small wonder, then, that Climacus believes that such communication will be a work of art. He says:

The subjective thinker has a form, a form for his communication with other men, and this form constitutes his style. It must be as manifold as the opposites he holds in combination.... As he is not himself a poet or ethicist or dialectician, his form cannot be that of either directly. His form must first and last relate itself to existence, and in this connection he will have at his disposal the poetic, the ethical, the dialectical, and the religious.... The person of the abstract thinker is irrelevant to his thought. An existential thinker must be pictured as essentially thinking, *but so that in presenting his thought he sketches himself.*[27]

In presenting his thought to another human being, the individual must not forget that he is an existing individual for whom existence is the decisive thing. "But existential reality is incommunicable," Climacus claims, "and the subjective thinker finds his reality in his own ethical existence." [28] It seems that we have come to a dead end. The existing individual must sketch himself in presenting his thought, yet existential reality is incommunicable. The subjective thinker finds his reality in his own ethical existence, yet he may wish to communicate with another.

There is one road out of this impasse:

When reality is apprehended by an outsider it can be understood only as a possibility. Everyone who makes a communication, in so far as he becomes conscious of this fact, will therefore be careful to give his existential communication the form of a possibility, precisely in order that it may have a relationship to existence. A communication in the form of the possible compels the recipient to face the problem of existing in it, so far as this is possible between man and man.[29]

It might be thought that by telling someone that one has really done such-and-such, that person will be helped to make a decision. Just the

---

[26] *Ibid.*, p. 69.
[27] *Ibid.*, p. 319. (Italics mine.)
[28] *Ibid.*, p. 320.
[29] *Ibid.*

reverse, Climacus argues. One must evoke the latent possibility "in terms of the ideal man" rather than the actuality of some actual man:

It is everlastingly untrue that anyone was ever helped to do the good by the fact that someone else really did it; for if he ever comes to the point of really doing it himself, it will be by apprehending the reality of the other as a possibility. When Themistocles was rendered sleepless by thinking about the exploits of Miltiades, it was his apprehension of their reality as a possibility that made him sleepless. Had he plunged into inquiries as to whether Miltiades really has accomplished the great things attributed to him, had he contented himself with knowing that Miltiades had actually done them, he would scarcely have been rendered sleepless. In that case he would probably have become sleepy, or at the most a noisy admirer, but scarcely a second Miltiades. Ethically speaking, there is nothing so conducive to sound sleep as admiration of another person's ethical reality. And again ethically speaking, if there is anything that can stir and rouse a man, it is a possibility ideally requiring itself of a human being.[30]

If there is to be communication between existing individuals with respect to essential knowledge, it will have to stress the possible. In this way, the maker of the communication maintains his own relationship to the thought as an existing individual (for the possibility he evokes applies to him) and the recipient is compelled to face the problem of existing in the possibility evoked.

These, then, are the general principles which must govern the process of communication between existing individuals. In the final section of this chapter, we shall see how Climacus incorporates these principles in his own authorship. The problem of communicating with someone who has possibly forgotten what it means to exist is more complex. To that problem, and to the directives Climacus issues concerning it, we turn next.

C. THE ART OF REMINDING

Communication between two existing individuals is an art. A still more demanding art is communication between an existing individual and someone who is caught in a forgetting. Climacus has scattered a number of hints about the practice of the art of reminding throughout the *Postscript*. In this section, we shall ferret out and develop these clues and then show how they can be put to work in connection with one of the forgettings discussed in the previous chapter.

In the first place, the author of the communication must preserve his identity as an existing individual. Nothing is gained if he, too, begins

[30] *Ibid.*, pp. 321-22.

to speak in an absent-minded way. Climacus gives this piece of advice to an individual who encounters a man who identifies himself with the philosophical standpoint of mediation:

> But it is important not to direct the polemic to the wrong point, and hence not to begin in a fantastic objective manner to discuss *pro* and *contra* whether there is a mediation or not, *but to hold fast to what it means to be a human being.*[31]

Secondly, the author of the communication must clarify to himself in a second reflection his own relationship to the content of his communication. He must understand what he hopes to achieve through it. Is he seeking to emancipate the recipient from his confusion or to bind the recipient to himself? Does he seek to accuse the recipient, put him in the wrong, or to free him?

Third, the author of the communication must have a well-developed sense for the situation of the recipient:

> In connection with this task of becoming essentially subjective, it is necessary to take into account the scope of the reflective presuppositions that the subject has to interpenetrate, *the weight of the objectivity* he has to throw off;...[32]

By "objectivity," Climacus means an individual's commitment to tasks in the area of objective reflection. For example, in order to do science, an individual must abandon his own personal concerns and his own limited point of view in order to see things from the scientific point of view. He must immerse himself in the community's way of thinking and its modes of expression. The more deeply he becomes involved in the life of the scientific community and its mode of existence, the greater will be the hold of these ways of speaking. From the subjective point of view, such a man labors under a heavy burden; the heavier it is, the harder it will be for a man to get out from under it.

The first step, in communicating with someone laboring under such a burden, is to attempt to restore the man to his status as an existing individual. Thus Climacus advises the use of "a powerful formula of incantation" when one encounters a philosopher who wants to approach everything *sub specie aeterni:*

> In this connection it will perhaps again appear how necessary it is to take special precautions before entering into discussion with a philosophy of this sort: *first to separate the philosopher from the philosophy,* and then as in cases of black magic,

---

[31] *Ibid.,* p. 177. (Italics mine.)
[32] *Ibid.,* p. 62. (Italics mine.)

witchcraft, and *possession by the devil, to use a powerful formula of incantation to get the bewitched philosopher transformed into a particular existing human being, and thus restored back to his true state.*[33]

Further on in the *Postscript,* Climacus gives the reader a sample of the formula mentioned above. He refers to "...*the formula of exorcism* against speculative philosophers...: 'May I have the honor to ask with whom I have the honor to converse; is it a human being, etc.?'" [34]

Climacus' choice of metaphor is interesting. He would have the reader deal with someone laboring under a forgetting as one might deal with a person who is *possessed by a spirit*. In such cases, the voice that one hears from an individual is not his own but the voice of the spirit who has taken possession of him. The purpose of exorcism is to drive the spirit from the individual, thus restoring the individual back to his true state and giving him back his own voice. In New Testament times, Jesus and His disciples cast out many a spirit. Sometimes they met with a very obdurate spirit which could be expelled "only by prayer and fasting." [35]

Although many men no longer believe in cases of possession by the Devil (such beliefs are accounted prescientific and therefore part of the mythology of the New Testament [36]), they are yet comfortable with locutions such as "the scientific spirit" or "the spirit of philosophy." As we saw in the last chapter, the budding scientist must do more than master certain skills. He must become "infected" (one might even say "possessed") by the spirit of the scientific community.[37] He must learn to speak with its voice.[38] But if that spirit takes hold in him with such force that he loses a sense for the sound of his own voice; if every time he speaks, it is the community's spirit that speaks through him; would this not be similar to cases of demonic possession? And what of the philosopher?

---

[33] *Ibid.*, p. 324. (Italics mine.) Cf. Kenneth Hamilton, *The Promise of Kierkegaard,* The Promise of Theology Series, ed. Martin E. Marty (Philadelphia and New York, 1969), p. 48.

[34] *Post.*, pp. 466-67. (Italics mine.)

[35] Matthew 17:20.

[36] For a close look at Bultmann's critique of the New Testament and its mythology, cf. H. A. Nielsen, "Bultmann's Philosophical Troubles," *Dialogue,* VIII (1970), pp. 635-45.

[37] Cf. Chapter V, p. 150.

[38] *Ibid.*, p. 151.

...his task consists in getting more and more away from himself so as to become objective, thus vanishing from himself and becoming what might be called the contemplative energy of philosophy itself.[39]

Climacus' counsel is that one should deal with such cases very carefully:

On must therefore be very careful in dealing with a philosopher of the Hegelian school, and, above all, *to make certain of the identity of the being with whom one has the honor to discourse.* Is he a human being, an existing human being? [40]

If one discovers that one is speaking to an individual who wishes to represent "philosophy" or "science" and is unable to speak in his own name with his own voice. then one must attempt to drive the spirit out of the man.

Climacus provides an example of how one might begin such an "exorcism":

"But viewed eternally and from the divine standpoint, and especially theocentrically, there is no paradox; true speculative philosophy does not therefore remain at the standpoint of the paradox, but takes a step in advance and explains it." "May I ask to be permitted a little piece; I beseech the gentlemen not to begin again in this style, for I have already said that I cannot enter into a discussion with over-earthly and under-earthly beings."[41]

The other party to this discussion would speak as one who is *sub specie aeterni.* Such a man has forgotten what it means to *exist* as an individual human being. Climacus refuses the gambit and counters with one of his own designed to "separate the philosopher from the philosophy." This is the first step in getting a man restored to his status as an existing individual.

It is understandable, then, that Climacus would favor the dialogue as one form of communication well-suited to dealing with absent-minded beings:

If we could only get the dialogue introduced again in the Greek manner, for the purpose of testing what we know and what we do not know, the entire ingenious affectation that clusters about recent philosophy, its artificiality and unnaturalness, would soon disappear. It is not by any means my opinion that Hegel should be asked to talk with a day-laborer, and that it would prove anything if the latter could not be made to understand him;... But this is not what I mean, and my proposal does not in the slightest resemble an idler's attack on science. But let a philosopher

---

[39] *Post.,* p. 54.
[40] *Ibid.,* p. 271. (Italics mine.)
[41] *Ibid.,* p. 194.

of the Hegelian school or Hegel himself enter into conversation with a cultivated person, who has made himself competent dialectically through having existed,...[42]

The dialogue allows the existing individual to use his own voice. If he does this artfully, it can also open the way for his interlocutor to become aware of the voices coming from his own mouth. The dialogue has other savory features. It has patience built into it. While the treatise hurries along to its conclusion, a dialogue can move no faster than its slowest participant. Climacus imagines what a dialogue between Hegel and Socrates might have been like:

Imagine Socrates in conversation with Hegel. With the help of the notes he will soon have Hegel on the hip; and as he was not accustomed to being put off by the assurance that everything will be made clear at the end, not even permitting a continuous speech lasting for five minutes, to say nothing of a continuous development lasting through seventeen volumes of print, he would put on the brakes with all his might—merely to tease Hegel.[43]

The dialogue form then seems to be a very appropriate one for dealing with a forgetting. The time has come for us to attempt to put Climacus' suggestions to work on an actual forgetting. Prior to that, however, we want to cite an example of a dialogue which stands at the furthest possible remove from the one we shall offer. In his *Basic Modern Philosophy of Religion,* Frederick Ferré constructs a dialogue which he introduces in these words:

Matching style to purpose, we shall see what might happen in the course of a friendly argument between a pair of reasonably well matched debaters, Theophilus and Skepticus. Both of these characters have a good general knowledge of the sciences, but they cannot agree on the question whether it is still reasonably justifiable to retain belief in God. The relatively unsophisticated remarks of their friend, Simplicius, will serve to start the apples of philosophical discord rolling.[44]

Simplicius tosses out the first apple:

Simplicius: ..., you might as well give in and admit that there is a religious reality behind the visible structure of things.... Why don't you admit it?... It seems to me that you ought to come in out of the rain!

Skepticus: Thanks for the suggestion, but I'd rather be drowned in the open than choked to death by the mob.... Far from luring me in from the rain, your argument makes me want more than ever to keep my distance from your house of fallacy.[45]

[42] *Ibid.,* p. 291.

[43] *Ibid.,* p. 297.

[44] Frederick Ferré, *Basic Modern Philosophy of Religion* (New York, 1967), p. 301.

[45] *Ibid.,* pp. 302-303.

So the dialogue continues for some thirty pages, with each discussant contributing an apple of discord from time to time. We find barbs like these strewn along the way: "your reductionist biasses"; [46] "Now look me in the eyes, Theophilus,..."; [47] "I know the arguments you have in mind, and they are all quite capable of being countered. Try me." [48] The communications in this dialogue are as direct as one could find. The fur is flying. Each contestant is putting as much pressure as he can on the other. Each wants to put the other in the wrong. Such pressure is not the gentle kind of handling which is conducive to self-discovery.

We begin our own dialogue with a text which we discussed before as one which might be symptomatic of a forgetting:

MacPherson: The scientist cannot believe that these miracles or unnatural events really occurred; there is no verifiable evidence, and they do not fit into the pattern of knowledge we now have of the physical world. [49]

The "events" referred to here by MacPherson would be, for example, some of those reported in the New Testament. Climacus, too, sees difficulties in the New Testament texts, but of a different sort. From his point of view, MacPherson's difficulties are not the real ones but rather a kind of illusory difficulty which bespeak a forgetting. We have already indicated the nature of the forgetting involved. Let us then imagine how Climacus might continue the dialogue. The hope is that the forgetting will declare itself if the situation is arranged dialectically so as to make this possible. Climacus' first move must be "to separate the scientist from the science." He might begin in this fashion.

Climacus: I agree with you that there are difficulties in believing the events related in the New Testament. But tell me, who is this "we" you mentioned?

MacPherson: The physicists and other scientists whose business it is to discover and articulate the laws that govern the physical world.

Climacus: What you are saying, then, is that you scientists cannot incorporate these reported happenings into the vision you have of the physical world. They just don't fit, is that it?

MacPherson: That's it in a nutshell.

Climacus: As for myself, I'm no scientist. I don't see what you see. My knowledge of these laws is meagre, so I'm not in a position to say, with respect to the events

---

[46] *Ibid.,* p. 304.
[47] *Ibid.,* p. 310.
[48] *Ibid.,* p. 312.
[49] Cf. Chapter V, pp. 156-57.

reported in the New Testament or any others, whether they do or do not fit into a vision which I don't have. I trust you understand. At the same time, I must admit that had I been present at any of them, I should have been completely baffled. A man is dead one minute and the next minute he is alive again. I wouldn't have known what to think. But then, you must be patient with me; for you are dealing with an ignoramus who doesn't even begin to understand what happens when a light switch is thrown.

MacPherson: It is well to recognize one's ignorance and one's limitations. But you must be careful not to confuse two events so very different as throwing a switch and a man supposedly coming back to life after he is really dead. You really shouldn't mention them in the same breath even. What happens when a light switch is thrown is perfectly intelligible. But a man coming back to life or changing water into wine by an act of will—such things, we know, just cannot happen.

Climacus: I am sure that the difference is quite clear to someone with your background. But that "we" does not include someone like myself.

MacPherson: That may be, but I certainly trust that you are not implying that because the difference isn't clear *to you* (as you are fond of saying), it therefore does not exist. That would be a most lamentable kind of ego-centrism. From the scientific point of view, the difference is crystal-clear. I'm inclined to say that if you cannot see the difference, that is the worse for you. Perhaps you should brush up on your science a bit; you might find that you would not be so inclined—as you seem to be—to even consider accepting as fact the myths and legends of a bygone time. You wouldn't be so gullible.

Climacus: It's a terrible thing to be thought gullible, isn't it? Your suggestion that I could do with a refresher course in science is interesting. The trouble is that I'm not sure my brain would accommodate me. But something else, too. A moment ago you said that it is a good thing to recognize one's own limitations and ignorance. That thought occurred to me some while ago. And it struck me that were I to devote myself to science without first securing an understanding of myself that I would be guilty of a kind of recklessness. I find it hard to concentrate on more than one task at a time, you see. So I thought that my ignorance of myself ought to have first claim on my energies. I know that individuals more gifted than I am are able to chip away at both sorts of ignorance simultaneously. But as I am still busy with that first task, I'm afraid I couldn't follow your suggestion. Still I marvel at those of you who can do both.

MacPherson: I'm beginning to feel like a very privileged man. I'd have to agree that the scientist perhaps has the advantage. Not only does a knowledge of science decrease one's gullibility-quotient, if I may put it that way; but science has made significant strides in presenting us with a comprehensive view of man. The two fit together quite well, so I don't feel the pinch that you do.

Climacus: Yes, I've heard about the great advances that have been made in this very century in sociology, psychology, and anthropology. I respect the view of the authorities. I hope you won't think it bold if I say, however, that it seems to me that this new knowledge does not remove the unknowing which has me in its clutches.

MacPherson: The way you emphasize the word "me" and this unknowing of yours leads me to think that you think of yourself as somewhat singular. I must inform you that the laws of behavior apply to both of us. They are quite general.

Climacus: Yes, but if these laws have the generality you say they have, it is difficult for me to see how they could help me in endeavor to understand myself as the particular individual that I am. *That* is where my unknowing begins.

MacPherson: I find it hard to believe what I'm hearing. Surely you are not suggesting that because these laws are general, they cannot be of service to individuals! You have only to read the barest amount before you discover that there are myriads of people who are living better lives today because of advances in psychology, for example.

Climacus: I certainly have no intention of denying that. How could I? My point was the much less sweeping one that it did not seem to me that these laws could free me from the particular unknowing that I am working on. I realize that, from the point of view of the scientific community, I am just like any other human being and am subject to the same laws. But this way of looking at myself could hardly cure the ignorance I am afflicted with. It seems to me that my only hope is to pay attention to myself. From this point of view, any inroads which I might make into psychology would in fact be detours. For I would have to take my attention from myself. Though I would presumably know more about man-in-general, I would be none the further ahead with respect to my task.

MacPherson: It seems to me like a very boring kind of life—sitting around thinking about oneself all the time. *Chacun a son goût,* as they say. But we seem to have wandered from our point of departure which had to do with the scientist's unwillingness (and your apparent readiness) to accept as fact the happenings related in Scripture.

Climacus: I'm glad you had sense enough to get us back on the track. But the digression was not completely useless. I think I can understand now why the scientific community—devoted as it is to a thorough understanding of all phenomena—must be dissatisfied with some New Testament texts. Those texts, if admitted, would be monstrous ruptures in the community's vision of the flow of events. But the community is by nature committed to healing all such ruptures. So I can see why the community must reject such texts. What I am wondering is why you also reject them.

MacPherson: That seems to me to be a very peculiar question.

Climacus: Yes, but I'm hoping you won't deny me an answer.

MacPherson: I'll do what I can. I take it we agree that science is concerned with knowledge and understanding and that it puts it claims, in the form of laws and theories, to the test. "To accept a new fact, [the scientist] must first be provided with carefully documented background information. He is especially reluctant to believe anything that appears to conflict with theories that have accurately described the relationship of previously verified events. He tends to believe what he has seen or what other trained observers have seen, provided all such events fit together in a natural way and can be correlated by general rules. Essentially all other reported events he classes as exceptions to the order observed in nature and therefore of doubtful verity." [50] Thus the scientist must consider the events reported in Scripture as of doubtful verity. It seems fair to suggest that his conclusions should be accepted by all reasonable men. Thus as both a scientist and—I hope—a reasonable man. I accept the community's verdict.

Climacus: I think I might agree once I understand what such acceptance amounts to. Obviously, I cannot claim the expertise which is necessary to appraise a scientific theory. For I cannot even claim to understand any scientific theory. From your fine description a moment ago, I have a rough idea of what such understanding and acceptance involve for the scientist. But I cannot see from that what these terms would mean outside of that community of scientists. What, for example, would accepting a scientific theory involve for one such as myself? It is not easy for me to grasp the thought that I have any duties or obligations in this realm.

MacPherson: Couldn't you consult one of the many popularizations written for people like yourself? They explain these theories in language which everyone with some education can understand.

Climacus: I've looked at a few of these in my time. I hope you will be appreciative when I say that I am skeptical of calling what one gets as a result of reading one of these popularizations an "understanding." It certainly seems to differ mightily from what the community calls "understanding."

MacPherson: Yes, there are significant differences. In can't deny that it irks me a bit when a layman begins to speak in an authoritative voice about "Relativity Theory" or "Heisenberg's Uncertainty Principle."

Climacus: Then we are agreed that neither acceptance nor rejection of a scientific theory would seem to be a realistic possibility for someone outside of the scientific community. Of course, I can say that I "accept" the community's theories in the sense that I acknowledge the competence and the authority of those qualified to render a verdict. But then I can't see that any scientist would be particularly interested in whether I accept the community's verdict or not. It certainly doesn't affect your work one way or the other. Nor does it seem to me in any way meritorious if I do offer such acceptance.

MacPherson: I think we are at one on this point. Whether through luck or by choice, you are unable to "understand" the community's theories and hence in no position to accept or reject. You cannot see things the way a scientist does. Let me ask you this: Do you think that those of us who have this ability—and I won't deny that some element of luck is involved; some have it, some don't—and can see the world from the community's points of view ought to suspend our critical faculties when we come across a New Testament text—or any other kind of supposedly "baffling" events?

Climacus: I can't presume to tell you what to do or what not to do.

MacPherson: Come now, a little honesty, if you please. Aren't you in fact suggesting that when I read certain passages from the New Testament, I ought to forget all about the scientific progress of the last two thousand years? That I ought

[50] H. G. MacPherson, "What Would a Scientific Religion Be Like?" *Saturday Review,* August 2, 1969, p. 44.

to prescind from the knowledge we now have of the ways of the physical world and approach those texts just as a first-century Galilean might have? "..., modern man cannot be expected to shut his mind to all that has happened in the last thousand years." [51] It seems to me one of the salutary effects of science that it has helped to rid the world of a certain amount of myth and magic and to provide some insulation against the credulity which might have captured a Galilean two thousand years ago. So I ask you: Are you asking me to suspend my scientific sensibilities when I read the New Testament? If so, then I might just as well go in for astrology, mysticism, and every other species of tomfoolery!

Climacus: I'd be the last to deny that one likes to insulate himself against nonsense and the like. And no one in his right mind likes to be thought gullible or foolish, especially when he has devoted a good measure of his time and talent to the hard work and the clear thinking, no-nonsense ways of science. So I can well appreciate your sensitivity at what you take to be an invitation to be called gullible. You think that if you were to discard your "scientific sensibilities," you would immediately become vulnerable to every sort of nonsense and absurdity invented by the human mind. Science is your protection against this fate. If you were to separate yourself from the scientific point of view, you would perhaps become the laughing-stock of your colleagues. "Poor old MacPherson," you can hear them saying. "He's gone in for those Christian myths." Your fear is that your reputation would suffer.

MacPherson: I can practically guarantee it.

Climacus: I understand your plight.

MacPherson: I wonder whether you do or not. Because I have to get back to the main point here. It sounds to me like you think that my reason for rejecting the New Testament texts in question is that I'm afraid my reputation would suffer if I accepted them. But the reason, as I have said several times, is that those texts report events which we know *cannot have happened* as reported.

Climacus: It must be a wonderful thing for a man to be able to state with such authority that certain things cannot happen. Such powers of understanding are far in advance of my own. I seem to be destined to go through life with no such protection against the baffling and the un-understandable.

MacPherson: Please don't misunderstand me. There are things which I don't understand, too. I never said that I, personally, understand everything. When I said a moment ago that we know that certain things cannot have happened, it wasn't just myself speaking; it was the collective voice of the scientific community.

Climacus: I see, you are reminding me that there is a considerable difference between "MacPherson" and "Science" and that when you said a moment ago that certain things cannot have happened, although it was your voice I heard, you were really speaking as one authorized by training and competence to make pronouncement in the name of Science. I think you have made a very helpful distinction and I'm sorry that it took me so long to see it. I think I can understand

---

[51] MacPherson, *op. cit.*, p. 44.

very clearly now why Science must reject these New Testament texts. But now I'd like to address a question to you personally: What view do you take of those texts? What is your opinion? You can speak with your own voice now without fear of misunderstanding.

MacPherson: Personally, I haven't any opinion. I just don't think about them. I let the community speak for me and that is the end of it.

Climacus: I gather, then, that you have struck some sort of agreement and understanding with yourself about which situations will get a response from you personally and which will get the community's response, filtered through your voice. I would be very interested in hearing more from you about this agreement you have with yourself, as it seems the kind of thing that might save a man from a good deal of unnecessary agonizing. But that will have to wait for another occasion.

The art of communication requires knowing not only how to start a dialogue and keep it going, but also when to break it off. The dialogue can end here. Climacus has done as much as he can (though it is not much) *to arrange the situation dialectically* [52] so that MacPherson can now, if he chooses, continue the dialogue in the privateness of his own interior. He may then discover whether he has given the community a roving commission to speak for him or not. He may find that he has in effect given such a commission, although he was not aware of it. This might lead him to rethink that license. He may find that his fears of being thought gullible go deeper than he cares to admit publicly. He may learn that he values his own existence just in so far as it is different from the ordinary, just in so far as it is special because of the extras he happens to possess. He may find that he has become so accustomed to speaking with the voice of the scientific community that his own voice rarely gets exercise. All of these, or none of them, are *possible*.

From Climacus' point of view, the important feature is that a number of *possibilities* have been brought to light. No pressure of any kind has been applied to MacPherson to admit defeat. But suppose Climacus' reply to MacPherson's opening statement had been:

You simpleton! You're suffering from a severe case of absent-mindedness (though you don't know it). You've forgotten what is means to *exist*. That's your problem!

Such a *direct* accusation would naturally have served to put MacPherson, or anyone else for that matter, on the defensive. This would militate against the desired result of getting MacPherson to look carefully at his own existence.

[52] Cf. above, p. 175.

The dialogue that we have constructed is *indirect* in the sense that it has been guided by the thought that MacPherson is the victim of a species of forgetting, though this is never directly stated. Climacus, as we have imagined him, has been careful not to put MacPherson on the defensive, not to force him to admit in the presence of another human being an admission which he can most profitably make to himself alone. Climacus has withdrawn himself in order to be out of the way. How things go with MacPherson will depend upon "the weight of the objectivity he has to throw off." [53] There is no reason to think that one conversation will enable him to throw that weight off, especially if he has become accustomed to it and perhaps rather comfortable with it. It is, however, a beginning.

In the *Postscript,* Climacus effects a real disappearing act. To its nature and significance, as well as to several unanswered question about the *Postscript* itself, we shall now turn.

D. CLIMACUS' WITHDRAWAL

Climacus, as we have seen, has enunciated a number of principles which he believes should govern the process of communication between existing individuals. How does he put these principles into operation in his own authorship?

Climacus tells us that once he had understood that the misdirection of speculative philosophy was rooted in the fact that men had forgotten what it means to *exist*, it likewise became clear to him that an indirect form of communication was necessary.[54] He says:

If men had forgotten what it means to exist religiously, they had doubtless also forgotten what it means to exist as human beings; this must therefore be set forth. But above all it must not be done in a dogmatizing manner, for then the misunderstanding would instantly take the explanatory effort to itself in a new misunderstanding, as if existing consisted in getting to know something about this or that.[55]

Climacus thus exhibits his "awareness of the form of the communication in relation to the recipient's possible misunderstanding." [56] A direct communication would become one more item on the menu of speculative

---

[53] Cf. above, p. 183.
[54] *Post.,* p. 216.
[55] *Ibid.,* p. 223.
[56] *Ibid.,* p. 70. Cf. above p. 180.

philosophy, thus compounding the problem rather than alleviating it. He says:

> Only one who has some conception of the enduring capacity of a misunderstanding to assimilate even the most strenuous effort of explanation and still remain the same misunderstanding, will be able to appreciate the difficulties of an authorship where every word must be carefully watched, and every sentence pass through the process of a double reflection.[57]

But just as he was about to embark on such an authorship which would call attention to what it means to *exist, Either-Or* was published. In an appendix entitled "A Glance at a Contemporary Effort in Danish Literature," Climacus reviews the pseudonymous production (along with "Magister Kierkegaard's *Edifying Discourses*") up to and including *Stages on Life's Way*. He finds that all of these works, both in respect of their content and their form, are quite compatible with his own analysis. Climacus believes that the pseudonymous authors are in agreement with his thesis that subjectivity is the truth [58] and that existence is the decisive thing.[59] More to the point of our discussion here are Climacus' reflections on the form of these works. Particularly important for understanding the *Postscript* are the notions of a "contrasting form" and the experiment.

The following passage provides a lead for understanding what a contrast-form is:

> Let a teacher in relation to the essential truth (for otherwise a direct relationship between teacher and pupil is quite in order) have, as we say, much inwardness of feeling, and be willing to publish his doctrines day in and day out; if he assumes the existence of a direct relationship between the learner and himself, his inwardness is not inwardness, but a direct outpouring of feeling; the respect for the learner which recognizes that he is in himself the inwardness of truth, is precisely the teacher's inwardness. Let a learner be enthusiastic, and publish his teacher's praises abroad in the strongest expressions, thus, as we say, giving evidence of his inwardness; this inwardness is not inwardness, but an immediate devotedness; the devout and silent accord, in which the learner by himself assimilates what he has learned, keeping the teacher at a distance because he turns his attention within himself, this is precisely inwardness. Pathos is indeed inwardness, but it is an immediate inwardness, when it is expressed; but *pathos in a contrary form* is an inwardness which remains with the maker of the communication in spite of being expressed, and cannot be directly appropriated by another except through that other's self-activity: the contrast of the form is the measure of the inwardness. The more complete the contrast of the form, the greater the

[57] *Ibid.*, p. 223.
[58] *Ibid.*, p. 248.
[59] *Ibid.*, p. 251.

inwardness, and the less contrast, up to the point of direct communication, the less the inwardness.[60]

If an individual is to express himself on the subject of the essential truth, he cannot do so directly and immediately. He must take an indirect path. He must express himself in such a way as to retain his own inwardness and at the same time force the recipient to become active. In a direct communication, the thought and the expression of the thought are immediately related. But in an indirect communication, the thinker's thought and his expression of it are filtered through a number of considerations. Hence the expression will appear (to the author) to contrast with the thought rather than to match it. Yet this is necessary if the communication is to achieve its intended effect of setting the recipient in action as an existing individual.

It might be said that a contrast-form exhibits its point instead of stating it directly. Climacus credits Johannes *de Silentio* (the pseudonymous author of *Fear and Trembling*) with having grasped this idea:

The contrasting nature of the form is absolutely necessary for every production in this and similar spheres. In the form of a direct communication, in the form of a shriek, "fear and trembling" is of no great moment; for the direct form of communication shows that the direction is outward, culminating in the shriek, not inward into the abyss of inwardness, where alone fear and trembling are really fearsome, while if expressed, the fearsomeness remains only if the expression is given a deceptive form.[61]

Presumably, *de Silentio's* thought is that real faith is a matter of "fear and trembling." It can safely be assumed that most people, in their lucid moments, know this. But if this thought is expressed directly, in a treatise, for example, the reader will be led to appropriate this thought as an item of knowledge. "That is an excellent work," the reader may think to himself. "I can hardly wait for his next one." Presumably, however, the point behind the communication was for the reader to appropriate the thought as a possibility for himself as an existing individual. The fault here was not really the reader's; for the direct form of communication has such misunderstanding built into it (though it is quite legitimate in other spheres—mathematics, history, and such). The author did not give the process of communication enough thought. Had he done so, he might have seen the need for a slight deception. He would not have stated his

---

[60] *Ibid.*, p. 217. (Italics mine.)
[61] *Ibid.*, p. 234.

thought and his purpose directly.[62] He would have used a form that would inch his reader towards his own existence, where alone fear and trembling are real. The deception would enter in with the fact that this was his purpose, though he would not have called it by name.

We get a better grip on the idea of a contrast-form if we consider Socrates. Climacus says:

Socrates was an ethical teacher, but he took cognizance of the non-existence of any direct relationship between teacher and pupil, because the truth is inwardness, and because this inwardness is precisely the road which leads them away from one another.[63]

Now how does Socrates express himself? It was, Climacus says, because he understood that inwardness is the truth that he was so happy about his favorable outward appearance.[64] But what sort of visage did Socrates have?

..., he was very ugly, had clumsy feet, and, above all, a number of growths on the forehead and elsewhere, which would suffice to persuade anyone that he was a demoralized subject. This was what Socrates understood by his favorable appearance...[65]

Socrates was no dashing fellow who cut a fine figure, yet he reckons this an asset. Why?

Why was this old teacher so happy over his favorable appearance, *unless it was because he understood that it must help to keep the learner at a distance*, so that the latter might not stick fast in a direct relationship to the teacher, perhaps admire him, perhaps have his clothes cut in the same manner.[66]

Socrates' appearance is an advantage because it keeps the learner at a healthy distance. It is thus compatible with "the subtle principle that the personalities must be held devoutly apart from one another, and not permitted to fuse or coagulate into objectivity." [67] But this is one expression of the principle that inwardness is the truth. Socrates' appearance

---

[62] Climacus refuses to make any pronouncement about *de Silentio*'s purposes: "How things really are with Johannes *de Silentio* I cannot of course tell with certainty, since I do not know him personally; and even if I did, I am not precisely disposed to believe that he would wish to make a fool of himself by giving a direct communication. *Post.*, p. 234.

[63] *Post.*, p. 221.

[64] *Ibid.*

[65] *Ibid.*, p. 222.

[66] *Ibid.* (Italics mine.)

[67] *Ibid.*, p. 73. Cf. above p. 180.

helps to prevent the learner from establishing a direct relationship. It might even prompt someone to say: "He is such an ugly man. How can he possibly have anything worthwhile to say?" A learner would have to overcome any fondness for externalities if he is to learn from Socrates. It will require seriousness of purpose and earnestness to get close to him. But these are the match-sticks which can ignite the ethical flame.

Then there is the matter of Socrates' irony:

Through the repellent effect exerted by the *contrast*, which on a higher plane was also the rôle played by his irony, the learner would be compelled to understand that he had essentially to do with himself, and that the inwardness of the truth is not the comradely inwardness with which two friends walk arm in arm, but the separation with which each for himself exists in the truth.[68]

In their tendency to repel the would-be learner, Socrates' form and his irony help to prevent a direct and immediate relationship between the two. They are thus conducive to the learner's coming to understand that inwardness is the truth and to Socrates' maintaining this understanding within himself. This is what is achieved by the contrast-form in the realm of the written word.[69]

The author of *Repetition*, Constantine Constantius, made use of this form:

In this book there is no dogmatizing, far from it; this is precisely what I had wished, since it was in my view the misfortune of the age to have too much knowledge, to have forgotten to exist, and what inwardness is. Under such circumstances *it is desirable that an author should know how to withdraw himself*, and for this purpose a confusing contrast-form is always usable.[70]

A "confusing" contrast-form (which must be distinguished from a "confused" one) would be one which keeps the reader off-balance, thus preventing him from establishing a direct relationship to the book, summarizing it in one sentence, etc. The particular contrast-form used in *Repetition* is the experiment:

Repetition was called "a psychological experiment" on the title-page. That this was a doubly reflected communication form soon became clear to me. By taking place in the form of an experiment, the communication creates opposition for itself, and the experiment establishes a yawning chasm between reader and author, posits the

---

[68] *Ibid.*, p. 222.

[69] Interesting in this connection are Climacus' reflections on the Lessing-Jacobi affair. Cf. *Post.*, pp. 91-97.

[70] *Post.*, p. 235. (Italics mine.)

separation of inwardness between them, so that an immediate understanding is rendered impossible.[71]

An "experiment," since it makes no claims, is difficult to appropriate directly.

In *Repetition*, Constantius introduces the reader to a young man in the early pages. "It was about a year ago I began to bestow serious attention upon a young man with whom already I had had some contact...," he writes.[72] The reader will thus assume that there actually is such a young man. But at the very end of the essay, Constantius leads the reader to think that this young man is really his own invention: "The young man whom I have brought into being is a poet." [73] What, then, is the reader to think? Is there such a young man or not? "It's all a bit confusing," the reader may think to himself.

Yet this confusion is not accidental. Walter Lowrie demonstrates one sort of reaction:

In the same way Frater Taciturnus in the *Stages* would make one believe at the end that the young man, Quidam, whom he had depicted so realistically, and also the diary which he fished out of the lake, were figments of his imagination. Of course such *mystification* is characteristic of S.K.'s "intriguing pate," but in this instance *it is clear enough* that he was intent upon establishing an alibi, that is to say, he desired to distract attention from *the only too obvious autobiographical* character of this work by representing that this very real young man had no historical existence but was merely his invention, or rather that he was even more remote from reality, being the invention of the character whom he invented, Constantine Constantius.[74]

Lowrie offers a simple explanation. By calling the work an experiment, Kierkegaard is simultaneously enabled to indulge his fondness for mystification and to cloak the autobiographical character of the work. This appraisal witnesses to the poverty of the historical approach in dealing with such intricate subjects as the form of a communication. Climacus' explanation of why an author might utilize an experiment is superior to Lowrie's:

The experiment constitutes the conscious, challenging recall of the communication, which is always of importance for an existing individual who writes for existing individuals, to prevent the situation being altered so as to become that of a prater writing for praters.[75]

[71] *Ibid.*

[72] Søren Kierkegaard, *Repetition*, trans. with intro. and notes Walter Lowrie (New York, Evanston, and London, 1964), p. 35.

[73] *Ibid.*, p. 134.

[74] Walter Lowrie, "Editor's Notes," *Repetition*, p. 142, *n.* 93. (Italics mine.)

[75] *Post.*, p. 235.

The experiment can have the effect of "recalling" the individual to his own existence by pushing the reader away from the author. An experiment leaves no coattails for the reader to latch on to. Climacus explains the point in greater detail:

> If a man were to stand on one leg, or pose in a queer dancing attitude swinging his hat, and in this attitude propound something true, his few auditors would divide themselves into two groups; and many listeners he would not have, since most men would give him up at once.[76]

And so when an author avoids the conventional literary forms (the systematic treatise, the encyclopedia, the *Zeitschrift*) for communication and uses instead an experiment, many a reader will not be bothered. An earnest effort would be required to open the cover. Then:

> The one class would say: "How can what he says be true, when he gesticulates in that fashion?" The other class would say: "Well, whether he cuts capers or stands on his head, even if he were to throw handsprings, what he says is true and I propose to appropriate it, *letting him go*." [77]

So with a work like *Repetition,* the reader who makes his way through the work and finds that it is an experiment will fall into one of two groups. Either he will say: "Anyone who contrives in such a fashion cannot have anything worthwhile to say." Or he may say: "What difference does it make whether he has invented the young man in question or described a real one. I propose to make what I can from the work, forgetting about its author."

The importance, generally, of the contrast-form is that it establishes a distance between author and reader. The experiment, as one type of contrast-form, has additional assets:

> So also with the experiment. If the utterance is earnest in the writer, he preserves the earnestness essentially for himself; if the recipient apprehends it as earnest, he does it essentially by himself, and this precisely is the earnestness.... The interposition of the experiment is favorable to the inwardness of the two in its tendency *away from one another in inwardness. This form completely gained my approval,* and I thought also to discover therein that the pseudonymous authors constantly had *existence* in view, and thus maintained an indirect polemic against speculative philosophy. *When a man knows everything, but knows it by rote, the experimental form is a good instrument of exploration; one may tell him even what he knows in this form, and he will not even recognize it.*[78]

---

[76] *Ibid.,* pp. 235-36.
[77] *Ibid.,* p. 236. (Italics mine.)
[78] *Ibid.* Climacus italicizes "existence" and "away from one another in inwardness." The other italics are added for emphasis.

Hopefully our extended discussion of the contrast-form and the experiment as a communication-form will enable us to understand why these forms gained Climacus' approval.[79]

Recall that Climacus' analysis of the relationship between philosophy and Christianity culminated in several thoughts. He came to the conclusion that the relationship between the two was in fact a mis-relationship: in reducing faith to a relative moment, speculative philosophy vitiates Christianity. The reason, in turn, for this is that because of the great increase in knowledge, men had forgotten what it means to *exist*. They are unable to understand that Christianity is "not a doctrine but an existential communication expressing an existential contradiction." [80]

The *Fragments* was Climacus' first response to the situation. "The reader of the bit of philosophy presented in the *Fragments* will remember," Climacus states, "that the piece was not doctrinal but *experimental*." [81] Climacus uses an experiment to show that Christianity and philosophy are at loggerheads on every crucial issue. Had he stated this belief dogmatically, in a treatise, it would be appropriated as an item of knowledge. Hence the need for an indirect form. The experiment is such a form which, moreover, has the added feature that one can use such a form to tell a man what he already knows, and he will not recognize it. Those to whom the *Fragments* addresses itself would surely think that they "knew" what Christianity was. The very word would trigger a whole set of responses. Thus Climacus abstained from mentioning Christianity by name (until the very end [82]) and from using the Christian terminology. This move was designed to gain breathing space for the author and the reader both and to give the reader a chance to draw the conclusion *for himself* that Christianity and philosophy are different. Referring to his *Fragments,* Climacus writes:

Whether I succeeded, in this little piece, in the task of indirectly connecting Christianity with existence, and by the use of an indirect form was enabled to bring it to the attention of the informed reader, whose misfortune perhaps it was that he was too well informed, I shall not attempt to decide.[83]

---

[79] Such forms make the reviewer's task very hazardous. Climacus can therefore understand why the pseudonymous authors have asked not to be reviewed (*Post.,* p. 252) and also why these authors "are fully justified in contenting themselves with a few actual readers" (*Ibid.*).

[80] *Post.,* p. 339.

[81] *Ibid.,* p. 323. (Italics mine.)

[82] This is explained in the *Postscript.* Cf. pp. 323-29.

[83] *Post.,* p. 244.

If Climacus was successful, his reader will find himself facing another question: "How does one become a Christian?" In the *Postscript*, Climacus again uses the experimental form to raise this question. He states:

Whether there really exists or has existed such a religious person..., whether all are religious or no one is, I do not propose to decide, nor would it be at all possible for me to decide.... But surely I may be permitted the satisfaction of sitting here and experimenting, to see how such a religious individual would conduct his life, without in speculative fashion committing myself to the paralogism of inferring existence from the hypothetical...; much less concluding from my hypothetical thinking that it is myself, by virtue of the identity of thought and being. My experiment is as innocent as possible, far, far from affronting anyone; for it is not so personal as to say about anyone that he is a religious person, and it does not offend anyone by denying that he is religious. *It establishes the possibility that everyone is religious—* with the exception of those who cannot be offended,...[84]

Climacus' experiment decides nothing and has no result which a reader can appropriate directly. It raises a possibility (the aim of any communication between existing individuals [85]) and places a "yawning chasm" [86] between the author and the reader which enables each to investigate the possibility in his own inwardness.

Both the *Fragments* and the *Postscript* are ticketed with the same phrase: "*proprio Marte, propriis auspiciis, proprio stipendio.*" [87] Climacus writes both of them "on his own behalf." They are both, in an important sense, self-serving; for "the problem concerns myself alone; partly because, if it is properly posed, it will concern everyone else in the same manner;..." [88] The *Postscript* exhibits the difficulties—*as seen through the eyes of one man*—involved in becoming a Christian, showing them to be even greater than the ones involved in becoming subjective. Climacus states:

My opinion is that religiousness A (within the boundaries of which I have my existence) is so laborious that it is always enough of a task. My purpose is to make it difficult to become a Christian, yet not more difficult than it is,... This is my purpose—in such a sense, that is to say, as an experimenter who does everything for his own sake can be said to have a purpose.[89]

---

[84] *Ibid.*, p. 457. (Italics mine.)
[85] Cf. above pp. 181-82.
[86] *Post.*, p. 235. Cf. above p.
[87] *Frag.*, p. 3; *Post.*, p. 6.
[88] *Post.*, p. 20.
[89] *Ibid.*, p. 495.

But now the *Postscript* begins to look very much like a direct communication. It has a statement of the author's purpose and his conclusion. What is to prevent the reader from appropriating this work directly, as an item of knowledge?

The *Postscript* also contains an appendix which bears the subtitle: "For an Understanding with the Reader." In it, Climacus describes the kind of reader he would hope to have:

> He understand at once and line by line; he has the patience not to skip over subordinate clauses or to hasten from the woof of the episode to the warp of the table of contents; he can hold out as long as the author;...[90]

Unfortunately, Climacus' fate seems to have been to attract a very different sort of reader—one who is not able to hold out as long as the author. Without some such assumption, it is difficult to account for the fact that this remarkable little appendix (which contains some very important words) has gone virtually unnoticed.

Climacus begins by reaffirming his standpoint as a humorist, claiming to be "content with his situation at the moment, hoping that something higher may be granted him,..." [91] We are now in a position to see claerly that there is hard logic in the fact that it is a humorist who raises the question of how to become a Christian and makes the claim that men have forgotten what it means to *exist*. That is, given the theory of the existence-spheres, let us inquire: In which sphere of existence are such questions appropriate? Could they, for example, have been raised by someone in the aesthetic sphere? No, because such an individual is too involved in the pursuit of pleasure—a pursuit which deprives him of that sense of himself as an existing individual which gives the question (How do I become a Christian?) its anchor. The individual in the ethical sphere knows what it means to *exist* and hence could conceivably raise the question. But he is totally occupied in the task of existing and does not have the leisure time necessary to speculate, for example, about the relationship between philosophy and Christianity. The Christian, as such, is engaged in holding fast to the Teacher.

To undertake the projects carried out in the *Fragments* and the *Postscript,* an individual would have to know what it means to *exist* (else he could not make the claim that men have forgotten what this means); he would have to have read a fair amount of the philosophy of that time (else he could not hope to analyze the relationship between speculative

---

[90] *Ibid.,* p. 548.
[91] *Ibid.,* p. 545.

philosophy and Christianity); and he would have to live on the boundary
of the ethical sphere (else he could not seriously entertain the possibility
of becoming a Christian); he would have to understand what it means
to exist in time and yet have enough leisure to undertake an authorship.
Who is such an individual? In terms of the theory of the spheres of
existence, he is a humorist. He alone fulfills these requirements.

Let us turn, for a moment, to Kierkegaard. In "A First and Last
Declaration," he says this:

My pseudonymity or polynymity has not had a casual [sic] ground in my person
(certainly it was not for fear of a legal penalty,...), but it has an *essential* ground
in the character of the *production*,... which is bounded only ideally by psychological
consistency,...[92]

Our study has never denied that Kierkegaard is ultimately responsible
for the *Postscript*. He is responsible for it in the sense that he brought
it into existence to serve a purpose. But his reflections about that purpose
convinced him that it could best be served with the use of pseudonymous
points of view. It was, then, no jejune fondness for mystification nor yet
the desire to conceal his own personal life that led him to use the Climacus-
pseudonym in order to analyze the relationship between philosophy and
Christianity and to raise the problem of becoming a Christian. Our
analysis suggests rather that he did so, as he said, in order to meet the
requirement of psychological consistency—to insure a fit between the
"what" and the "how." [93]

In the appendix, then, Climacus reaffirms his standpoint as a humorist.
He states that he is "completely taken up with the thought how difficult
it must be to be a Christian;..." [94] The indirect message here is this: If
the reader thinks that being a Christian is a relatively easy matter, then
there is an important difference between his thinking and Climacus'. But
Climacus leaves the matter there. If a reader should want to discover
where the disagreement lies, he must pursue the matter himself.

The *Postscript*, then, raises the question of how one becomes a
Christian, yet not in the ordinary way:

In the aloofness of the experiment the whole work has to do with me myself, solely
and simply with me.... I ask only for my own sake, yes, certainly that I do, or
rather I have asked this question, for that indeed is the content of the whole work.
Let no one put himself out to say that *the book is entirely superfluous* and quite

---

[92] *Declaration*, p. 551.
[93] *Post.*, p. 544.
[94] *Ibid.*, p. 545.

irrelevant to the times—unless in the end he has to say something, for in that case he pronounces the wished-for judgement, which indeed I have already passed upon the author.[95]

Climacus is perfectly willing to agree with a reader who would indict him for writing a book which is superfluous. But let us not be over-hasty in interpreting his readiness. For on the next page, we read these words:

So then the book is superfluous; *let no one therefore take the pains to appeal to it as an authority; for he who thus appeals to it has eo ipso misunderstood it.*[96]

These are strong words. What kind of book is this if one cannot appeal to it, cite its pages, quote its author? Does this mean that an individual who says "As Climacus says in the *Postscript,...*" has misunderstood the work? On the next page, Climacus "goes further":

As in Catholic books, especially those of an earlier age, one finds at the back of the volume a note which informs the reader that everything is to be understood conformably with the doctrine of the Holy Catholic Mother Curch—*so what I write contains also a piece of information to the effect that everything is so to be understood that it is understood to be revoked, and the book has not only a Conclusion but a Revocation.*[97]

This may sound like gibberish, yet Climacus is confident that the right kind of reader will understand him. Such a reader:

...can understand that understanding is revocation; he can understand that to write a book and revoke it is something else than not writing it at all; that to write a book which does not claim importance for anybody is something else than leaving it unwritten,...[98]

How are we to understand this Revocation? How is the reader to "understand that understanding is revocation"? We propose the following interpretation.

Recall that in the second section of this chapter, we quoted *The Point of View* to the effect that "...the indirect method...arranges everything dialectically for the prospective captive, and then...withdraws..., so as not to witness the admission which he makes to himself alone..." [99] Climacus' Revocation bears striking similarities to such a withdrawal. In

---

[95] *Ibid.* (Italics mine.)
[96] *Ibid.,* p. 546. (Italics mine.)
[97] *Ibid.,* p. 547 (Italics mine.)
[98] *Ibid.,* p. 548.
[99] *POV,* pp. 25-26. The answer to the question as to whether the *Postscript* is direct or indirect communication is implicit here.

order to understand this, we reintroduce the metaphor cited in Chapter I. In the original preface to his *Fragments,* Climacus had written:

...; I feel a little like a poor lodger who has a little room in the attic of a huge build-ing which is constantly being enlarged and beautified while to his terror he thinks he discovers that the foundation is cracking (changed to: *thinks he discovers a mis-understanding which, however, no one is concerned about);...*[100]

The huge building of this metaphor symbolizes the sphere of objective thought and knowledge. The fact that he places himself in a little room in the attic signifies Climacus' acknowledgement that he, too, is involved in objective thought. Yet his involvement is different in kind both from that of one helping to enlarge and beautify the structure and that of one who would tear it down. Though he dwells temporarily in this little room, his real home is elsewhere—a simple single-occupancy dwelling.

Climacus "thinks" he has seen a crack in the foundation of this huge edifice. Less metaphorically, Climacus believes that due to the great increase in knowledge, men have forgotten what it means to *exist.* What caused this rupture, Climacus does not say. Perhaps it was the fact that this magnificent building was never supposed to be a home for so many men. It began as a statue, an avocation. Through a mis-understanding, many men now think of it as their home. This is what it means to forget: each man has a home of his own.

Now suppose Climacus decided to share his thoughts with someone. Suppose that "...whenever he communicated his doubts to someone he perceived that his speech, because of its departure from the prevailing fashion, was regarded as the bizarre and threadbare costume of some unfortunate derelict—..." [101] Such a man is up against real difficulties. If he wishes to communicate anything at all on this point, he must proceed with caution. Climacus has said:

I will be quite frank about it; my conception of communication by means of books is very different from what I generally see put forward respecting it, and from what seems silently to be taken for granted. The indirect mode of communication makes communication an art in quite different a sense than when it is conceived in the usual manner: that the maker of the communication has to present something to the attention of one who knows, that he may judge it, or to the attention of one who does not know, that he may learn something. But no one bothers himself about the next consideration, that which makes communication dialectically so difficult, namely, that the recipient is an existing individual, and that this is essential.[102]

[100] Thulstrup, *Commentary,* p. 153. Cf. Chapter I, pp. 32-33.
[101] *Post.,* p. 59.
[102] *Ibid.,* pp. 246-47.

In an earlier section of this chapter, we discussed certain principles which must govern the process of communication between existing individuals.[103] One of those was to the effect that the author of the communication must consider the possible effects of his communication on the recipient. He must understand, as best he can, the circumstances of the recipient.

In light of these reflections, let us ask: To whom might Climacus communicate his doubts? Presumably it would be very difficult to get the attention of those who are busily engaged in the task of enlarging the structure. If he could, it is not very likely that they would give him the time he might need to communicate his doubts. Presumably his best chance of getting a hearing would be with those who have not yet assumed an active role in the enlarging and beautifying, but who have the interest and the skills which will enable them to take such a role at some future time. We might call these the apprentices, recalling that Climacus has described his readers as "those who deem themselves possessed of leisure and talent for a deeper inquiry." [104]

How is Climacus to go about getting a hearing? He says:

To stop a man on the street and stand still while talking to him, is not so difficult as to say something to a passer-by in passing, without standing still and without delaying the other, without attempting to persuade him to go the same way, but giving him an impulse to go precisely his own way. Such is the relation between one existing individual and another, when the communication concerns the truth as existential inwardness.[105]

Recasting these thoughts in terms of the metaphor we are using, we can see that Climacus must dismiss any thought of picketing the construction site. Brute force is no solution either. If he attempts to seize the apprentice and carry him away, this may simply increase the young man's determination.

The apprentice, it may be assumed, must do a fair amount of reading in order to prepare for his future tasks. It is here that Climacus would have to make contact with him. That is to say, Climacus might author a book which contains *his* reflections about this magnificent structure. It would contain a blueprint which shows where the foundation is cracking—or better, where he thinks the crack is to be found. It might contain in addition a description of two other buildings, perhaps more

[103] Cf. above pp. 176-82.
[104] *Post.*, p. 152, *n.* Cf. Chapter I, p. 32.
[105] *Post.*, p. 247.

humble in their conception and style. The description of the first of these would make clear the author's conviction that every individual has the task of building such a dwelling and living in it. It is to be his own home, but one that he alone can build. For this, in a sense, is how Climacus describes the task of *existing* as an individual human being. The other dwelling is also a single-occupancy dwelling. Building it is an even more difficult task and one that Climacus does not claim to have achieved. For this, in a sense, is how Climacus described the task of becoming a Christian. (The reader might recognize this second dwelling as one which other architects have described as one floor—not the top one either—of the huge edifice under construction.)

There is no guarantee that any of the apprentices will read such a work. If one of them does, he will not find it easy reading. He will need "courage and strength" [106] if he is to persist through to the end, for such a work is certain to challenge his most basic convictions. In the end, he comes upon the Revocation. He receives, that is to say, "an impulse to go precisely his own way." [107] For how else can he discover whether or not there is a crack in the foundation? If this is to happen, he must at some point put this work down in order to *see for himself*. In the beginning, the apprentice had to make an effort to take this contrary work seriously. Now he must make an effort to lay the work down. For as long as his attention is riveted on the work, he will never discover the crack in the structure. The *Postscript,* we may say, suggests where to look and how to go about it. But the reader must do the looking for himself.

Less metaphorically, one *understands* the *Postscript* only when he is ready to dispense with it, when he sees that it is superfluous, that it cannot possibly do his work for him. In this way, finally, he will understand that "understanding is revocation." In order to understand the *Postscript,* its reader must come to see how unimportant and superfluous it truly is.

In light of this discussion, we can now appreciate the sense and significance of the term "mimic" in the sub-title of the *Postscript*. First, the term is descriptive. Climacus, using himself by way of illustration, is acting out or "miming" the difficulties involved in the decision to become a Christian. He chooses this form rather than a systematic discussion, for it enables him to keep one eye on existence—his own

---

[106] *Ibid.,* p. 167.
[107] Cf. above p. 206.

existence. The reader may thereby be encouraged to do the same. Climacus' reflections may serve as a kind of example.

But, secondly, the term is also an admonition—a warning to the reader. Climacus knew that in becoming an author he was taking a considerable risk. The reader's attention and interest will, for the moment at least, be focussed on something other than his own existence— i.e., on the *Postscript*. Yet a considerable part of Climacus' goal is to get his reader to take a careful look at his own existence. We have seen this paradox several times. In terms of the metaphor used in the introductory section of this chapter, we could say that Climacus' task was to prepare a meal for the man who loves eating—a meal which will get him to stop eating, at least for a while.[108] Preparation of such a meal would call for great skill, since few cookbooks would contain a recipe for a meal which would both satisfy and inhibit a man's appetite. Special ingredients would have to be added. Less metaphorically, Climacus' had the task of writing a book for a reader who loves to read and to think, who perhaps enjoys this too much. The *Postscript* contains several "ingredients" which may serve to check his craving, while yet giving him "an impulse to go his own way." [109] One of these is the Revocation, in which Climacus, in effect, takes the book away. Another is this term "mimic," which presumes to warn the reader that the problems and difficulties treated in the pages of the *Postscript* are only *imitations* of the real ones which are to be found in the reader's own existence. By terming the *Postscript* "a mimic composition," Climacus is saying—both to himself and to his reader—"Don't mistake this for the real thing." "More than this no one can require, either before or after." [110]

The *Postscript*, then, can best be described as a work which "arranges everything dialectically for the prospective captive, and then—withdraws..." [111] It is indirect, offering no result to which the reader can attach himself. As Climacus says, the indirect method reaches its goal slowly:

But speed is of no value whatever in connection with a form of understanding in which the inwardness is the understanding. To me it seems better to reach a true mutual understanding in inwardness separately, though this might take place slowly.

---

[108] Cf. above pp. 173-74.
[109] Cf. above p. 206.
[110] *Post.*, p. 547.
[111] Cf. above p. 175.

Indeed, even if this never happened, because the time passed and the author was forgotten without anyone having understood him, to me it seems more consistent not to have made the slightest accommodation in order to get anyone to understand him, first and last so tending to his own self as not to make himself important in relation to others,... If he acts in this manner he will have the solace in the day of judgement, when God is the judge, that he has indulged himself in nothing for the sake of winning someone, but with the utmost exertion has labored in vain, leaving it to God to determine whether it was to have any significance or not.[112]

In the next chapter, we shall assess the significance of Climacus' labors.

[112] *Post.,* p. 247.

CHAPTER VII

CONCLUSION

The aim of this study has been to present the fundamental insights of the *Concluding Unscientific Postscript* into human existence. Before our eyes throughout has been this one question: What does it mean to exist as an individual human being? We have deliberately departed from the traditional method of interpretation in that we have attributed this work not to Kierkegaard himself but to its pseudonymous author— Johannes Climacus. We must now ask: What is the philosophical value of Climacus' analysis of human existence?

The philosopher will not find that Climacus offers any new insights into human existence. The philosopher undoubtedly knows that each human being has responsibilities to himself which he alone can meet and that he must meet them within the limited time and with the limited powers he has at his disposal. This is the basic insight of the *Postscript*. Climacus is pleased to acknowledge that this is "neither more nor less than what pretty much every man knows," since he does not claim to be a teacher, but rather a learner, in the art of existence.

What, then, is there of philosophical value here? We answered this question partially at the end of Chapter III. Climacus develops and refines this basic insight in such a way as to expose a dangerous philosophical tendency—the tendency to apotheosize philosophical reflection and knowledge. Not every man can reflect about world-history and the course of Absolute Spirit. But every man can reflect upon himself as an individual human being and upon the course of his life. Climacus calls this kind of reflection "subjective thinking," and his insistence that this is the form of thinking that a man must use in order to meet his responsibilities to himself exposes the tendency of philosophers to absolutize philosophical reflection. The most direct (and most dangerous) result of this tendency is the notion that a truly human existence is possible for some—but not all—human beings. Climacus opposes this notion by "holding fast to what it means to be a human being," by placing himself in what we have termed *the basic human posture* and insisting that the possibility of a truly human existence is open to every human being.

In the last two chapters, we have unfolded another dimension of Climacus' treatment of human existence. We can best summarize and appraise this dimension by first considering a metaphor which he himself uses often. Consider, then, the activity of eating. A man must eat in order to live. But more than this, eating can also be pleasurable. Who has not experienced the joys of a midnight snack? Once in a while, however, a man eats too much. He gets indigestion; cramps set in—Nature's little reminders that moderation is the best policy. So we learn the art of eating moderately. Those who do not—those for whom over-indulgence is a way of life—grow fat, develop various illnesses, even die.

All of this is true of thinking as well. A man must think in order to live. Yet thinking has its pleasures. Are we to say, however, that overindulgence is not a danger here, too? We may concede that philosophical reflection is the highest of human activities—comparable to French cuisine in the gastronomic order—and yet hold that it can be overdone. A man can have *too much knowledge,* Climacus would remind the philosopher. He calls the illness which results from this excess "forgetting what it means to exist" and describes many of its symptoms. Thus Climacus would have us attend to an individual's manner of speaking. If he is forever saying "we" and "our age" and "philosophy," this can be a sign that he has lost the ability to say "I," to speak with his own voice as an existing individual. In detecting and describing this illness to which philosophers are susceptible, Climacus has rendered an important service to philosophy.

There is a certain irony here. Normally the thinker's concern is that his powers of reflection may prove inadequate to the difficult tasks he has set for himself. Climacus would warn him of the dangers of being successful. For the path of objective reflection is an endless one—"from China to Persia, then to astronomy, and on to the veterinary sciences," as Climacus would say. Yet all the while he is engaged in these tasks, his own existence and its tasks may go unattended. Climacus insists that thinking must be seen as the activity of the individual human being. As such, it is or ought to be subject to a decision, to "the inspection of the ethical." The thinker must relate his activities to his own existence. For no matter how glorious his goal, the thinker remains always an existing individual with the same responsibilities to himself that other individuals have.

Yet Climacus realizes the very limited nature of what one man can do for another in those matters wherein each man has essentially to do with himself. None of these insights have any value unless the individual puts them to work in his own existence. The author of the *Postscript* had no illusions about his labors and their possible significance. This is the real force of his Revocation at the end. Climacus has arranged the situation dialectically for his reader and then withdrawn. The *Postscript* may enable its reader to "separate the philosopher from the philosophy," to begin to recover—if he believes he has lost it—his own voice as one individual human being. But this can happen, Climacus is aware, only if the individual puts the *Postscript* down in order to look for himself. Once the reader has returned to existence as his scene, however, the *Postscript* is no longer needed.

It is interesting, then, to compare the *Postscript* with a work like the *Critique of Pure Reason,* of which Kant wrote:

It is, at the same time, a powerful appeal to reason to undertake anew the most difficult of all duties, namely, self-knowledge, and to institute a court of appeal which should protect the just rights of reason, but dismiss all groundless claims, and should do this not by means of irresponsible decrees, but according to the unalterable laws of reason. This court of appeal is no other than the *Critique of Pure Reason.*[1]

We have already seen Climacus' opinion of the *Postscript:* "So then the book is superfluous; let no one therefore take the pains to appeal to it as an authority; for he who thus appeals to it has *eo ipso* misunderstood it."[2] The contrast could hardly be more striking.

The philosopher to whom Climacus seems closest in spirit is Wittgenstein. Climacus' Revocation calls to mind one of the final paragraphs of the *Tractatus Logico-Philosophicus:*

My propositions serve as elucidations in the following way: anyone who understands me eventually recognizes them as nonsensical, when he has used them—as steps—to climb up beyond them. (He must, so to speak, throw away the ladder after he has climbed up it.)[3]

Both Climacus and Wittgenstein want to emancipate the reader from misunderstandings. As different as those misunderstandings are, the

---

[1] Immanuel Kant, *The Critique of Pure Reason,* trans. F. Max Müller, 2nd. ed. (Garden City, 1961), p. 21.

[2] *Post.,* p. 546.

[3] Ludwig Wittgenstein, *Tractatus Logico-Philosophicus,* trans. D. F. Pears and B. F. McGuinness (London, 1961), p. 151 (6.54).

approach is strikingly similar. Each puts his own thoughts on paper only to withdraw them in the end. Each maintains that the reader who understands what he has read will have no further need of it. Having finished the *Tractatus,* Wittgenstein quit philosophy. The *Postscript,* too, was a finishing touch. Kierkegaard intended to end his authorship at this point and to become a priest in the Lutheran church. Although he subsequently resumed the authorship, Kierkegaard never returned to philosophical issues in the manner of the *Postscript.* Climacus is never heard from again, and from 1847 on the authorship is devoted almost entirely to Christian issues.

Wittgenstein did return to philosophy, and his latter philosophy still displays similarities to Climacus'. Both wish to stimulate the reader to do his own thinking:

It is not impossible that it should fall to the lot of this work, in its poverty and in the darkness of this time, to bring light into one brain or another—but, of course, it is not likely.
I should not like my writing to spare other people the trouble of thinking. But, if possible, to stimulate someone to thoughts of his own.[4]

Referring to another work (but in a way that makes it clear that the same applies to his own), Climacus says: "If is thus left to the reader himself to put two and two together, if he so desires; but nothing is done to minister to a reader's indolence." [5] Both Climacus and Wittgenstein treat the reader as potentially the victim of an illness whose cure is arduous business and requires patience. "In philosophizing," Wittgenstein says, "we may not terminate a disease of thought. It must run its natural course, and *slow* cure is all important." [6] Speaking of the medicine he is prescribing, Climacus says:

...when one takes medicine, one is accustomed...to getting a *douceur* along with it. I am so far from failing to understand this, that if I were (as being a *subjective* author I am not) objectively convinced of the medicine I offer, and believed that it did not depend simply and solely upon the way in which it is used, so that the way is really the medicine, I should be the first to promise my readers a reasonable *douceur*...in order in this way to instill in them the strength and courage required for reading my books.[7]

---

[4] Wittgenstein, *PI,* p. x.

[5] *Post.,* pp. 264-65.

[6] Ludwig Wittgenstein, *Zettel,* ed. G. E. M. Anscombe and G. H. von Wright, trans. G. E. M. Anscombe (Oxford, 1967), #382.

[7] *Post.,* pp. 166-67.

Finally, both Climacus and Wittgenstein are critical of the philosophy they know best. Both insist that philosophy has limits and must, if it is to remain a human activity, acknowledge those limitations. For Wittgenstein, that limit is what he calls "forms of life." For Climacus, it is "the existing individual." To these, philosophizing must wed itself; to these, it must always return *to look and see.* Yet it is the very conspicuousness of these limiting points that makes them hardest to grasp:

The aspects of things which are most important for us are hidden because of their simplicity and familiarity. (One is unable to notice something—because it is always before one's eyes.) [8]

Climacus puts it this way:

For so men speak: in one moment they know everything, and in the next moment they do not know it. And this is the reason it is regarded as folly and singularity to bother one's head about it, and to attend to the difficulties; because everyone knows it. But what everyone does not know, so that it counts as differential knowledge, that is a glorious thing to be concerned with. What everyone knows on the other hand, so that the difference is merely the trivial one of *how* it is known, that is a waste of effort to be concerned about—for one cannot possibly become self-important through knowing it. [9]

It is perhaps fitting to allow "Magister Kierkegaard" a word or two. In a report written just after the *Postscript* was sent to press, he writes:

Without being able to appeal to revelations or anything of the kind, I have understood myself in having to stress the universal in a botched and demoralised age, in making it lovable and accessible to all others who are capable of realising it, but who are led astray by the age to chasing after the unusual and the extraordinary. [10]

We have detected just such a stress throughout this study of the treatment of existence given in the *Postscript*. Still Kierkegaard was not at all optimistic. For he adds in the margin of the above:

My merit in literature is that I have set forth the decisive qualifications of the whole compass of existence with such dialectical clarity and so originally as has not, so far as I know, been done in any other literature; neither have I had any books to help me nor upon which to draw for advice. Secondly, the art with which I have communicated it, its form, its logical accomplishment; but no one has time to read and study seriously and to that extent my production is for the moment wasted, like putting exquisite dishes in front of peasants. [11]

---

[8] Wittgenstein, *PI,* #129.

[9] *Post.,* p. 80.

[10] Dru, *Journals,* #(600); VII A 126.

[11] Dru, *Journals,* #601; VII A 127.

The *Postscript* is certainly one of these "exquisite dishes." Yet one is aware of how distressing such a judgment might be to an author who asked that no one appeal to him. Still if this study has helped to make that work—and the ideal which it serves—more accessible, then perhaps "Magister Kierkegaard" will put in a good word for us with Johannes Climacus.

BIBLIOGRAPHY

A. BIBLIOGRAPHIC

Himmelstrup, Jens. *Søren Kierkegaard International Bibliografi.* Copenhagen: Nyt Nordisk Forlag, 1962.

B. PRIMARY SOURCES

1. *Danish:*

Kierkegaard, Søren. *Samlede Vaerker.* Edited by A. B. Drachmann, J. L. Heibert and H. O. Lange, 3rd ed. with text and notes revised by Peter P. Rohde, and with a terminological dictionary by Jens Himmelstrup. 20 vols. Copenhagen: Gyldendalske Boghandel, Nordisk Forlag, 1962-64. Vols. 7, 20.

2. *German:*

Kierkegaard, Søren. *Gesammelte Werke.* 26 vols. Dusseldorf and Koln: Eugen Diedrichs Verlag, 1950-1962. Abt. 16.

3. *English:*

a. Works by Kierkegaard

Attack Upon Christendom. Translated by Walter Lowrie. Boston: Beacon Press, 1959.
The Concept of Dread. Translated by Walter Lowrie. Princeton: Princeton University Press, 1957.
Concluding Unscientific Postscript to the Philosophical Fragments. Translated by David F. Swenson and Walter Lowrie. Princeton: Princeton University Press, 1941.
Edifying Discourses. 2 vols. Translated by David F. and Lillian Marvin Swenson. Introduction by Paul Holmer. Minneapolis: Augsburg Publishing House, 1962.
Either/Or. 2 vols. Vol. I translated by David F. and Lillian Marvin Swenson. Vol. II translated by Walter Lowrie. Both revised by Howard A. Johnson. Garden City, New York: Doubleday, 1955.
Fear and Trembling and The Sickness Unto Death. Translated by Walter Lowrie. Revised edition. Garden City, New York: Doubleday, 1959.
Johannes Climacus or *De Omnibus Dubitandum Est* and *A Sermon.* Translated with an Assessment by T. H. Croxall. London: Adam and Charles Black, 1958.
On Authority and Revelation. Translated and edited by Walter Lowrie. Introduction

by Frederich Sontag. New York: Harper and Row, 1966.

Philosophical Fragments. Translated with an Introduction by David F. Swenson. New Introduction and Commentary by Niels Thulstrup. Translatio1 revised and Commentary translated by Howard V. Hong. Princeton: Princeton University Press, 1962.

The Point of View for My Work as an Author and Related Writings. Translated with an Introduction and Notes by Walter Lowrie. Newly edited with a preface by Benjamin Nelson. New York: Harper and Brothers, 1962.

Repetition. Translated with Introduction and Notes by Walter Lowrie. New York: Harper and Row, 1964.

Stages on Life's Way. Translated by Walter Lowrie. Princeton: Princeton University Press, 1955.

b. Journals and Papers

The Diary of Søren Kierkegaard. Edited by Peter P. Rohde. Translated by Gerda M. Anderson. New York: Philosophical Library, 1960.

The Journal of Søren Kierkegaard. A selection edited and translated by Alexander Dru. London: Oxford University Press, 1959.

The Last Years Journals: 1853-1855. Edited and translated by Ronald Gregor Smith. New York: Harper and Row, 1965.

Søren Kierkegaard's Journals and Papers. Vol. I, A.-E. Edited and translated by Howard V. and Edna O. Hong, assisted by Gregor Malantschuk. Bloomington, Indiana: Indiana University Press, 1958.

C.   SECONDARY LITERATURE

1. *Books:*

a. Works on Kierkegaard

Arbaugh, George E. and George B. *Kierkegaard's Authorship.* London: George Allen & Unwin, 1968.

Bohlin, Torsten. *Kierkegaards dogmatische Anschauung in ihrem geschichtlichen Zusammenhange.* Translated into German by Ilse Meyer-Lüne. Gütersloh: Bertelsmann, 1927.

Collins, James. *The Existentialists. Chicago: Regnery,* 1950.

—. *The Mind of Kierkegaard.* Chicago, Regnery, 1953.

Croxall, T. H. *Kierkegaard Commentary.* New York: Harper and Brothers, 1956.

—. *Kierkegaard Studies.* New York: Roy Publishers, 1956.

Dewey, Bradley. *The New Obedience: Kierkegaard on Imitating Christ.* Introduction by Paul Holmer. Washington: Corpus Publications, 1968.

Diem, Herman. *Kierkegaard: An Introduction.* Richmond: John Knox Press, 1966.

—. *Kierkegaard's Dialectic of Existence.* Translated by Harold Knight. London and Edinburgh: Oliver and Boyd, 1959.

Dupré, Louis. *Kierkegaard as Theologian. London:* Sheed and Ward, 1964.

Garelick, Herbert. *The Anti-Christianity of Kierkegaard.* The Hague: Martinus Nijhoff, 1965.

Geismar, Eduard. *Lectures on the Religious Thought of Søren Kierkegaard.* Minneapolis, Augsburg Publishing House, 1937.

Gill, Jerry H., ed. *Essays on Kierkegaard*. Minneapolis: Burgess Publishing Company, 1969.

Haecker, Theodor. *Søren Kierkegaard*. Translated by Alexander Dru. London: Oxford University Press, 1937.

—. *Kierkegaard the Cripple*. Translated by C. Van O. Bruyn. London: Harvill Press, 1948.

Hamilton, Kenneth. *The Promise of Kierkegaard*. The Promise of Theology Series. Edited by Martin E. Marty. Philadelphia and New York: J. B. Lippincott Company, 1969.

Harper, Ralph. *The Seventh Solitude*. Baltimore: Johns Hopkins Press, 1967.

Hirsch, Emanuel, *Kierkegaard-Studien*. 2 vols. Gütersloh: C. Bertelsmann, 1930-33.

Henriksen, Aage. *Methods and Results of Kierkegaard Studies in Scandinavia*. Copenhagen: Ejnar Munksgaard, 1951.

Johnson, Howard A. and Thulstrup, Niels, eds. *A Kierkegaard Critique*. New York: Harper, 1962.

Jolivet, Regis. *Introduction to Kierkegaard*. Translated by W. H. Barber. London: Frederick Muller, Ltd., 1950.

LeFevre, Perry D. *The Prayers of Kierkegaard*. Phoenix Books. Chicago: University of Chicago Press, 1963.

Lowrie, Walter. *Kierkegaard*. 2 vols. Harper Torchbooks. New York: Harper and Brothers, 1962.

Malantschuk, Gregor. *Kierkegaard's Way to the Truth*. Translated by Mary Michelsen. Minneapolis: Augsburg Publishing House, 1963.

Patrick, Denzil, *Pascal and Kierkegaard*. 2 vols. London: Lutterworth Press, 1947. Voll. II.

Perkins, Robert L. *Søren Kierkegaard*. Richmond: John Knox Press, 1969.

Price, George. *The Narrow Pass*. London: Hutchinson & Co., 1963.

Roubiczek, Paul. *Existentialism: For and Against*. Cambridge: Cambridge University Press, 1964.

Ruttenbeck, Walter. *Søren Kierkegaard: Der Christliche Denker und sein Werk*. Berlin and Frankfurt: Trowitzsch and Sohn, 1929.

Schrag, Calvin O. *Existence and Freedom: Towards an Ontology of Human Finitude*. Evanston: Northwestern University Press, 1961.

Sikes, Walter. *On Becoming the Truth*. St. Louis: Bethany Press, 1968.

Sponheim, Paul. *Kierkegaard on Christ and Christian Coherence*. New York and Evanston: Harper and Row, 1968.

Swenson, David F. *Something about Kierkegaard*. Minneapolis: Augsburg Publishing House, 1945.

Thomas, J. Heywood. *Subjectivity and Paradox*. Oxford: Basil Blackwell, 1957.

Thompson, Josiah. *The Lonely Labyrinth: Kierkegaard's Pseudonymous Works*. Carbondale: Southern Illinois University Press, 1967.

Thomte, H. Reidar. *Kierkegaard's Philosophy of Religion*. Princeton: Princeton University Press, 1949.

Warnock, Mary. *Existentialist Ethics*. New Studies in Ethics. Edited by W. D. Hudson. London: MacMillan and Co. Ltd., 1967.

Wild, John. *The Challenge of Existentialism*. Bloomington: Indiana University Press, 1955.

Wyschogrod, Michael. *Kierkegaard and Heidegger.* New York: The Humanities Press, 1954.

b. Works on Science

Ardrey, Robert. *African Genesis.* Laurel Edition. New York: Dell Publishing Company, 1961.

Barzun, Jacques. *Science: That Glorious Entertainment.* New York: Harper and Row, 1964.

Benjamin, A. Cornelius. *Science, Technology and Human Values.* Columbia: University of Missouri Press, 1965.

Boas, George. *The Challenge of Science.* Seattle: University of Washington Press, 1965.

Braithwaite, R. B. *Scientific Explanation.* Harper Torchbooks. New York: Harper and Brothers 1960.

Bronowski, Jacob. *The Common Sense of Science.* Pelican Books. Harmondsworth: Penguin Books, 1960.

—. *The Identity of Man.* Garden City: The Natural History Press, 1966.

Bube, Richard H., ed. *The Encounter Between Christianity and Science.* Grand Rapids: W. B. Eerdmans Publishing Company, 1968.

Bunge, Mario. *Metascientific Queries. Springfield:* Charles C. Thomas, 1959.

—. *Scientific Research I: The Search for System; Scientific Research II: The Search for Truth.* Studies in the Foundations, Methodology and Philosophy of Science. Edited by Mario Bunge. Vol. III. New York: Springer-Verlag, 1967.

Colborn, Robert, ed. *The Way of the Scientist.* New York: Simon and Schuster, 1962.

Conant, James B. *Modern Science and Modern Man.* Doubleday Anchor Books. Garden City: Doubleday, 1952.

—. *Science and Common Sense.* New Haven: Yale University Press, 1966.

d'Abro, A. *The Evolution of Scientific Thought.* 2nd ed. New York: Dover Publications, 1950.

Danto, Arthur and Morgenbesser, Sidney, eds. *Philosophy of Science.* Preface by Ernest Nagel. Meridian Books. Cleveland and New York: World Publishing Company, 1960.

Darwin, Charles. *Autobiography.* Edited by Nora Barlow. London: Collins, 1958.

Edwards, Frank. *Stranger than Science.* New York: Bantam Books, 1959.

Eiduson, Bernice T. *Scientists: Their Psychological World.* New York: Basic Books, 1962.

Einstein, Albert. *Essays in Science.* Translated by Alan Harris. New York: Philosophical Library, 1950.

—. *Out of My Later Years.* New York: The Wisdom Library, 1950.

Gerth, H. H. and Mills, C. Wright, eds. *From Max Weber: Essays in Sociology.* New York: Oxford University Press, 1958.

Hagstrom, Warren O. *The Scientific Community.* New York: Basic Books, 1965.

Hanson, Norwood Russell. *Patterns of Discovery: An Inquiry into the Conceptual Foundations of Science.* Cambridge: Cambridge University Press, 1958.

Harrison, James. *Scientists as Writers.* Cambridge: Massachusetts Institute of Technology Press, 1967.

Heim, Karl. *Christian Faith and Natural Science.* Harper Torchbooks. New York: Harper and Brothers, 1953.

220 BIBLIOGRAPHY

Hoyle, Fred. *Man in the Universe.* New York and London: Columbia University Press, 1966.

—. *Of Men and Galaxies.* Seattle: University of Washington Press, 1964.

Huxley, Julian. *Man in the Modern World.* Mentor Books. New York: The New American Library, 1948.

—. *The Human Crisis.* Seattle: University of Washington Press, 1963.

Kaplan, Norman, ed. *Science and Society.* Chicago: Rand McNally, 1965.

Kuhn, Thomas S. *The Structure of Scientific Revolutions.* 2nd ed. International Encyclopedia of Unified Science. Edited by Otto Neurath. Vol. II. Chicago: University of Chicago Press, 1970.

Lakatos, Imre and Musgrave, Alan, eds. *Problems in the Philosophy of Science.* Proceedings of the International Colloquium in the Philosophy of Science, London, 1965. Vol. 3. Studies in Logic and the Foundations of Mathematics. Edited by A. Heyting, A. Robinson, P. Suppes, and A. Mostowski. Amsterdam: North-Holland Publishing Company, 1968.

Luck, J. Murray, ed. *The Excitement and Fascination of Science.* Palo Alto: Annual Reviews, 1965.

Lundberg, George, *Can Science Save Us?* 2nd ed. New York: Longmans, Green and Company, 1961.

Margenau, Henry. *Open Vistas: Philosophical Perspectives of Modern Science.* London and New Haven: Yale University Press, 1961.

Maslow, Abraham. *The Psychology of Science.* New York: Harper and Row, 1966.

Planck, Max. *Scientific Autobiography.* New York: Philosophical Library, 1949.

Platt, George. *The Excitement of Science.* Boston: Houghton, Mifflin Company, and Cambridge: The Riverside Press, 1962.

Polanyi, Michael. *Personal Knowledge: Towards a Post-Critical Philosophy.* Harper Torchbooks. New York: Harper and Row, 1964.

—. *Science, Faith and Society.* Phoenix Books. Chicago: University of Chicago Press, 1964.

Pollard, William G. *Physicist and Christian.* New York: The Seaburg Press, 1959.

Price, Derek J. de Solla. *Science Since Babylon.* New Haven: Yale University Press, 1961.

Rushdoony, Rousas John. *The Mythology of Science.* Nutley: The Craig Press, 1967.

Sarton, George. *The Life of Science.* New York: H. Schuman, 1948.

Scheffler, Israel. *Science and Subjectivity.* Indianapolis, New York, and Kansas City: Bobbs-Merrill Company, 1967.

Schilling, Harold K. *Science and Religion.* New York: Charles Scribner's Sons, 1962.

Schilpp, Paul, ed. *Albert Einstein: Philosopher-Scientist.* 2 vols. New York: Harper and Brothers, 1949. Vol. I.

Schrödinger, Erwin. *Science and Humanism.* Cambridge: Cambridge University Press, 1951.

Shapley, Harlow; Rapport, Samuel; and Wright, Helen, eds. *A Treasury of Science.* New York: Harper and Brothers, 1943.

Storer, Norman W. *The Social System of Science.* New York: Holt, Rinehart, and Winston, 1966.

Sullivan, J. W. N. *The Limitations of Science.* Mentor Books. New York: The New American Library, 1949.

Terrell, D. B. *Logic: A Modern Introduction to Deductive Reasoning.* New York:

Holt, Rinehart, and Winston, 1967.

Toulmin, Stephen. *Foresight and Understanding: An Enquiry into the Aims of Science.* Foreword by Jacques Barzun. Bloomington: Indiana University Press, 1961.

—. *The Philosophy of Science.* Harper Torchbooks. New York: Harper and Brothers, 1960.

Waddington, C. H. *The Scientific Attitude.* Pelican Books. London and Aylesbury: Penguin Books, 1948.

Watson, James D. *The Double Helix.* Signet Books. New York: The New American Library, 1968.

Whitehead, Alfred North. *Science and the Modern World.* New York: MacMillan, 1948.

Young, J. Z. *Science and the Individual: Are They in Conflict?* Catham: Ruari MacLean Associates, 1967.

Ziman, John M. *Public Knowledge: The Social Dimension of Science.* Cambridge: Cambridge University Press, 1968.

Zwicky, Fritz. *Discovery, Invention, Research through the Morphological Approach.* New York: MacMillan, 1969.

c. Historical and General Works

Alexander, W. M. *Johann Georg Hamann: Philosophy and Faith.* The Hague: Martinus Nijhoff, 1966.

Allison, Henry E. *Lessing and the Enlightenment.* Ann Arbor: University of Michigan Press, 1966.

Aquinas, St. Thomas. *In Aristotelis Librum De Anima Commentarium.* 4th Marietti Edition. Edited by P. F. Angeli M. Pirotta, O. P. 1959.

Aristotle. *De Anima. The Student's Oxford Aristotle.* Translated and edited by W. D. Ross. 6 vols. London, New York and Toronto: The Oxford University Press, 1942. Vol. III.

Ayer, A. J. *Language, Truth and Logic.* New York: Dover Publications, n. d.

Burnet, John, ed. *Platonis Opera.* 5 vols. Oxford: The Clarendon Press, 1902. Vols. II, IV.

Cassirer, Ernst. *The Philosophy of the Enlightenment.* Translated by Fritz C. A. Koelln and James P. Pettegrove. Boston: Beacon Press, 1960.

Chesterton, G. K. *What's Wrong with the World.* London, New York, Toronto and Melbourne: Cassell and Company, 1912.

Clive, Geoffrey. *The Romantic Enlightenment.* New York: Meridian Books, 1960.

Descartes, Rene. *Meditations on First Philosophy. The Philosophical Works of Descartes.* Translated by Elizabeth S. Haldane and G. R. T. Ross. 2 vols. New York: Dover Publications, 1955. Vol. I.

Dunne, John S., C.S.C. *The City of the Gods: A Study in Myth and Mortality.* New York: MacMillan, and London: Collier-MacMillan Ltd., 1965.

Edwards, David L., ed. *The Honest to God Debate.* Philadelphia: The Westminister Press, 1963.

Ferguson, John. *The Wit of the Greeks and Romans.* London: Frewin, 1968.

Ferré, Frederick. *Basic Modern Philosophy of Religion.* New York: Charles Scribner's Sons, 1967.

Hamann, Johann Georg. *Socratic Memorabilia.* Translated with commentary by James C. O'Flaherty. Baltimore: Johns Hopkins Press, 1967.

Hamilton, Edith and Cairns, Huntington, eds. *The Collected Dialogues of Plato.* New York: Pantheon Books, 1961.

Hegel, Georg Wilhelm Friedrich. *Reason in History: A General Introduction to the Philosophy of History.* Translated with an Introduction by Robert S. Hartman. New York: The Liberal Arts Press, 1953.

—. *The Phenomenology of Mind.* Translated by Sir James Baillie. 2nd ed. London: George Allen and Unwin, 1964.

Heidegger, Martin. *Being and Time.* Translated by John Macquarrie and Edward Robinson. London: SCM Press, 1962.

James, William. *Pragmatism.* Meridian Books. Cleveland and New York: The World Publishing Company, 1955.

Kant, Immanuel. *The Critique of Pure Reason.* Translated by F. Max Müller. 2nd ed. Dolphin Books. Garden City: Doubleday, 1961.

—. *The Critique of Pure Reason.* Translated by Norman Kemp Smith. New York: St. Martin's Press, and Toronto: MacMillan, 1965.

Langer, Susanne K. *Philosophy in a New Key.* Mentor Books. New York: The New American Library, 1962.

Leibniz, Gottfried Wilhelm von. *Theodicy.* Translated by E. M. Huggard. Edited with an Introduction by Austin Farrer. London: Routledge and Kegan Paul, 1952.

Lessing, Gotthold Ephraim. *On the Proof of the Spirit and of Power. Lessing's Theological Writings.* Translated with an Introduction by Henry Chadwick. London: Adam and Charles Black, 1956.

Locke, John. *A Discourse of Miracles. The Works of John Locke.* 10 vols. Germany: Scientia Verlag Aalen, 1963. Vol. IX.

—. *An Essay concerning Human Understanding.* Collated and Annotated with Prolegomena, Biographical, Critical, and Historical by Alexander Campbell Fraser. 2 vols. New York: Dover Publications, 1959.

Locke, John. *The Reasonableness of Christianity as Delivered in the Scriptures. The Works of John Locke.* 10 vols. Germany: Scientia Verlag Aalen, 1963. Vol. VII.

Malcolm, Norman. *Ludwig Wittgenstein: A Memoir.* Oxford Paperbacks. Oxford: The Oxford University Press, 1962.

Moore, G. E. *Philosophical Papers.* New York: Collier Books, 1962.

—. *Philosophical Studies.* The International Library of Psychology, Philosophy and Scientific Method. Edited by C. K. Ogden. Totowa: Littlefield, Adams & Company, 1965.

—. *Some Main Problems of Philosophy.* New York: Collier Books, 1962.

Plato. *The Republic of Plato.* Translated with an Introduction by Francis MacDonald Cornford. New York and London: Oxford University Press, 1964.

Quine, Willard Van Orman. *From a Logical Point of View.* 2nd ed. Harper Torchbooks. New York and Evanston: Harper and Row, 1963.

Russell, Bertrand. *The Art of Philosophizing and Other Essays.* New York: The Philosophical Library, 1968.

Schweitzer, Albert. *The Quest of the Historical Jesus.* Translated by W. Montgomery. New York: MacMillan, 1957.

Smith, Ronald Gregor. *J. G. Hamann, 1730-1788: A Study in Christian Existence with Selections from His Writings*. London: Collins, 1960.

Tindal, Matthew. *Christianity as Old as the Creation*. London, 1730.

Toland, John. *Christianity not Mysterious*. London, 1702.

Voysey, Rev. Charles, ed. *Fragments from Reimarus*. London and Edinburgh: Williams and Northgate, 1879.

Wittgenstein, Ludwig. *Lectures and Conversations on Aesthetics, Psychology and Religious Belief*. Edited by Cyril Barrett. Oxford: Basil Blackwell, 1966.

—. *Philosophical Investigations*. Translated by G. E. M. Anscombe. 2nd ed. Oxford: Basil Blackwell, 1953.

—. *Tractatus Logico-Philosophicus*. Translated by D. F. Pears and B. F. McGuinness. Introduction by Bertrand Russell. The International Library of Philosophy and Scientific Method. Edited by A. J. Ayer. London: Routledge & Kegan Paul, 1961.

—. *Zettel*. Edited by G. E. M. Anscombe and G. H. von Wright. Translated by G. E. M. Anscombe. Oxford: Basil Blackwell, 1967.

2. *Articles:*

Allison, Henry E. "Christianity and Nonsense." *Review of Metaphysics*, XX (1967), 432-460.

Broudy, Harry S. "Kierkegaard on Indirect Communication." *Journal of Philosophy*, LVIII (1961), 225-233.

Cavell, Stanley. "Existentialism and Analytic Philosophy." *Daedalus*, XCIII (1964), 946-974.

Collins, James. "Three Kierkegaardian Problems." *The New Scholasticism*, XXIII (1948), 370-416; XXIII (1949), 147-185.

—. "Kierkegaard's Critique of Hegel." *Thought*, XVIII (1943), 74-100.

Crites, Stephen D. "The Author and the Authorship: Recent Kierkegaard Literature." *Journal of the American Academy of Religion*, XXXVIII (1970), 37-54.

Durfee, Harold A. "The Second Stage of Kierkegaardian Scholarship in America." *International Philosophical Quarterly*, III (1963), 121-139.

Gerber, Rudolph J. "Kierkegaard, Reason and Faith." *Thought*, XLIV (1969), 29-52.

Goudge, T. A. "Memorial for Fulton Henry Anderson, M.A., Ph.D., Ll.D., D.Litt., F.R.S.C." *Dialogue*, VII (1969), 92-93.

Hall, Thor. "Theological Table-Talk." *Theology Today*. XXVII (1970), 71-80.

Herbert, Robert. "Two of Kierkegaard's Uses of Paradox." *The Philosophical Review*, LVI (1961), 41-55.

Holmer, Paul. "Kierkegaard and Theology." *Union Seminary Quarterly*, XII (1957), 23-31.

—. "Kierkegaard and Religious Propositions." *Journal of Religion*, XXXV (1955), 135-146.

Klemke, E. D. "Some Misinterpretations of Kierkegaard." *Hibbert Journal*, LVIII (1959), 259-270.

Larsen, Robert E. "Kierkegaard's Absolute Paradox." *Journal of Religion*, XLII (1962), 34-43.

Lowrie, Walter. "Existence as Understood by Kierkegaard and/or Sartre." *Sewanee Review*, LVIII (1950), 379-401.

—. "Translators and Interpreters of Kierkegaard." *Theology Today,* XII (1955), 312-327.

McInerny, Ralph. "Ethics and Persuasion: Kierkegaard's Existential Dialectic." *The Modern Schoolman,* XXXIII (1956), 219-240.

—. "Kierkegaard and Speculative Thought." *The New Scholasticism,* XL (1966), 23-35.

Mackey, Louis. "The Loss of the World in Kierkegaard's Ethics." *Review of Metaphysics,* XV (1962), 602-620.

—. "Philosophy and Poetry in Kierkegaard." *Review of Metaphysics,* XXII (1969), 316-333.

McKinnon, Alistair. "Kerkegaard's Irrationalism Revisited." *International Philosophical Quarterly,* IX (1969), 165-176.

—. "Kierkegaard, Paradox and Irrationalism." *Journal of Existentialism,* VII (1967), 401-416.

—. "Kierkegaard's Pseudonyms: A New Hierarchy." *American Philosophical Quarterly,* VI (1969), 116-126.

MacPherson, H.G. "What Would a Scientific Religion be Like?" *Saturday Review,* August 2, 1969, 44-47.

Nielsen, H. A. "Bultmann's Philosophical Troubles." *Dialogue,* VIII (1970), 635-645.

Ramsey, P. "Existenz and the Existence of God." *Journal of Religion,* XXVIII (1948), 157-176.

Searles, Herbert. "Kierkegaard's Philosophy as a Source of Existentialism." *Personalist,* XXIX (1948), 173-186.

Thulstrup, Niels. "Theological and Philosophical Kierkegaardian Studies in Scandinavia, 1945-53." Translated by Paul Holmer. *Theology Today,* XII (1955), 297-311.

Walker, Jeremy. "Kierkegaard's Concept of Truthfulness." *Inquiry,* XII (1969), 209-224.

3. *Unpublished Materials:*

Holmer, Paul. "Kierkegaard as Critic." Mimeo., n.d.

—. "Kierkegaard and Philosophy." Mimeo., n.d.

Magel, Charles. "An Analysis of Kierkegaard's Philosophical Categories." Unpublished doctoral dissertation. Philosophy Department, University of Minnesota, 1960.

Martin, George A. "An Interpretive Principle for Understanding Kierkegaard." Unpublished doctoral dissertation. Philosophy Department, University of Notre Dame, 1969.

INDEX